The
BRITISH
AIRCRAFT
CARRIER

Paul Beaver

'The Fleet Carrier—the most impressive fighting machine the world has ever seen.
This one ship can unleash a greater variety of lethal weapons
with a greater destructive power, at longer range, than any man o' war in history.'

Admiral of the Fleet Lord Hill-Norton, GCB
Seapower, BBC tv, February 1981

The BRITISH AIRCRAFT CARRIER

Paul Beaver

PSL

Patrick Stephens
Wellingborough, Northamptonshire

Title page *The large number of arrestor wires needed aboard an axial deck carrier can be seen in this photograph of a Firefly landing on the Canadian carrier* Magnificent. *The aircraft has taken the third of 14 wires and the deck handlers are racing to unhitch the plane so that it may taxi forward and park* (RCN/DND).

First published March 1982
Second edition September 1984
Third edition May 1987

British Library Cataloguing in Publication Data

Beaver, Paul
    The British aircraft carrier.—3rd ed.
    —History
    I. Title
    623.8'255'0941   V874.5.G7

    ISBN 0-85059-877-X

Patrick Stephens Limited is part of the Thorsons Publishing Group

Printed in Great Britain.

Contents

Dedication

For my parents, who first aroused my interest in aircraft carriers at one of Portsmouth's Navy Days, and who did not realise just what they had let themselves in for.

Above *This is how the conventional aircraft carrier began. A view of* Argus *taken during the later weeks of World War 1, as emphasised by the dazzle paintwork* (Fleet Air Arm Museum).

Below *The ultimate fixed-wing carrier after a three year refit,* Ark Royal, *equipped with 'the world's best mini-air force' of Phantoms, Buccaneers, Gannets and Sea Kings, steams through the Mediterranean on her last deployment before decommissioning. On the bow catapult a Gannet AEW3 prepares for launch, with its wings still folded* (Fleet Photographic Unit).

Introduction to the Third Edition

When I set out to compile this book on the British aircraft carrier, the demise of *Ark Royal (IV)* had only been a few months before and the prospects for the future looked rather bleak, even with the advent of the revolutionary Sea Harrier 'jump jet' and the commissioning of *Invincible*. On the day the first edition was published, the Argentine invasion of the Falkland Islands caused a dramatic change in the fortunes of the aircraft carrier and today, four years later, I have great confidence in the three CVSs now in service. In fact, there are signs of a carrier revival amongst the maritime powers and although the United Kingdom will never be in a position to give its Royal Navy another fully-fledged £1,000 million fleet carrier again, the age of the carrier is not dead.

This revised third edition of *British Aircraft Carrier* reflects the changes in posture, thinking and attitude towards the aircraft carrier, together with some new appendices material comparing naval aircraft—the life blood of any carrier—and some specially-drawn illustrations by Ian Commin and the late Bob Downey, who also worked so hard on producing the photographs for the first edition; sadly Bob was killed in October 1985.

Acknowledgements

In compiling the information for this account of the British fixed-wing aircraft carrier, I have tried wherever possible to seek out people 'who were there' and this has not always been easy because in the end I found it impossible to talk to everyone who volunteered to have their brains picked. Many people were able to delve deep into the past by the use of personal diairies, log books, etc, and to recall with clarity the event or events which needed to be confirmed. To all of them, I am very grateful, and especially to those who read through particular chapters, for their time, interest, patience and support: Admiral Sir Frank Hopkins, KCB, DSO, DSC; Admiral Sir William O'Brien, KCB, DSC; Admiral Sir Derek Empson, GBE, KCB; Admiral Sir Desmond Cassidi, KCB; Admiral Sir Anthony Griffin, GCB; Vice Admiral Sir Donald Gibson, KCB, DSC, JP; Vice Admiral Sir Conolly Abel Smith, GCVO, CB; Vice Admiral Sir Richard Smeeton, KCB, MBE, FRAeS, DL; Rear Admiral A.S. Bolt, CB, DSO, DSC[+]; Rear Admiral D.R.F. Cambell, CB, DSC: Rear Admiral H.C.N. Goodhart, CB, FRAeS; Rear Admiral A.D. Torlesse, CB, DSO; Rear Admiral H.C.N. Rolfe, CB, MA; Rear Admiral J.O. Roberts, CB; Rear Admiral P. Gick, CB, OBE, DSC[+]; Captain George Baldwin, CBE, DSC[+], RN (Rtd); Captain Eric Brown, CBE, DSC, AFC, FRAeS, RN (Rtd); Captain Alan Leahy, CBE, DSC,

RN (Rtd); Captain Duncan Lewin, CB, DSO, DSC, RN (Rtd); Captain D.T. McKeown, RN (Rtd); Captain Keith Leppard, CBE, RN (Rtd); Captain M.J. Button, RN (Rtd); Captain Antonio Dutra; Braz. N.; Captain Mortimer Neame, DSO+, RN (Rtd); Captain J.H. West, RN (Rtd); Colonel J.G. Boulet, CF; Commander Peter Libby, RN; Commander Dennis White OBE, MRAeS, RN (Rtd); Commander Peter Carmichael DSC, RN (Rtd); Commander V.G. Sirett, RN; Commander N. Cambell, RN (Rtd); Commander Charles Lamb, DSO, DSC, RN (Rtd); Commander Dennis Bourne, RN (Rtd); Lieutenant Colonel Peter Hicks (Rtd); Lieutenant Commander J.B.A. Hawkins, RN; Lieutenant Commander Richard Swift, RN (Rtd); Lieutenant Commander Cyril Poutney, RNVR (Rtd); Lieutenant Commander Charles Wines, RN (Rtd); Lieutenant Commander Douglas Hale, RN (Rtd); Lieutenant Commander Jack Waterman, RD, RNR (Rtd); Lieutenant Commander J.B.A. Hawkins, RN, Lieutenant Commander P.G. Wilkins, RN (Rtd); Lieutenant Commander Alex Brown, RN (Rtd); Major Douglas Holmes (Rtd); Lieutenant 'Tug' Wilson, RN; Lieutenant Rod Safe, RN; Lieutenant B.A. Kenyon, RN; Len Lovell; Harry Liddle; Owen Cathcart-Jones; Ken Sims; Jack Bryant; Michael Howe; H.H. Sainsbury; Sir Edward Singleton; N.E.D. Parkinson; Ann Lance; Bob Downey; H.E. Skinner, OBE; Charles Sherwin, CB; Ray Sturdivant; Rob Roseveare; Peter George; Robert Taylor; C. Bristow; Norman Hanson, DSC; H.J. Bricknell; Charles Stevens; D. Barnett; William West; Robert Shopland; Miss M.W. Thirkettle; Ian Garnett; Graham Swanson; Bryan Philpott; R.B. Wigg; B.G. Blampied; R.L. Ward; Douglas Rough and Robert Baillie.

The following organisations kindly provided factual and photographic assistance: Australian War Memorial; British Aviation Research Group; Brown Bros Ltd; Canadian Forces (in London, Halifax and Ottawa); Culdrose Aero Park; Fleet Air Arm Museum; Fleet Air Arm Officers Association; Fleet Photographic Unit; Harland & Wolff; MacTaggart Scott & Co Ltd; Ministry of Defence (Navy); Naval Historical Section; Office of the Flag Officer Naval Air Command; Public Archives of Canada; Royal Australian Navy; Royal Navy; HMS *Bulwark* Association; HMS *Daedalus*; HMS *Seahawk*; HMS *Heron* and British Aerospace.

I am particularly grateful to those who have so kindly read extracts from the manuscript and made such helpful comments—in particular I would like to thank Captains Baldwin and Lewin for steering me clear of several minefields, and to Rear Admiral Cambell for keeping my head above water in the pre-1945 period. Special mention must be made of the sterling efforts by the original typists: Lyn Greenwood (who also prepared the index), Eileen Farnham, Pat Kennedy and my wife, Ann.

Sources

In a book which relies on facts to tell its story, it is important that the facts are accurate and relevant. Wherever possible the facts, especially the dates mentioned in this book, have been checked against more than one source, often by verifying the script with one, or several, individuals who were actually there. I have also consulted many leading works.

The illustrations have been gleaned from many sources, particularly the Fleet Air Arm Museum at Yeovilton, Somerset, and from the personal albums of former officers and ratings of the Royal Navy. I am particularly indebted to those who have allowed me access to their collections. Wherever possible I have indicated the exact source of each photograph, but with the passage of time, and the fact that many fine illustrations had to be copied directly from the pages of albums, this becomes very difficult. I hope sincerely that if I have mis-credited a photograph, the photographer whose art is involved will forgive me. I am particularly indebted to the Royal Navy for the use of their copyright materials.

Reference works consulted include the following, and these could form further reading for those interested in pursuing this fascinating topic: *Jane's Fighting Ships*; *British Naval Aircraft* by Owen Thetford (Putnam); *Pictorial History of the Fleet Air Arm* by John Rawlings (Ian Allan); *Carrier Pilot* by Norman Hanson (Patrick Stephens Ltd); *Wings on my Sleeve* by E.M. Brown (Airlife); *Four Ark Royals* by Michael Apps (Kimber); *British Aircraft Carriers* by W.D.G. Blundell (MAP); *Aircraft Carriers* by David Brown (MacDonald & Janes); *Aircraft Carriers* by Norman Polmar (Doubleday); *Aircraft Carriers* by Antony Preston (Hamlyn); *Rise & Fall of the Aircraft Carrier* by Bernard Ireland (Marshall Cavendish); *Air Power & the Royal Navy* by Geoffrey Till (Janes); *Ark Royal* by Paul Beaver (Patrick Stephens Ltd); *Fleet Air Arm Song Book*; *Carrier Air Groups—HMS Eagle* by David Brown (Hylton Lacy); *On the Surface* by F.W.W. Hollingham (HMS *Hermes*); *Air Facts & Feats* by Taylor & others (Guiness); various Commissioning Books of HM Ships; *Warships of World War II* by Lenton & Colledge (Ian Allan); *War in a Stringbag* by Charles Lamb (Arrow); *Taranto* by Newton & Hampshire (New English Library); various Aircraft and Warship Profiles (Profile Publications); *The Forgotten Fleet* by John Winton (Michael Joseph); *Action this Day* by Sir Philip Vian (Muller); *Flashing Blades over the Sea* by John Milne (Maritime Books); *Escort Carriers* by Kenneth Poolman (Ian Allan) and *Carrier Air Operations* by David Brown (Ian Allan).

Journals consulted include: *Air Pictorial; Aircraft Illustrated; Airfix Magazine; Aviation News; British Aviation Review;* FAAOA Newsletter; *Flight; Flight Deck; Fly Navy;* International Plastic Modellers' Society Magazine; *Marines Internationales; Navy News; Navy International; Random Thoughts; Ships Monthly; TAGS; World War II* and *The Manchester Engineer.*

Paul Beaver
Old Basing, Hampshire, June 1986

Chapter 1

In the beginning

The carrier story begins just before the end of World War 1—with the commissioning of the first flush-deck aircraft carrier, named *Argus*. To get this enormously important event in perspective, we should go back a year to September 1917. Following the sad and untimely death of the gallant young squadron commander, Ernest Dunning, a very important recommendation of the Committee of Inquiry into Naval Aviation, was that ships engaged in flying should have a 'landing-deck' of at least 300 feet (91.4 m) in length and the full width of the ship, in effect, a flushed deck running from the bows to the stern and from one beam to the other.

This requirement was immediately implemented on a converted Italian passenger liner, *Conte Rosso,* later renamed the *Argus,* which had been laid down in 1914 and subsequently purchased by the Admiralty. Conversion to a carrier design without any flight deck obstruction had begun in August 1916 and the ship was eventually launched in December 1917, displacing 14,000 tons (14,225 tonnes). The engine exhausts were ducted beneath the flight deck and, to con the ship when not at flying stations, a chart house on a hydraulic lift was provided. *Argus* was to become a perennial and, although obsolete by the middle 1930s and relegated to training in 1942, she was not scrapped until 1946.

The previous 'aircraft carrier', the former light battlecruiser, *Furious*, had used a centrally trunked funnel which gave it the appearance of a conventional warship of the period, except that it had a flattened stern. The obvious flying-off and landing-on problems which this caused led to the deliberate design of a flush deck in *Argus*—the 'flat iron' of every early naval aviator, and a few hundred 'temporary gentlemen' of World War 2 who learned to deck land on her. *Furious* herself, having been re-constructed for aircraft twice, was taken in hand for a third time and when she emerged in 1925 she was also a flush decker but she was the last of her type—for the next generation of aircraft carriers would have island superstructures.

So the story of the carrier begins with *Argus* in 1918 and goes on through the inter-war years of uncertainty, the campaigns of World War 2, the advances of the immediate post-war period, the halcyon days of the carriers in the 1950s, and early 1960s, ending with the decommissioning of Britain's last conventional fixed-wing aircraft carrier in 1978. Sixty glorious years where time and again Britain led the world in achievement and in technical expertise.

*　　　*　　　*

The take-over of the Royal Naval Air Service (RNAS), effectively the whole of Naval aviation, by the Royal Air Force (RAF) on that much lamented day—April Fool's Day 1918—has always been seen as a great blow not only to Naval aviation, but also to the development of the aircraft carrier.

Whilst the United States Navy (USN) was busily trying out new weapons and tactics against war-retributive Kaiserliche Marine Warships, the Board of the Admiralty were still enthralled, it seems, by the seaplane (we have Winston Churchill to thank for that name, rather than the more favoured 'hydroplane' quoted at the time). In 1919 the Admiralty were proposing a Flying Squadron attached to the fleet and comprising *Furious,* plus six seaplane carriers. Quite where *Argus* would fit in was not discussed. Their Lordships went on to say that naval aircraft were best suited to attacking bases ashore 'rather than against forces operating in the high seas'. These ideas persisted in theory throughout the 1920s and 30s, but in practice very little training was carried out against land targets and the fleet practised both torpedo and conventional bombing against warships.

In 1919 the element of the RAF which undertook Naval flying (the Fleet Air Arm (FAA) was not formed until 1924), comprised one spotter-reconnaissance squadron, a fighter squadron and half a torpedo-bomber squadron—a far cry from the 3,000 aeroplanes which the RNAS could muster in 1918. Between the formation of the RAF and the founding of the FAA, the naval aeroplane lost its superiority over its land-based counterpart and the new FAA was almost starting from scratch. Apart from the actions in the Mediterranean and a few scouting flights for the Home Fleet, the bulk of the Royal Navy had not seen their air service in action during the war—their main battleground being the Western Front alongside the Royal Flying Corps. It was, therefore, not surprising that there was almost apathy amongst the gunnery, navigation, and communication branches of the 'senior' Service.

With the advent of the flush deck aircraft carrier, capable of landing and of launching biplane fighters and multi-role aircraft, various technical problems had to be overcome, not least how to stop or slow down the landing run of such aircraft as the small Sopwith Pup then in regular service. A primitive start to the long saga of arrester gear was tried on *Furious* in the early days of flight deck trials and consisted of longitudinal wires stretched along the deck, raised a few inches by wooden pegs, with the aircraft destined to operate from the aircraft carrier, fitted with skids instead of wheels. To these skids were attached small hooks which could catch the wires and thereby slow down the forward movement of the aircraft, but which were more suited to keep the aircraft running straight. This was considered to be somewhat better than the transverse wire system, the forerunner of what we now know as arrester wires.

Either of these systems would be employed with a crash barrier, a suspended system of ropes from a folding gantry, which would prevent the aeroplane landing on from going over the ship's bow. This barrier, though still seen on the later carriers, had changed shape and content several times, from the steel barrier of World War 2 to the nylon flexible barrier of the 1950s, to be finally displaced by that marvellous invention, the angled flight-deck. Early attempts at landing resulted in all sorts of problems and, initially, though aircraft could be launched, they could not return; some were even recovered by ditching in the sea and being hoisted aboard.

As World War 1 drew to a close, the British Grand Fleet who, still smarting

The next carrier to be completed in the conventional mould was Furious, *a ship which had already seen a great deal of the early experiments by the Royal Naval Air Service. This particular view shows the carrier in 1933 whilst flying off Fairey IIIFs. Note the palisades forming a fence along the flight deck to prevent an aeroplane, running along the deck, from swinging over the side* (RN via H. Liddle).

from their unsuccessful bid to destroy the German High Seas Fleet at the Battle of Jutland two years earlier, were planning a major torpedo raid on the German harbours which were the havens of the mighty battlecruisers and battleships of the Kaiserliche Marine. Spearheading the intended attack on the German High Seas Fleet would be a force of 20 Sopwith Cuckoo torpedo bombers. These aircraft were the first wheeled torpedo bombers, and it was envisaged that they would be embarked in *Argus,* from where they would deliver an 18 inch (45.72 cm) torpedo apiece, but the armistice came before either the Cuckoo or the *Argus* could be tried in action. The Cuckoo was from the same stable as the ubiquitous Camel, Pup and 1½ Strutter designs which the Admiralty had used during the war in the initial aircraft carrier trials.

Without doubt a landmark in British naval aviation design, the Cuckoo was unusual as a torpedo bomber, because it was a single seat aircraft with a maximum speed of 103 mph. It first entered service at East Fortune in Scotland and the pilots were trained to be operational in *Argus* by the Autumn of 1918. Cuckoos did, however, go on to serve in the British aircraft carriers *Argus, Eagle* and *Furious,* with 210 Squadron, until withdrawn from service in April 1923. This was not, however, before the Imperial Japanese Naval Air Service had taken a significant interest in the torpedo carrying aeroplane, and they developed the state of the art to a degree which was to become famous less than 20 years later, when torpedo carrying aircraft attacked a small Pacific island and finally brought the United States into World War 2.

The aircraft carriers which we have mentioned so far had, it will be remembered, not been built as such, but were converted from other designs. The Admiralty, after a fairly slow start, was now keen to press ahead with the aircraft carriers as a weapon of war.

In 1917—a significant year for naval aviation—the Royal Navy took over the hull of a suspended Chilean battleship, provisionally named *Almirante*

Cochrane, which was formally renamed *Eagle* in February 1918. Just a month earlier the keel had been laid for the world's first aircraft carrier to be designed from the start to operate aircraft. The *Hermes,* as she was later named, featured a full length flight deck but, unlike *Argus* and *Furious,* she overcame the problem of venting exhausts by having a normal enclosed funnel, but arranged in the superstructure on the starboard side of the ship. This design feature, to become known as the 'island', was a dominant characteristic of all aircraft carriers built in later years.

Other ingenious features destined for the *Hermes,* were incorporated in the design of the *Eagle*—she too had an island superstructure, but with one difference—she was the only conventional aircraft carrier in the Royal Navy to feature two funnels in the island superstructure. She also had a larger hangar than *Hermes* and so was more useful in later years when larger Naval aircraft arrived on the scene. *Eagle* was launched in June 1918, again too late to see war service in that earlier conflict, but she was to give sterling service in the Mediterranean theatre during 1940-42.

The first deck landing aboard *Argus* is credited to a Sopwith 1½ Strutter, flown by Wing Commander Bell Davies, VC (later a Vice Admiral who returned to the RN as a captain in World War 2). Both Bell Davies and the 1½ Strutter flew numerous test flights from carrier decks using both wheels and skids in the development of both arrester gear and the aircraft carrier in general, and the aeroplane had already become the first two-seat aircraft to be launched from a British warship. The design went on to test flotation bags and similar devices which were to be the forerunners of flight safety equipment carried by Naval aircraft to the present day.

Another aircraft equipped with hooks on the axle bar to negotiate the fore and aft arrester wires on the carrier deck of such ships as *Argus* was the Nieuport Nightjar, which also had the distinction of being the first of a new generation of single-seat carrier fighters, when it entered service with the fleet in 1921. Another contemporary was the Parnall Panther, which had the distinction of being the first British Aircraft designed specifically for carrier operations. Although it was not a successful design, it did see service with the fleet's spotter reconnaissance flights in *Argus* and *Hermes* until withdrawn from front-line service in the middle of the 1920s, to be replaced by the Fairey IIID. The Nightjar which had superseded the famous Sopwith Camel, was itself replaced in service by the Fairey Flycatcher in 1924, but not before it had taken part in that small war in Turkey which was also the first operation in which the *Argus* was deployed—the Chanak crisis of 1922.

The Fairey IIID mentioned above was a two-seater reconnaissance aircraft, another of the peacetime designs which was equipped for catching the longitudinal arrester wires. It was a somewhat unsatisfactory system leading to the claim that aeroplanes made only one successful landing out of six in *Argus.* This ludicrous method of aiding the recovery of naval aircraft was eventually abandoned in the mid-1920s in favour of the transverse system although, for some time into the 1930s, aeroplanes were capable of landing aboard carriers with no wire across the deck and with no brakes. In fact, as late as 1940, an aircraft not equipped for flight deck operations was able to land on carriers at sea. One has only to recall the most gallant and successful attempt by RAF pilots to land aboard *Glorious* with their Hurricanes during the Norwegian campaign which was sadly all to no avail as *Glorious* was sunk by naval gunfire

from German capital ships, a matter of hours later. Later during the siege of Malta the reinforcements flown off the evergreen *Argus* were land-based aircraft, again operated from the carriers.

A naval aviator, who later commanded the light fleet carrier *Vengeance* in the Pacific, Captain Mortimer Neame, looks back with fond memories of his first carrier, *Argus*, which he joined in the Solent flying a Blackburn Blackburn. This aircraft was a fleet spotter which normally carried an observer in a cabin below the pilot, the latter sitting in the open air. The way that the Fleet Air Arm was organised in those days meant that when aircraft left the parent ship to go ashore for leave periods and more intensive flying than they could find at sea, the observers usually stayed on board the ship, as they were very much considered to be primarily naval officers, whereas those flying the aircraft were joint RAF/RN officers. So Neame was alone, when he approached *Argus*. He saw the low speed flag was flying and this meant that the ship was making only, perhaps, 12 knots, into a 20 knot wind, giving 32 knots over the deck. This meant that he would have to land at a lower speed, because in those days there was no arrester gear and no way of stopping the Blackburn other than by landing on and running into the wind. As he circled, the ship put up the flag 'affirmative', there being no radio contact between carriers and aircraft until sometime later. It was also his first landing operationally on a flight deck and as he was joining the ship he had all his gear aboard the aircraft. Crossing the stern, the difference in the airflow caused his aircraft to drop a matter of six inches, and this was enough for it to catch the rounddown, stall and crash back on to the quarter deck. Captain Neame was very lucky because, despite an open cockpit, he was able to walk away. The only thing he lost was his best cap!

On the bridge of the *Argus* they could not see what had happened, because it was for'ard and below the level of the flight deck, and thought he had probably gone into the sea, only to be confronted with a rather white-faced young aviator who came to report that he had joined. The downdraught from the hangar, which had caused this crash, was to catch many young pilots when they were flying at a very slow speed with no room to manoeuvre. They were only able to continue their approach, sometimes to disaster.

The whole sequence of carrier flying in those days (1927-29) was somewhat of a hotch-potch arrangement, where carriers would turn into wind and when there was sufficient wind, hoist the affirmative flag for the aircraft circling to land on. The actual approach was at a relative speed of about 15 knots (27.8 kph)

Top left *Britain's only twin-funnelled conventional aircraft carrier was* Eagle *which was famous for its Spanish language engine room instruments which harped back to its days of construction as the Chilean battleship,* Almirante Cochrane. *In this photograph* Eagle *can be seen at the Royal Naval anchorage of Wei Hai Wei on China's Yellow Sea coast* (via H. Liddle).

Centre left *Even with a completely flush deck like that of* Argus *or* Furious *it was still possible to go wrong when landing on without any real means of stopping the aeroplane. Mind you, the speeds were so slow that it was possible for the aircrew to evacuate their errant machines before they took the plunge, as in this shot* (Lieutenant Commander R. Swift).

Left *The light aircraft carrier* Hermes *was the first of its type to be designed from the start to operate aeroplanes from an uninhibited deck. Although too small to operate a truly effective air group, the ship did have a fine reputation as a good and happy ship* (H.J. Bricknell).

In the early days of carrier flying, the Admiralty's planners envisaged that a torpedo-carrying aeroplane, like this Blackburn Dart (1923–33), would attack and slow up an enemy warship so that it could be finished off by a battleship or battlecruiser, as illustrated in the background (Owen Cathcart-Jones).

because the aircraft's normal landing speed was 45 knots (83.3 kph), and normally the ship would be trundling along at 20 knots (37 kph) in a 10 knot (18.5 kph) wind. There were, of course, no navigation aids, not even a radio and the pilot was very definitely his own master, and it was very simple to fly the aircraft, like the Blackburn Blackburn or the Avro Bison. The pilots very rarely swopped types of aircraft and there was little cross-operating—one was either trained as fighter pilot, reconnaissance pilot or torpedo pilot.

After some time aboard *Argus,* 'Morti' Neame joined *Furious* where Wing Commander Collishaw, the famous Canadian Ace, was the senior RAF officer. *Furious* could carry 33 aircraft, and she too had no arrester wires and, as the aircraft had no brakes, it was often the practice of the flight deck crew to leap up across the deck to a slowing aircraft, drag it to a halt and help it to manoeuvre to a lift, so that it could go below and the deck would then be clear for the next pilot to land on. It was a painfully slow operation, but it moved very slickly, as the aircraft returning from a sortie would position themselves to land every one minute or so, so that the flight deck was constantly in use.

Chapter 2

Flying for fun

Although the War of Intervention, in Northern Russia, in 1919, led to the deployment of the seaplane carrier *Pegasus,* it was not until 1922 that a 'flat-top' went to war stations, though no shots were fired in the Anglo-Turkish confrontation of the Chanak Crisis, and the *Argus,* the carrier deployed, was only used as an aircraft transport for the RAF. It is no wonder then, that in 1921 when Lord Chatfield reported to the Admiralty that new equipment such as catapults and arrester gear should be developed, his words of wisdom fell on deaf ears. For a further 20 years the doctrine that the big gun was the major weapon of the fleet held sway.

In the early years after the war, Britain tried to maintain the neutrality of the area around the Dardanelles against the threats of the Turkish nationalists. Prompt action in September 1922, including the despatch from Leuchars via *Argus* of 203 Squadron, flying Nieuport Nightjars, helped keep the peace. *Argus* returned to the UK in December, bringing home the remaining aircraft of 203 Squadron (the Nightjar having proved to be unsuccessful in the Near East theatre). *Argus* rejoined the Atlantic Fleet (later known as the Home Fleet) until her refit in 1925-26, when anti-torpedo bulges were added to her underwater hull, thus enabling her to remain in service for a few more years; in the event she did not decommission until 1946.

Perhaps the most significant event of the early post-war era was the signing, in December 1921, of the Washington Naval Treaty which limited the size and scope of the major navies of the world, including the Royal Navy. The tonnage quota allowed under the terms of the Treaty led to the conversion of two light battlecruisers into aircraft carriers. The two ships, named *Courageous* and *Glorious,* had been designed initially for shallow water coastal bombardment in 1907 and, because of their light armour, they were mothballed when completed in 1916. Their conversions took some time to take place and the result was that they were not commissioned until 1928 and 1927 respectively.

The additional tonnage allowed under the Washington Treaty (1921) would be taken up by the construction of four small 17,000 tonne carriers between 1926-35. This programme was, however, to suffer from the mid-20s defence cuts and the keel laying of the first unit was deferred for some time. In 1924, the tentative plan evolved to cater for the up-grading of the carriers in the RN was to run for ten years (1925-35) and envisaged that *Furious, Glorious* and *Courageous* would be completed in 1925, 1927 and 1928 respectively. *Argus,* the world's first flush-decker, would be phased out, as would the *Hermes* (completed in 1923); *Eagle* would be scrapped in 1939.

The Admiralty did not at the time consult the Air Ministry, but it was obvious that the larger aircraft coming into service would need larger carriers if they were to be used in an efficient manner. It is interesting to reflect that the first of the larger carriers, *Ark Royal,* was not completed until 1937 and that at the time of the Treaty, *Hermes*—the first specifically designed aircraft carrier—was still three years from commissioning! Luckily for the Royal Navy, the need to convert and to retain aircraft carriers was championed by Lord Beatty who constantly stressed their need to the Admiralty. The three subsequent units of the *Ark Royal* Class were cancelled in favour of the armoured fleet carrier designs of the *Illustrious* Class. These same cuts saw the retention of *Argus, Eagle* and *Hermes,* so that the RN entered World War 2 with seven carriers. More distressing was the fact that the RN had been denied the opportunity to work up tactics and expertise in carrier operations. The Spring Cruise of 1929 saw *Furious, Courageous* and *Eagle* working together for the first time, although actual cross-deck operating was an exercise element of the future. Various evolutions were carried out, but nothing seemed to be able to impress the Admiralty—World War 2 was still ten years away.

The hazards of flying during this period can be amply illustrated by a small yet significant incident during one of the two combined fleet exercises. The carriers had been divided between the Atlantic and Mediterranean Fleets and their aircraft were used on long patrols of up to four hours duration, flying in pairs. During one sortie, now remembered with some relief by A.D. Torlesse (then a

Left *In 1925, the converted battle-cruiser,* Courageous, *re-joined the fleet, but this time as an aircraft carrier. With a main flight deck running three-quarters of the ship's length, and a lower flying off deck which allowed for faster launching operations, both she and her sister-ship,* Glorious, *were welcome additions to the fleet. As a point of interest, the two accelerators on the forward end of the flight deck are noteworthy* (Fleet Air Arm Museum).

Above right Glorious *spent many happy years in the Mediterranean Fleet before the war and is seen here steaming through a calm sea during flying operations. The aeroplane over the carrier is a Fairey IIIF—one of the most popular of the Fairey biplane designs* (via Lieutenant Commander R. Swift).

Lieutenant (O) and now a retired Rear Admiral) involved the problem of inadequate radio equipment. One of the pair on this particular sortie developed engine trouble, serious enough to necessitate an immediate ditching. Torlesse's radio in the surviving aircraft would not play the game and he could not raise the 'friendly' fleet. Luckily by changing to the other frequency of the exercise, he was able to contact the 'enemy' and one of their destroyers collected the downed aircrew who were rather bedraggled by that time. In the days of otherwise primitive search and rescue procedures, a ditching at sea, away from the carrier and her consorts, could have so easily been the end of that particular aircrew. Nevertheless, these exercises, in Admiral Torlesse's own words were 'very good because of the training they gave on reconnaissance and shadowing'—the main role of the torpedo-bomber-reconnaissance aircraft embarked in carriers at this time.

During earlier exercises off Singapore, *Eagle* was allocated to the 'attacking' force in similar exercises but, at the end of the day, the torpedo bombing successes of its aircraft were partially discounted by the 'battleship-minded' Admirals of the day. In 1931, *Glorious'* torpedo-bombers scored nine hits on battleship targets just to prove how vulnerable the big guns were to the actions of aircraft operating from what was essentially a mobile airfield.

The Combined Fleet Exercises carried out in the Mediterranean in 1933 gave the three fleet carriers a chance to demonstrate their talents again, but luckily the threat of carrier-borne aerial assault was at last being taken seriously. RN surface units, though, were still going to sea during the first couple of war years with pitifully weak anti-aircraft armament, and the development of the torpedo-bomber was not speeded along as it should have been. Such are the problems of a Navy in peacetime.

It is a popular misconception, perpetrated probably by those senior ranks unconnected with the Fleet Air Arm, that the air branch of the Royal Navy did not have a good working relationship with the Royal Air Force. In fact it would probably be truer to say that the Fleet Air Arm was on far better terms with the RAF than with other branches of the Navy. It should, of course, be remembered that Fleet Air Arm pilots also held a Commission in the Royal Air Force and,

Showing the flag literally. Eagle *was in the South China Seas during the Sino-Japanese War and, in order to prevent mis-identification, three large Union Jacks were painted on her flight deck* (H. Liddle).

for example, a Lieutenant RN would be a Flying Officer in the Royal Air Force. By December 1931, however, only 11 flights* out of the 26 operational were commanded by RAF officers.

The Fleet Air Arm was a very exclusive club of about 200 members at most and perhaps the antagonism felt towards it by other more staid traditional branches was that it was doing something that little bit more glamorous in the peacetime Navy. They were not by any means the cream of the Navy, and in fact bright young officers were not encouraged to fly. Several of those early flyers who rose to places of distinction within the Royal Navy considered themselves to be rebels, fed up with the formality of the quarter deck and preferring the dashing, fun-filled existence of flyers who were not subject to interference from other branches. The aircraft carrier's role, in the 1930s especially, was that of showing the flag with limited fleet exercise. During these exercises, the air branch was utilised, but not in any particularly useful manner. In fact, the pilots were encouraged to 'swan off somewhere', while the fleet got down to the real job of exercises, manoeuvres and gunnery. During the typical commission a pilot may come back after three months at sea with only 40 hours in his log book to show for the time spent either in the Mediterranean or else with the Home Fleet.

The transfer of responsibility from the Royal Air Force to the Royal Navy for the Fleet Air Arm in the autumn of 1938, was not really a victory for the pilots and observers who flew the aircraft. It was, to a certain degree, the changeover of ownership that made life somewhat more unpractical for the flyers in that they had been used to RAF Wing Commanders in charge of the shore stations— men who were used to flying themselves—and they now found that the Captains of Naval Air Stations could be anything from gunnery officers to navigators, with no flying experience. This is in direct contrast to the naval aviation side of the US Navy who benefited because all senior officers were encouraged to learn

* Naval 'flights' became 'squadrons' in 1933.

Despite the menacing look of all those whirling propellers, there were relatively few fatal accidents aboard the early carriers. The Nimrods (foreground) and Ripons of Glorious *are prepared for the day's flying* (via Lieutenant Commander R. Swift).

to fly if they wanted to, hence the nickname 'Pensacola Admirals'. Any senior officer who wanted a carrier command, or indeed any operational command in naval aviation, had to be a pilot.

The story is often told by Fleet Air Arm pilots of those days, although the name, date and place involved cannot be identified here of the senior officer who went to lecture at a Naval Air Station, and was speaking of the constant battle between the Admiralty and the Air Ministry to keep control of naval aviation. During the period for questions afterwards, the young naval pilot got up and said that he had learnt to fly with the Royal Air Force, had in fact been seconded to an RAF Squadron for a time, and had enjoyed a close working relationship with the RAF. He then, rather tongue in cheek, posed the question: 'At what rank does a naval pilot have to get to to fall out with the Royal Air Force?'.

There has always been a lot of talk of the Royal Air Force being able to carry out the duties of Naval air crew and therefore do away with the need for the Fleet Air Arm. In 1936 they even tried switching the squadrons just to prove to the Admiralty that the RAF could deck land and could in fact fight an aeroplane at sea as well as anyone else.

43 Squadron, Royal Air Force, based at Tangmere in Sussex, and flying the famous Hawker Fury fighter, were due to trade mounts with 800 Naval Air Squadron, in *Courageous*, flying a mixed Hawker Nimrod/Osprey air element. This would have been an extremely interesting experiment had not two problems arisen. One was the Abyssinian crisis which sent 800 and *Courageous* scurrying into the Mediterranean (Alexandria), and two, that the Air Ministry attempted to keep all the aces up their sleeve by posting all available ex-Fleet Air Arm pilots (and in 1930 there was a ratio of 50-50 RAF-Fleet Air Arm pilots at sea) to 43 Squadron! This continual contention that the RAF could do the Fleet Air Arm's job was again raised in the 1960s by the incoming Labour

One of the most popular fleet fighters of the RN was the Fairey Flycatcher. This particular machine, from 401 Flight, is seen taking off from the lower flying off deck of Furious—*straight out of the hangar!* (Rear Admiral Cambell).

Government who used it to argue that it was prudent to disband the Royal Navy's carrier force. A decision which some feel we shall live to regret.

In the early 1930s, a number of naval pilots elected to cross-qualify as naval observers. One of the first was Henry Rolfe, who, impressed by the professionalism of the observers with whom he had served, decided to take the course. Until World War 2, observers tended to be appointed to particular ships rather than to an individual squadron. Designated a Lieutenant (P) (O), officers like Rolfe were sure that a comprehensive view of naval aviation could only benefit carrier aviation, which was still in the doldrums.

Normally, when an observer was appointed to a particular ship, he would team up with a particular pilot and they would fly as a team throughout the commission. Although 'scotched by the war', there was a scheme to form a specialist squadron composed entirely of dual trained pilot-observers (to be known as, for example, Lieutenants (F)). Even as an observer, Rolfe still kept his air time up by flying Swordfish when his squadron, 814, was ashore for a while at Freetown.

*   *   *

Let us take a look at the individual carriers. Although completed initially in 1917, *Furious* comes into the story of British fixed-wing aircraft carriers in 1925, following a four-year refit and reconstruction to produce a flush-decked design. She then displaced 22,800 tonnes and was capable of carrying 33 naval landplanes. In her overall length of 786 feet (239 metres), there were two aircraft lifts to enable the air complement to be struck below when not flying.

The actual completion of *Furious* was seriously delayed by economic pressures, but the carrier was to have a distinguished, almost charmed, life. In 1925 she began service with the Atlantic Fleet which lasted until a major refit at Devonport in 1930. During this time, Rear Admiral Torlesse, then a newly qualified naval observer, recalls that the ship had aboard a pigeon loft and the birds were taken aloft by aircrew: 'some of the homing pigeons even managed to find their way back to ship!'. In November 1931 she was ready for sea again and this time joined the Home Fleet, with which *Courageous* was already operating. Apart from a six month stint in the Mediterranean during 1934, the 'Covered Wagon', as she was known by those who served in her, stayed with the Home Fleet until the outbreak of war. The hostilities found her in Rosyth.

William West joined the ship at Devonport in August 1937, as a Petty Officer, Gunner's Mate, and he recalls what it was like to serve in an aircraft carrier just before war broke out. 'When I joined *Furious* in August 1937, she was Training Carrier, Home Fleet, and carried 33 Fairey Swordfish aircraft and two DH Tiger Moths. Her attendant destroyer was *Shikari* which followed closely astern whenever flying was taking place. *Furious* was commanded by Captain Clayton (the younger brother of Tubby Clayton, the Toc H Padre of World War 1) and her complement was about 1,200 of whom about 375 were RN and the remainder RAF.

'*Furious* had a completely flush flight deck extending over most of her length but had a large metal fencing that could be raised when not flying to afford wind protection to those on deck. Also towards the fore end of the flight deck was a small navigating housing that could be raised to deck level when not flying. Her navigating position was a small bridge on the starboard side extending out from and just below the flight deck. A similar structure on the port side was the flying control position. The funnel ducts extended along each side immediately below the flight deck to a position just before the quarter-deck and this was the reason why the aft end of the ship was painted black.

'Soon after I joined we sailed for the Firth of Forth which was to be our base for the next three months. After clearing the harbour our aircraft flew on from a shore base and once in the Forth there was little time for anything but flying. We sailed out to sea on a Monday morning and returned to the Forth on a Friday night or Saturday morning, depending on progress made during the week. The ship steamed up and down the wind continuously during daylight hours with aircraft flying on and off whenever we were steaming into the wind. Each trainee deck-landing pilot had to complete so many landings and take-offs with an instructor and then repeat the procedure alone. When considered proficient he had to do it all over again with weighted bags to represent the extra weight of a torpedo. Later with an observer and TAG aboard, formation flying was practised.

'During my time in *Furious**, we experienced only three accidents but only two of these were fatal. On the first occasion a Flight Sergeant Pilot came in to land and missed the arrester wires. He tried to accelerate to take off again but his engine cut out and the plane slithered across to the starboard side just near the navigation position and fell into the sea. The pilot stepped out of the cockpit into the inflatable dinghy that burst from the top of the fuselage and didn't even get his feet wet! *Shikari* picked him up and also was smart enough to get hooks into the plane from a special crane fixed on her forecastle. Part of the wings and the fuselage were cut away but the engine was salvaged and returned to *Furious.*

'The second happening was when a Captain in the Marines was bringing his plane in to land and apparently lost flying speed and plunged into the sea just

* Author's note: By tradition one is always 'in' a warship, never 'on'.

astern of the ship. Nothing of this plane or pilot was seen again. The third occurrence happened when three planes were doing formation flying some distance from the ship and for some unknown reason one dived into the sea and was lost despite a thorough search by *Furious* and *Shikari.* As a result of a refit, a small island was constructed on the starboard side of the flight deck to provide a home for fighter direction and what was then known as 'RDF' (later to be known as radar). I think *Furious* was only the third ship to be thus fitted. The other two were *Rodney* (a battleship) and a County Class cruiser. The only other happening of any note during this rather short commission occurred during the Munich Crisis when the ship steamed up through the North Sea completely darkened and with half the armament constantly manned. The other carriers in service at this time, *Argus, Courageous, Eagle, Glorious* and *Hermes*, were still feeling the pinch of economic cuts, but were still able to go to sea, even if they were considered to be very much the eccentric element of His Britannic Majesty's Navy.'

Glorious spent three years attached to the Mediterranean Fleet between 1930-33 carrying Hawker Nimrod fighters, and Blackburn Ripon torpedo bombers. Radar had yet to be invented so the safety of aircraft out of sight of the ship was dependent on the radio Direction Finding (D/F) receiver, because the ship was often almost invisible in haze, especially to aircrew in an open cockpit. Simply explained, the aircraft would carry a transmitter, operated in the Nimrod by the pilot and in the longer range Ripon by the telegraphist air gunner (a rating member of the aircrew). The ship's portable radio receiver, with its internal aerial, would be tuned and the aerial rotated until a minimum signal was detected. The two positions of minimum signal giving the direction of the transmitter, a sensing device on the *Glorious'* D/F receiver would indicate which bearing was correct. A goniometer compass gave the bearing of the transmitter. About every half hour, an aircraft would transmit its callsign a few times, to enable the ship to take a bearing and place the data on the 'plot' to record the

The Blackburn Ripon saw service as a multi-purpose long-range torpedo-bomber-reconnaissance (TBR) aeroplane from 1929 until superseded by its larger brother, the Baffin, in 1935. During this time it served in Courageous, Furious *and* Glorious *in the Home and Mediterranean Fleets* (H. Liddle).

The Combined Fleet Exercises of 1932 saw Glorious *(left),* Furious *(top) and* Courageous *at Malta under the flag of devoted carrier Admiral, Sir Reginald Henderson, who, although not an aviator, was conscious of the need to develop the great potential of the aircraft carrier. In this view it is interesting to see the shape of* Courageous' *aircraft lift which can also be seen on the hangar deck below* (Fleet Air Arm Museum).

plane's progress. 'It was not at all unusual', says Richard Swift, a retired Lieutenant Commander who spent his early days of naval service in *Glorious'* DF office, 'to hear an aircraft returning to the ship signalling "am lost". Bearings would then be passed to him until he signalled "ship in sight".'

Courageous, Furious and *Glorious* were equipped with a lower flying-off deck, but its use was restricted to the nimble Flycatcher fighter which was flown directly out from the hangar. On the forecastle there was a very large hangar door but once, despite its weight, a stormy sea made a mess of the door and the hangar behind. Richard Swift recalls the most unpleasant feeling experienced several times in a Mediterranean storm, 'to be on the boat deck with, of course, no sky showing directly above and the outboard view restricted. When the *Glorious* was in a beam sea in bad weather, with a large top, the feeling was one of the whole vessel toppling over'.

Courageous had started life as a War Emergency Naval Building Programme battle cruiser, together with her close sister ship, *Glorious.* In June 1924 she was taken in hand for conversion at Devonport, from where she emerged in May 1928 as an aircraft carrier with a 480 feet (146.3 m) × 100 feet (30.5 m) flight deck and facilities for 50 aircraft. Her original complement consisted of six individual flights; two of Fairey Flycatcher fighters, two of Fairey IIIF spotter reconnaissance aircraft and two of Blackburn Dart torpedo bombers.*

Initially deployed to the Mediterranean, where she visited Greece and lifted men of the South Staffordshire Regiment from Malta to Israel (Palestine), *Courageous* did not return home until 1930. She then went into long refit to have the many recent advances in naval aviation incorporated and, although she

---

* In 1927, Squadron Leader T.B. Howe successfully landed a Dart at night on *Furious*—the first such recorded landing.

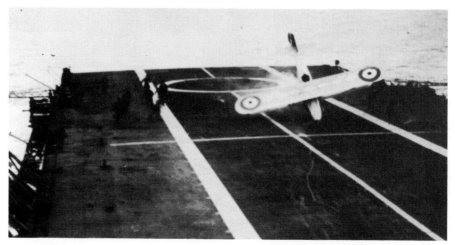

As a result of the first accelerator-assisted take-off from Courageous, *this Nimrod of 800 Squadron had a somewhat uncharacteristic recovery. This was the result of having its undercarriage smashed because of a fault in the accelerator mechanism* (RN).

visited Portugal in 1932, she was not in the public eye until the Naval Review of 1935. It was then that *Courageous* was involved in aircrew training and air equipment development, mainly in the Mediterranean. In 1936, she joined the Home Fleet as flagship and she carried out this role until replaced by *Ark Royal* in 1939, when she joined the Channel Force at Portland. *Courageous* was the first carrier to be lost in World War 2 when U-29 torpedoed her off Ireland on September 17 1939.

'In my days in *Courageous*, September 1934 to June 1936', wrote Commander Neville Cambell to the author, 'we had fighters, spotter reconnaissance and torpedo aircraft. I was in a Seal Squadron and so on our flying days we could be doing a navigation exercise, a formation high level bombing practice, a wireless exercise, anti-submarine spotting, acting as targets for a fighter attack on us, spotting for a battleship gunnery shoot, target towing for an HA* shoot by some ship and so on. The fighters would practise their dog fight tactics and the torpedo bombers would make a dummy attack on *Courageous* or some other ship and once or twice a cruise around or a live attack. So a 'usual' day's flying would contain a combination of the above with perhaps some dive bombing on a target towed astern by the ship.

'What was being practised as much as anything else was a speedy launching of a number of aircraft and, far more important, a speedy recovery. There were no barriers in the mid-1930s so the deck had to be clear before an aircraft could land. If we take just a flight of these aircraft to land on, they would circle the ship until the leader saw his squadron pennant hauled out on a boom on the port side; the flight would fly down the starboard side and break formation and the leader would go round to land; the other two would space themselves at what they hoped was the right interval for the next landings. All very similar to recent carrier work but, instead of R/T† or batsmen to help, one had to watch the deck

* HA stands for High Angle gunnery, basically anti-aircraft defence.
† Radio Telephone.

intently seeing how long the aircraft took to be taken on to a lift, folded, the lift lowered, the aircraft wheeled off and then the lift brought up again and the deck was clear. One aimed to be just short of the carrier as the heads of the handling party appeared above the deck as the lift came up with them. After a time one could judge it very well, provided there was no hitch getting the aircraft off the lift into the hangar; if one was too early then the following pilot should be reasonably close to land on next while the foiled one went round again. If one thinks of perhaps two squadrons to land on by this process, with the carrier steaming flat out away from the main fleet, one can appreciate how vital it was for very accurate landing drill—an accuracy I may say which was totally unnecessary then for the RAF squadrons ashore on the grass airfields.'

A unique incident took place in 1936 when two brothers, both naval aviators, were sharing a cabin in *Courageous*. One was a Sub-Flight Commander with 800 (Nimrod) Squadron, and the other was flying Fairey Seals—one of those typically versatile Fleet Air Arm biplane, spotter, reconnaissance aircraft. They were both in *Courageous* throughout the Abyssinian crisis in the middle of the 1930s.

During this time Seals and Nimrods frequently operated together for exercises. One such exercise was off Malta and it showed the bond between the two brothers. The incident occurred when Nimrods were practising fighter interceptions, flying in pairs to attack the Seals over the sea. Two Nimrods collided as a result of evasive action and crashed in flames, although one pilot was saved by an escorting destroyer. One brother in a Seal was keeping station on his formation leader, when he noticed a look of abject horror spread across the leading observer's face. Of course the pilots facing forward keeping station were not watching the Nimrod fighters attack—it would only be the observers who would have a chance to see them and to witness the appalling collision, but sensing what had happened he immediately obeyed the instruction for the flight to break formation, and turning, saw a column of smoke with the escort picking up the surviving pilot (who had incidentally nearly drowned as a result of his fearful burns and almost suffocating parachute canopy which had

With wings folded and wheels chocked, this Osprey is taken down Hermes' *forward lift, attended by a gaggle of RN/RAF ground crew* (via H.J. Bricknell).

dropped on top of him). The two brothers then immediately set about flying round the sky—one to find out if the other brother had been one of the aircraft in the crash, and the other to reassure his brother that he was OK. This incident shows how much naval aviators gained by the introduction of efficient voice radio. Despite the frail-looking aircraft at the time, Nimrods, Ospreys, Seals, Fairey IIID, etc, crashes were very rare, the major problem being engine failure. Break-ups in the air just did not occur and flight deck accidents were primarily due to human error.

*   *   *

The Abyssinian crisis of 1936 was fairly much of a non-event for the RN's carriers except that an idea was forming in the minds of the Flag Officer and his Staff Officers in the Mediterranean Fleet—an idea which would lead to the first successful naval aviation torpedo raid on a navy in harbour in history— Taranto. Naturally carriers were on the alert, in particular *Courageous* and *Glorious* who were at Alexandria, but in general nothing was allowed to affect the continuous rounds of exercises and courtesy calls on friendly nations.

Glorious had embarked three squadrons (812, 823 and 825), all trained in the relatively new art of night flying. In 1933 *Glorious* had begun the process of working up her Ripons, and later her Seals, with serious night flying exercises. At this time, she was also an undoubtedly happy ship; her problems were to come later during the first months of World War 2.

Hydraulic catapults called accelerators were first fitted in carriers in 1933/34 and they had a few teething problems. A good example, though, of the problems involved was an incident in January 1934, when a Nimrod from 800 Naval Air Squadron in *Courageous,* was placed aboard the starboard catapult for the very first accelerated launch. This catapult, a collapsible trolley of iron bar construction with various hooks and wheels, was used to launch the aeroplane in the flying position. It was similar in design to that used for the catapults of cruisers, except that, instead of having an explosive charge to propel the aeroplane forward, a hydraulic ram was used; the mechanism was that a wire attached to the trolley passed forward over a long sheave (pulley) at the fore end of the track and was attached to a hydraulic ram underneath the flight deck.

The pilot flying the Nimrod, about to experience his first catapult launch, was sitting waiting for the signal to be off, then down came the Deck Control Officer's flag and off sped the Nimrod into the air with a big bang and a rather alarming sinking feeling. But unperturbed, the pilot climbed and commenced some acrobatic manoeuvres, only to see the aircraft carrier turn out of wind and a stream of morse being flashed at him on the Aldis light. Like all pilots of the time, he had learnt not to rely upon the radio which was rather a cat's whiskers fine tune type, which was on the blink more often than not but he found difficulty in reading the sequence of morse dots and dashes. Eventually he did manage to tune the radio on to the ship's frequency and understood what had happened. It must be remembered that this was his first catapult launch and he had nothing to compare it with. He thought the big jolt on launching was the natural feeling felt when accelerated off the bow of a ship. What actually happened was the Nimrod's long undercarriage was lower than the sheave over which the propelling wire ran and so the axle had been smashed. This, of course, was seen from the ground but could not be seen by the pilot in his cockpit. The ship signalled the pilot to fly alongside the ship and ditch, but as it was January he was rather loath to do this, and eventually the Squadron Commander persuaded the Captain that it would be safe for him to bring the Nimrod back on to the deck, which he did.

Some ships are happy, whilst others are not so happy, and the first *Hermes* (for a second is still in service with the Royal Navy) was truly a happy ship. Former Marine Jim Bricknell served in *Hermes* on the China Station in the middle of the 1930s; his first ship and by far the one which holds his happiest memories of 15 years in carriers was *Hermes*. On reflection Jim feels that this was amazing for several reasons. 'She was small', he recalls, 'accommodation on the lower deck was uncomfortable and the mixture of RN and RAF personnel should have led to a troubled existence, especially in the hotter climes. Added to this the wardroom was quite blue-blooded (Commander, The Hon Pleydell Bouverie and First Lieutenant, The Hon Whitney-Smith) and the Captain was The Hon George Fraser. This should have widened the already existing gap between lower deck and the quarter deck', but didn't and despite all the theoretical minus points, Jim Bricknell remembers her as 'a grand ship with a grand ship's company'.

On the China Station, carriers, like other British warships, were painted white, with buff coloured upper works. Life aboard, although it could be hot, was pleasantly offset by the reception which awaited the ship's companies ashore. In those days, before World War 2, Britain was very much 'Great' Britain and the flag-showing visits mattered to all concerned, irrespective of rank in the Royal Navy. An American enlisted man was once heard to remark that whilst the US Navy tended to act as if they owned the whole Pacific seaboard, the Royal Navy did not really care who owned what because they were there because they were British.

Hermes in dry-dock showing her keen lines and jutting bow. As can be seen from this view, she did not have a very broad beam and so was not able to carry many aircraft, but her hull shape did allow for good sea-keeping. This was a great advantage in the vast tracts of ocean east of Suez where she spent most of her active life (RN via H.J. Bricknell).

The Royal Marines have always been associated with aircraft carriers, as gunners, pilots and, of course, as bandsmen. They provided a form of entertainment which was not only good for morale aboard ships in far away places, but also helped in showing the flag (via H.J. Bricknell).

Life aboard then was, in general, good—although discipline was strict. The food on the *Hermes* was, apparently, particularly good, due it seems to the single-handed efforts of the Warrant (Grocer) Supplies Officer, one 'Happy' Day, who never ceased to amaze the ship's company by producing choc-ices and even frozen lobster, irrespective of whether the carrier was at her home port of Hong Kong or not. Another special treat on holidays was known as grotters—soft drinks.

The China Fleet itself was a happy organisation, keen on sporting and competitions generally. The relationship between the RAF and RN personnel aboard the carriers was, to commence with it seemed, a joke, especially when the 'boys in light blue' went ashore dressed in riding breeches, puttees and Glengarry-type hats; plus their complete ignorance of all things Naval. Eventually the RAF ground-crews became as much a part of the ship's life as the Naval ratings. The fun era, one might even say the amateur era, was then in decline and a far more sinister era about to begin. Would the Fleet Air Arm and the nation's carrier forces be caught, unable to respond to the challenge of war in time?

Chapter 3

War clouds gather

The Royal Navy and Fleet Air Arm struggled through the defence cuts and restrictions of the 1920s and 1930s with six carriers—*Argus, Courageous, Eagle, Furious, Hermes* and *Glorious*. In 1937, things began to brighten up with the launching of one of the most famous warships of all time, *Ark Royal*. The third warship to bear the name was a 22,000 ton aircraft carrier with an armoured flight deck and capable of carrying 72 aircraft in two hangars. She was completed in late 1938 with two accelerators, three aircraft lifts and hydraulic arrester wires. The first flight deck safety barrier had also been installed in *Ark*. In all respects, she was a leap forward in aircraft carrier design and in her were sown the seeds of all the conventional fixed-wing carriers to follow, especially the *Illustrious* Class and the post-war fleet carriers.

Equipped with the Blackburn Skua and the faithful Fairey Swordfish, the *Ark* had worked up in time to be fully operational by September 1939. She replaced *Courageous* as the flagship of Rear Admiral Aircraft Carriers, Home Fleet and was based at Scapa Flow when war began. Within days, she was near missed by *U-39*, but this submarine herself became the first German submarine casualty of World War 2, when the Home Fleet's destroyer screen detected her and she was sunk following her unsuccessful torpedo attempt. At the end of September came the famous incident when a Heinkel HeIII was said (by the German Propaganda Minister, not by the Luftwaffe) to have sunk the carrier by bombing. A fact later disproved when she sailed into Rio de Janeiro during the hunt for *Graf Spee*. Her most famous exploit was in May 1941 when she joined the Home Fleet, together with other elements of the legendary Force H, to hunt for the German surface raiders *Bismarck* and *Prinz Eugen* in the North Atlantic. It was *Ark*'s Swordfish of 818 Squadron, led by Lieutenant Commander T.P. Coode, RN, which scored two torpedo hits on *Bismarck*'s after end which put her steering gear out of action and thus ensured her end by the closing fleet, under Admiral Sir John Tovey.

Ark resumed Mediterranean convoy work (see Chapter 8) and just how crucial her part was can be summed up in the words of Admiral Somerville: 'If I haven't got the *Ark* with me, I feel like a blind beggar without his dog'. Her end came at the hands of a U-Boat on November 13 1941, but not before she had been awarded the following Battle Honours: Norway—1940; Spartivento—1940; Mediterranean—1940-41; Bismarck—1941; and Malta Convoys—1941.

Following the take-over, by the RN, of the Fleet Air Arm, rapid evolutions and exercises were undertaken to find out just how effective the carrier air

squadrons were operationally. In March 1938, massed torpedo attacks by Swordfish of 810 and 820 Squadrons from *Courageous* and *Glorious* supported by Nimrods and Ospreys of 800 Squadron, were carried out against the 'Red' Battlefleet. These manoeuvres proved just how effective this form of attack was by breaking up the highly disciplined ranks of battleships and battlecruisers. Fourteen torpedo 'hits' were reported after attack runs by 27 aircraft during the first attack—a later attack was even more effective.

Later the same year *Courageous* launched another mock attack against the pride of the Royal Navy, the ill-fated battlecruiser, *Hood.* The Swordfish bombers deployed, successfully penetrated a fighter screen to reach their

Above *The first of the great British fixed-wing armoured fleet carriers which were laid down just before the outbreak of World War 2. Illustrated here, during her days with the BPF,* Illustrious *was later joined by five more carriers which were basically similar* (Fleet Air Arm Museum).

Left Ark *'s Ospreys and Swordfish ranged for flying during the shake-down cruise in November 1938* (Fleet Air Arm Museum).

objective. Although these attacks were only simulations, they did not say much for the fleet's anti-aircraft defences. It can be argued that this inadequacy was a legacy from the mistrust and attitudes of the Air Staff and Admiralty during and after World War 1. It is interesting to reflect that in the early months of the war, the *Ark Royal*, for instance, chose to rely on her AA guns for defence, rather than the Blackburn Skua fighter/dive bomber squadrons embarked. The Squadron Commander of one of the first Skua units was Lieutenant Dennis Cambell, who led 803 Squadron in *Ark Royal*, and he remembers that, after having sorted out teething troubles, the Skua was easy to fly, but nothing like fast enough to be a successful fighter, so perhaps this was the reasoning behind this seemingly reactionary idea.

By 1939, the ratio of fighters to TSRs/bombers was something like 1:5, and it is surprising to note the lack of impetus to update the fleet's weak fighter defences. The higher levels of the RN at that time displayed a lack of confidence in the carrier biplane fighters (Nimrods and Ospreys), exemplified by the decision, in 1936, to disembark all fighters from *Furious* and all but two from *Courageous,* during the Munich Crisis. It is true, however, that the fighter element of the Fleet Air Arm did have its supporters and the development of primitive radar (RDF) to direct fighters was commenced, at sea, in 1938. Unfortunately, in the development of the high performance monoplane fighter, the RN did not keep pace with friends and potential enemies abroad.

*　　*　　*

In the early 1930s the problems associated with safe deck landings became acute, for not only were carrier aircraft becoming heavier, but also their stalling speed—a critical moment when the aircraft ceases to fly because it loses lift—was increasing to the point where, even with the ship steaming into wind, a safe recovery was becoming more and more improbable. A carrier steamed into wind to reduce the relative speed of a landing aircraft over the flight deck. This, of course, had the added advantage of virtually eliminating drift or the sideways movement of the approaching aircraft; it was difficult enough to land directly down the axial deck without the added problem of crabbing towards the island or the deck edge to port.

In 1927, deck edge 'palisades' had been fitted to flight decks to prevent an aircraft which had either drifted or run off the centre line, from going directly in the 'oggin'. Aircraft, like the Blackburn Dart and Avro Bison, had been landing 'free' since 1925 and even though the accident rate was as high as 1 in 4 during the later half of that decade, casualties were light. The accident rate did, however, cause the writing off of many valuable airframes and in the days of only short ferry flight distances, this could prove embarrassing when a carrier was, say, off Hong Kong! The lack of wheel brakes on the aircraft also meant that they were almost uncontrollable on deck, and had a tendency to run over the side. The transition stage of deck landing was from thwartship wires, to longitudinal wires, to no wires whatsoever, hence the need to assist the pilot by the introduction of 'pallisades' on the *Courageous*—which proved more of a hazard than help to aircraft with any great wing-span.

Owen Cathcart-Jones, now resident in California, recalls his days in *Argus, Eagle, Furious, Hermes* and *Courageous*, as a pilot of a Fairey Flycatcher: 'Deck landing in the 1920s aircraft was comparatively easy due to slow landing speeds and fast steaming capacity of carriers. In fighters, we often used to side-slip on the approach to the deck to improve the forward view. It was not unknown for near simultaneous Flycatcher recoveries to be accomplished when the first aircraft would land as far aft as possible and go down the after-lift; as it was on the lift the second machine would fly over the lift and land further up the deck. We also did experiments with landing pontoon fitted Flycatchers on deck with a specially treated surface. In those days it might have been an advantage, but the fact of having pontoons so reduced the speed to render the aircraft valueless as a combatant machine'.

The Curator of the Fleet Air Arm Museum, Yeovilton, was, before being commissioned as a Pilot, a seaman deck handler in *Furious* in the 1930s. During this time, *Furious* was acting as a training carrier and, as well as having her own complement of aircraft, was used by various squadrons in the Fleet Air Arm for deck landing practice; aircraft seen aboard included Fairey Flycatcher, Fairey IIIF, Blackburn Baffin, Blackburn Ripon, Fairey Seal, the Hawker Osprey and the Hawker Nimrod.

Aircraft handling itself presented no great problems as the normal flying programme consisted of one detail in the morning and another in the afternoon. After launching operations, the deck handlers reverted to their ordinary jobs as seamen, before coming on deck again for the recovery of the aircraft which had been flown off. It was normal practice in those days, with the centrally placed aircraft lifts, for the aircraft returning to be unhooked from the arrester gear, moved forward and struck down either the forward or after lift into the hangar, the lift coming up again just in time for the next aircraft in circuit to land on. This landing cycle often was less than a minute and meant that tremendous teamwork and tremendous team spirit had to be evoked, so much so that the pilot had confidence enough to continue his approach even though he could see the deck either cluttered by an aircraft not yet struck down or else a gaping hole left by the deck lift in the down position.

The seamen used as deck handlers wore a conventional sailor's hat with a chinstrap, gym shoes, and a zipped one-piece flying suit, which made them look like 'rather comic athletes'. It was some time before the protective and more functional cloth helmet was evolved. Besides naval personnel on the deck, of course, there were also RAF personnel, as the Fleet Air Arm was at that time still the Fleet Air Arm of the Royal Air Force. They were mainly concerned with airframe and engine maintenance.

Casualties were very light during the time that 'Harpie' Cox was in *Furious*; there were only two crashes in his two-year period. During this two-year period as well, there were never any casualties among the deck handling party, although there can be no more dangerous place than a flight deck of an aircraft carrier. In the days of propeller aircraft and of a ship travelling at say 20 knots into a 30 knot wind, it was more than probable that somebody would be blown off their feet into the whirring 'fan', the propeller of an aircraft whose engine was being run up prior to take-off.

Contemporary records report that in the 1920s, to fly a loaded aircraft (fuelled and armed) on to the flight deck was impractical unless there was about 27 knots of true wind over the deck. True wind is the sum of natural wind speed plus the speed of the carrier. So in calm weather there would be for the ship the problems of eating up precious reserves of fuel, which even then was expensive, as well as the additional wear and tear on the ship's propulsion machinery. Not only did the carrier have to steam at high speed but, because of the lengthy process then used for recovering aircraft and clearing the deck for landing, she, and her screen of attendant destroyers, might have to take a new, and perhaps reverse, course from the rest of the fleet and so delay the passage for up to an hour. The menace of submarines to capital ships, such as the aircraft carrier, in these circumstances could not be discounted either.

In 1931 the Admiralty authorised the introduction of the American arrester wire system. Aircraft were immediately fitted with large hooks near their tails and these, after being lowered during the landing approach, connected with one of the several transverse wires stretched across the after end of the flight deck, a little forward of the rounddown. This development led to improvements in operating procedures which in turn led to larger, heavier aircraft being recovered at faster landing speeds and in less time than during the decade before. Added to this, of course, the carrier's Chief Engineer had less wear on his beloved ship's machinery which, in its turn, led to longer periods between refits and so the carrier was able to stay in commission longer.

Courageous, it seems, had the first wires fitted in the 1933/35 period. These were automatically resetting types using the energy stored within the system to re-align the wires after an aircraft had been disengaged. Only later, when aircraft larger than the frail-looking bi-plane fighters and torpedo bombers came into service, did the wires need to be powered. *Ark Royal III* could take a maximum weight of 2,000 lb (907.2 kg), the wartime carriers had the capacity for 11,000 lbs (4,989.6 kg) and eventually following 'Phantomisation', *Ark Royal IV* could cope with 40,000 lbs (18,144 kg) landing weights. Modern American aircraft types, perhaps those which would have been operating from CVA-01 by now but for the 'Healey axe' would have had a landing weight up to 65,000 lbs (29,484 kg), but, undoubtedly, the necessary improvements and developments in British arrester gear would have kept pace with the increase in aircraft landing weights.

It was about this time that the aesthetically pleasing and nimble Hawker fighters were introduced—the single seat Nimrod and the two-seat Osprey. These had been developed from the Hart light bomber of the RAF and were very popular with the Fleet Air Arm even though the pilot's view of the cockpit was pretty well obscured because of his relative position to the nose. This led to the introduction of a curved approach technique being developed: 'The Nimrod replaced the sturdy little Fairey Flycatcher, which had been the standard Fleet Fighter for some years and which finally phased out in 1934', writes Rear Admiral Dennis Campbell, whose Naval career spans the years 1925-60, many spent flying or testing Naval fighters.

'The first unit to be so re-equipped was 408 Flight, commanded by Lieutenant Commander E.M.C. Abel-Smith (now Vice Admiral Sir Conolly Abel-Smith) and the new aircraft were embarked in *Glorious* in the autumn of 1932, off Malta. The Nimrod was, like all Hawker fighter, very pleasant to fly, highly manoeuvrable and with docile landing characteristics. At that time our carriers had not been converted to the arrester-gear system, so good, slow landing behaviour was still highly important. By 1935, our carriers were being fitted with arrester gear and hydraulic "accelerators" and the Nimrods and Ospreys were modified with hooks and catapult spools.

'In 1934, all "Flights" were re-established in "Squadrons" and from then on all Fleet Fighter Squadrons had a mix of Nimrods and Ospreys (9 + 3 usually).

The CO usually flew an Osprey, his observer navigated the squadron and operated the W/T communication with the ship. The Nimrod only had a rather primitive radio, of "cat's whisker" standard—very difficult for the pilot to tune in. One interesting development was pioneered by the Nimrod—the technique of very steep dive bombing; cribbed, I must confess from the USA by way of the the Clark Gable film *Hell Divers*!'

*   *   *

The US Navy found that by stretching a stout wire fence across the deck, about midway along the island, with specially constructed wires and sheaves, damped down hydraulically, effectively prevented a rogue aircraft (ie, one which had not caught any of the arrester wires) from crashing into aircraft which could now be parked at the forward end of the flight deck. The hydraulic damping system allowed the barrier to be extended by an aircraft in proportion to the load exerted on it. The barrier could also be raised and lowered by remote control.

A system of vertical ropes had been tried in *Furious* before conversion to the flush deck design in 1918, but it had not been developed further by the Royal Navy. The new system was not fixed and after a safe landing, an aircraft would disengage from the wires, the barrier would be lowered and the aircraft, under its own power, would taxi forward to either park or be struck down via the forward lift into the hangar.

Like all good inventions, the crash barrier had its drawback. The pilot's margin of error was now reduced because he had to make sure that his aircraft touched down within 80 metres or so of the rounddown, otherwise he would not catch an arrester wire and would run forward into the heavy crash barrier— bending his aircraft and probably himself as well. A barrier crash also meant that the flight deck was blocked until the aircraft had been pulled out of its entanglement, and should there be no spare deck (another carrier or land airfield) within flying distance, the rest of the sortie might have to ditch because of their low fuel state. The barrier achieved its purpose, especially during the hectic war years, but it was not until the advent of the life-saving angle-deck in the 1950s that the pilot was again free to land on an unrestricted deck—a great psychological aid to safe landings.

Obviously then, something had to be done for the pilot and, in 1937, just before the introduction of the barrier, a specially trained team of deck landing qualified pilots was trained by the Royal Navy to control the landing approach of carrier aircraft. Simultaneously pilots were trained to follow the mandatory signals given by the 'batsman' or Deck Landing Control Officer (DLCO) and this system proved a great success until it too was superseded by the mirror landing aid invention of Commander Nick Goodhart. Standing on the port side of the flight deck, the batsman would watch the incoming aircraft and would give the pilots either the affirmative to continue their approach or else the appropriate signals to correct their speed, altitude and rate of descent on to the flight deck. Later, especially during the latter half of World War 2, one or two specially trained ratings were employed to assist the DLCO by checking that the incoming aircraft was able to land with wheels and hook down.

Very little appears to have been written previously about the actual design and construction of an aircraft carrier, from the point of view of the naval architects and shipbuilders especially. A great deal of patient and often enlightened paperwork had to go into the design of a carrier before the Deputy Director of Naval Contracts (as he used to be known) could write to the selected shipbuilder with the following request, in this case for *Hermes* in July 1943: 'I have to request that you will proceed with the construction and completion in all respects of one in number light fleet carrier for His Majesty's Navy'.

The author has been able to call upon former members of the Royal Corps of Naval Constructors on the staff of Director General (Ships), including Charles Sherwin, CB, a former Deputy Director. These professional officers were able to shed some light on the workings of the Department of Naval Construction and the design of aircraft carriers. The 'staff requirements', the opinion of Admiralty Board as to what exactly was required, was the first piece of paper to circulate. This was more than a mere statement of what is required, more than an idealised entry in *Jane's Fighting Ships*, for it contained various restrictions and alternatives, depending on a number of factors such as propulsion, number and type of aircraft and/or armament.

Following this statement, a series of sketch designs was prepared, which was basically a study of the type of ships which perform the tasks required by the Board. Often plans were redrawn several times because of a lack of finance or a change in equipment or perhaps the revolutionary re-designing of aircraft, such as the introduction of the jet. To a large extent, the designer had to use his judgement and a design which could be moulded and developed was necessary. Very often, it is said, these initial plans did not meet all the requirements of the Naval Staff, who may well have changed in character and composition since the original requirement was issued. Any re-designing would, of course, result in delay and additional cost to the project. A designer always had to keep the Staff's feet on the ground and advise whether or not a particular design or feature was feasible.

The ship's main dimensions were arrived at by selecting tentative figures which fitted together with weight and buoyancy equations. All this, at various stages, had to go to the Board for stage-by-stage approval. Their Lordships were not always realistic about finance and any changes at the top invariably led to a change of emphasis in the design of the carrier. Aircraft carriers had, in any case, a far longer design time than almost any other warship. The design of the aircraft themselves, carried out in a similar way, determined the equipment to be carried and the size and shape of the carrier, especially the hangar decks. The development of the fixed-wing aircraft carrier followed closely the increase in size and weight of the aircraft which it carried. In this connection, many designers and constructors felt that it was the development of large naval aircraft which eventually killed the fixed-wing carrier in the Royal Navy; we just could not afford larger and larger ships, especially in the near-sighted minds of certain politicians.

Even in the days of a mixed RAF/RN aircrew, although there may have been a controversy at the operational level as to who should control the carriers or where they should go tactically, there was not much interference in the actual design. In an aircraft carrier, the need for the flight deck to be able to cope with the aircraft embarked, played a fundamental part in the actual overall dimensions. The advent of the two-engined aircraft after World War 2 had a major influence on the design staff—the aircraft would need more room! Once confirmed on the drawing board that all the important topside features, the flight deck equipment, bomb lifts, aircraft lifts, would fit in above the all important hangar (or hangars in the case of larger carriers), the rest would follow. Naturally the wartime influence was considerable, but the early designs did not have that much in the way of previous experience to work on. *Ark Royal III*, a very successful inter-war design, was a one-off and contained two large hangars which could cope with a large number of aircraft at that time.

There were so many features to be considered and all the plans, drawings and calculations were checked and re-checked, amended and altered many times before the new ship's statement of particulars, together with costs, could be submitted to their Lordships. After deliberation, the Board would approve the drawing of large scale and detailed plans showing armour, machinery, power supply and distribution. Close contact was maintained with the various departments both at Bath, where Director General (DG) Ships had his establishment, and Whitehall. Documents were prepared and a competent and usually experienced shipbuilder chosen. Several companies figured prominently in the building of the great British fixed-wing aircraft carriers—Vickers-Armstrong at Barrow, Swan Hunter on Tyneside and Cammell Laird at Birkenhead.

Political problems often interfered, for better or worse (usually the latter) in carrier designs. For example, the building of the 'hangar and a half' fleet carriers *Implacable* and *Indefatigable*, was delayed by a directive in 1940, from the Prime Minister, Winston Churchill, who required that all shipyards should concentrate on the building of destroyers and other escort warships, so badly needed in the Battle of the Atlantic against the German U-Boat menace. *Illustrious, Victorious* and *Indomitable* were also on the stocks at this time and they were completed in May 1940, May 1941 and August 1941 respectively.

With the placing of a design contract, the shipbuilder and the main machinery contractor made a large contribution to the detailed design work. DG Ships and

Indomitable *was the last of the original* Illustrious *group with the more limited hangarage space. The whole class was a classic example of how well a mighty warship could look. This photograph shows* 'Indom' *at sea with Sea Hurricane fighters ranged on outriggers aft of the island* (Fleet Air Arm Museum).

After leaving the shipyard of Harland and Wolff, Formidable *is resplendent in her new camouflage colours but is as yet without any aircraft embarked. She spent most of her war service in the East Indies and Far East, apart from a period with Force H (1943) and the Home Fleet (1944). She was eventually scrapped in November 1953* (Harland & Wolff).

other departments provided expertise and were able to interpret the requirements of the Admiralty. Gradually more and more detail was produced and where necessary (or possible) adjustments were made to suit new and ever-changing circumstances.

Carrier designs can be said to have been trade-offs between aircraft and accommodation, especially for the aircrews. The '1½ Hangar' fleet carriers had to be such to allow for more accommodation for the large number of aircrew then in squadrons—pilot, observer(s) and telegraphist airgunner(s). Another debate which raged through the main life of the fixed-wing aircraft carrier, was whether or not to have armoured decks, bulkheads, etc. The US Navy was initially against such additional top-weight, but the advantages against bomb damage (eg, *Illustrious* in the Mediterranean) and later kamikaze attack (eg, *Formidable* back in action in hours after a hit in the Pacific) altered their opinion. Subsequently they designed and built a hybrid version of the armoured fleet carrier.

The US designs had a normal hull (armoured deck and belt), superstructure and hangar. This allowed the use of side lifts and the accommodation of a large number of aircraft. USN aircraft could even be run up in the hangar during maintenance without incapacitating everyone! British designs were based on a full hangar complement only and aircraft could not be run up in the hangar leading, one suspects, to a lower serviceability rate. The aircraft were, however, afforded a far greater protection against the enemy and the elements; fire fighting was also made easier in 'closed' hangars. In later years, there was another trade-off developing, that between 'open' (USN) and 'closed' (RN) designs. The light fleets, were, for example, still built with closed-type hangars.

In the middle of the war, the need for large carriers led to the design requirements being issued for a large class of carrier. The first two designs, *Gibraltar* and *Malta*, were planned with an open sided hangar in mind, plus an armoured deck and 'battleship' type armoured belts. Unfortunately these ships were cancelled before any real development could take place, although both *Ark Royal IV* (temporarily) and *Hermes* were later built with deck-edge lifts in the semi-open fashion.

The larger the carrier being designed and built, the greater the changes thrust upon the builders because of the developments, usually rapid, in naval air warfare and the general situation. Several carriers were practically built and then temporarily left, only to be completed when the technical changes had taken place. For example, *Hermes II* was, as we have seen, ordered in 1943, but her White Ensign was not finally hoisted until November 18 1959!

Not only did ships, especially aircraft carriers, take a long time to build, but they invariably seemed to need a major reconstruction at some time during their life. One only has to think of *Victorious* (1950-58), *Eagle* (1959-64) and *Ark Royal* (1967-70). These actual reconstructions were very similar to the original designs in terms of procedures and planning problems. Perhaps the most important element in any reconstruction was whether it could be carried out in time and within the budget allowed. Every single operation had to be planned in detail, time given and money allocated.

The ship was taken to sea to shake down the major components and this was a particularly testing time. *Ark III*, when on initial trials, nearly lost a rudder, but being, unusually, a three screw ship, she regained the builders' wharf. There followed a rather interesting discussion between the yard and the overseer! Naval constructors also produced instructions, suggestions and procedures in the event of mishaps at sea. The famous 'don't let any water into the ship, because that's what the enemy wants to do' (which had led, some people think, to the total loss of the *Ark Royal* off Gibraltar in 1941) was later disobeyed by the Captain of *Indomitable* off Italy during the Sicily landings and the carrier was saved to fight another day, by retiring to Virginia, USA, on an even keel.

The reason for the island superstructure being on the starboard side of the flight deck has intrigued people for some time, but the answer seems to be quite simple. It is apparently the 'natural' way round, as the early naval flyers told the Admiralty, when aircraft have a left-handed circuit pattern.

Chapter 4

New aircraft—old ideas

The development of Naval aircraft did not proceed as rapidly as their land-based counterparts between the wars. In real terms the performance of the Fairey Swordfish (entering service in July 1936) and the Fairey IIIF (1928) was almost identical, yet the latter's design had begun with the IIIC model during the final year of World War 1, and the former did not leave front-line service with the RN until 1945.

Much of the blame for this sad state of affairs can be placed firmly on the desks of the Air Ministry who, in the years 1924-37, had control of the Fleet Air Arm. Yet despite its apparent obsolescence the Fairey Swordfish, or TSR II as it was originally known, was to become the most famous naval aircraft of all time. The 'Stringbag'* as a London newspaper called it, on its introduction, was a superb deck landing aeroplane and is credited with destroying more enemy shipping than any other Allied type. It had already been noted that the Swordfish did not finish its front-line carrier until 1945, but it is not widely known that the Admiralty considered the design, by the normal run of things, to be obsolete by 1939! Another remarkable fact about this Fairey design was that it replaced its own replacement, the Fairey Albacore.

By September 1939, when the Nazi hordes began their conquest of Europe, there were 13 operational Swordfish squadrons in the Fleet Air Arm, the type having replaced those stalwart designs of Messrs Blackburn—the Shark and the Baffin, and Fairey's own forerunner, the Seal. As late as 1943, two further marks of the Swordfish had been introduced with strengthened wings for rocket

---

* *The Stringbag Song* (Tune: *My Bonnie lies over the Ocean*) From: *The FAA Songbook.*

My Stringbag flies over the ocean,
My Stringbag flies over the sea,
If it weren't for King George's Swordfish,
Where the hell would the Royal Navy be?
  Stringbag, Stringbag
  Oh, bring back my Stringbag to me, to me,
  Stringbag, Stringbag,
  Oh, bring back my Stringbag to me.
At Taranto and chase of the Bismarck,
In the battle of Cape Matapan,
'Twas the fish from the Swordfish that fixed 'em,
And those who could run, how they ran'.
  Stringbag, Stringbag,
  etc etc.

Known variously as the TSR II, the Stringbag and the Swordfish, this versatile aircraft is easily the most famous naval aeroplane of all time. Involved in all the early major actions including the Bismarck *operation and Taranto, the Fairey Swordfish won the hearts of all who flew in them. This flight is from 813 Squadron embarked in* Eagle *from 1937–40; K8400 is the squadron commander's aircraft* (H. Liddle).

projectiles and even RAF Coastal Command used them during the D-Day landings. Besides the Coastal Command units and training squadrons equipped with the Swordfish, 26 different operational naval air squadrons operated the aeroplane, including 860 Squadron, Royal Netherlands Navy. This unit, mainly engaged in operations aboard merchant aircraft carriers (see Chapter 8), was one of nine squadrons still flying 'Stringbags' on VE-day.

By 1938, two years after 825 Squadron had taken their mounts aboard *Glorious*, the Fairey Swordfish was the only torpedo-bomber in the Fleet Air Arm, equipping the following carrier units: 810 Squadron embarked in *Ark Royal*; 811 Squadron embarked in *Courageous*; 813 Squadron embarked in *Eagle*; 814 Squadron embarked in *Ark Royal*; 816 Squadron embarked in *Furious;* 818 Squadron embarked in *Furious*; 820 Squadron embarked in *Ark Royal*; 821 Squadron embarked in *Ark Royal*; 822 Squadron embarked in *Courageous*; 823 Squadron embarked in *Glorious*; 824 Squadron embarked in *Eagle*; 825 Squadron embarked in *Glorious*.

It was not until April 1940 that the venerable biplane saw action when 816 and 818 Squadrons, from *Furious*, carried out the first aboard torpedo-strike of the war, off the Norwegian coast. Only one hit was recorded on the German destroyers attacked, but it was a clear lesson as to what could be expected from the 138 mph (222 kph) biplane. Later, in the Mediterranean, the aircraft had to be used against Britain's ally during the campaign to prevent the magnificent and powerful French Fleet from falling into the hands of the Germans at Oran in French North Africa. 810 and 820 Squadrons flying from *Ark Royal* crippled the mighty battleship *Dunkerque*, again showing the way for a massed strike against enemy warships, whilst the fleet was safely out of range. A lesson, in fact, which modern politicians should be, but in reality do not seem to be, aware of today. Only weeks later, *Eagle*'s 813 Squadron was deployed ashore whilst

The fleet's first eight-gun fighter aircraft was the Fairey Fulmar and, although slow by comparison with the Axis day-fighters of the time, it was nevertheless far superior to its predecessors. In the hands of pilots like Charles Evans, Donald Gibson and Duncan Lewin, the RN's Fulmar squadrons gave the FAA a chance to hit back (Fleet Air Arm Museum).

their parent carrier underwent routine maintenance in Alexandria, Egypt. It was the time, August 1940, of great happenings in the Libyan desert, when the British 8th Army was pushing back the Italian forces. Led by a Royal Marines' pilot, Captain Oliver Patch, three Swordfish attacked and sank two submarines, a depot ship and a destroyer—four ships sunk with three torpedoes!*

In further chapters of this book, the Swordfish will appear again and again, especially in connection with its part in the Battle of the Atlantic, but what was it like to fly this most famous of naval aircraft? Former Lieutenant Commander Cyril Poutney replies, 'The Swordfish was a thoroughly reliable machine and indeed it had to be with but a single engine, the very trustworthy Bristol Pegasus radial, for flying hours on end at most times over the sea in all kinds of weather and but the deck of a carrier on which to land. As a pilot I found the Swordfish very pleasant and in general it could be well balanced for ease of flying control, though not a machine for "hands off" steadiness for more than a few moments at the most.

'I was returning to the *Ark Royal* with 816 Squadron after we had been on a fruitless search for some supposed Italian Naval ships in the Mediterranean. We were all armed with a torpedo and after extending our flying time to the utmost limit, it was almost dark. As matters became really urgent *Ark* broke radio silence to give us a bearing to return to the carrier and some pilots jettisoned their "tin fish" when they switched over to reserve on their petrol supply. I held on to mine and must count myself lucky because after landing on the deck in the dark, my engine stopped, having run out of fuel, and I could not taxi forward when

---

* It was later established that only two Italian warships had been destroyed at Bomba; a considerable propaganda coup had, however, been scored.

the crash barrier (the likeness of a large tennis net but made of steel wire), was lowered.'

Stories of the Swordfish's long sea legs are well known and it seems that on many occasions the aeroplane remained airborne for longer than the handbook said it should. One such incident took place during an anti-raider sweep by a Swordfish from *Eagle* in early 1941. Having passed through the Suez Canal, the carrier began sweeps at long range whilst on course for South Africa. Gordon Lambert started his Naval career at Ganges as a boy seaman and by 1941 was assigned to *Eagle* as a TAG. In the May 1977 edition of *TAGS*, the journal of the Telegraphist Air Gunners Association, he recalls the episode.* '. . . the Swordfish sighted a German supply ship almost at the farthest point of his patrol, the TAG, having made a sighting report, was told to shadow until a relief aircraft could take over. Eventually he returned to the ship long after his fuel supply should have been exhausted. On catching the arrester wire his engine cut out!'

This episode also illustrated another facet of the Swordfish—its ability to take 'punishment'. Apparently, the relieving aeroplane went rather too near the German vessel and had one of his wings almost completely shot away by the German gunners. As Gordon Lambert put it: 'Such was the wonder of the Swordfish that it made the return to the ship quite easily'.

As nimble and sleek as the Hawker Nimrod was, it had been, by 1938, in service for six years and its 195 mph (313.8 kph) speed was far below that of contemporary landplanes such as the RAF's Hurricane or the Luftwaffe's Messerschmitt Bf109. In 1938 then, the RN were given 38 navalised Gloster Gladiator biplane fighters, plus another 60 specially constructed Sea Gladiators to replace both Nimrods and Ospreys with the fleet. This was due to delay in receiving the two-seat Fairey Fulmar monoplane eight-gun fighter—a makeshift design needed to combat the growing menace of the land-based high performance fighter. It was not until February 1939, just a little over six months before the beginning of World War 2, that 801 Squadron received the Sea Gladiator for trials before embarking in *Courageous* that May. In later months, until replaced by the Grumman Martlet (the first of the American designed fighters to equip the Fleet Air Arm), the type was embarked in *Furious* (804 Squadron), *Glorious* (802 and 804 Squadrons), *Eagle* (813 Squadron)†, and *Illustrious* (813 Squadron)†. The Sea Gladiator's carrier-borne operations were mainly concentrated over Norway and in the Mediterranean, where its 245 mph (394.2 kph) speed gave the Fleet Air Arm's pilots a fair chance of scoring against the faster and more modern German and Italian fighters. It was, at best, though, a stop-gap arrangement.

The monoplane made its first appearance in the ranks of the RN in November 1938, when three Blackburn Skua dive-bombers/fighters of 800 Squadron, embarked for trials in the new British carrier, *Ark Royal*. This 225 mph (362 kph) two-seat aircraft was not without its teething troubles but it provided valuable monoplane experience for the Fleet Air Arm, which until then had been flying biplanes in the shape of the Hawker Nimrod, Hawker Osprey and the beautiful Gloster Sea Gladiator. To the Skua goes the distinction of the destruction of the first enemy aircraft to be destroyed by the Fleet Air Arm in

---

* Reprinted by kind permission of the Editor, Jack Bryant, himself a TAG during World War 2.
† 813 Squadron also operated Fairey Swordfish at this time.

The Royal Navy's first monoplane was the Blackburn Skua and the first squadron embarked in Ark Royal (III) *in May 1939. 803 Squadron later took part in the raid on and sinking of* Königsburg *off Norway, the first sinking of a warship by dive bombing. Although it performed well until the arrival of the Fairey Fulmar and Grumman Wildcat, the Skua was really outclassed as a fighter, even before the war started. Much of the credit for its successes off Norway and in the Mediterranean must therefore go to its aircrew* (Rear Admiral Cambell).

World War 2, a Dornier Do 18 flying-boat claimed by 803 Squadron which was operating from *Ark Royal* near Norway and the warship, *Konigsberg*, sunk by aerial dive-bombing. *Ark Royal* also provided the base for 800 Squadron to attack the French battleship *Richelieu*—known to FAA air crew as 'The Cardinal'—to prevent her falling into enemy hands in French West Africa.

Although designed as a dual role aircraft, it was used to good effect as a fighter in the Mediterranean by the FAA. Vice Admiral Sir Richard Smeeton, then a Lieutenant, had command of 800 Squadron in *Ark (III)* during the days of the air operations against the Italians in the Western Mediterranean and the actions against the Vichy French in Africa. He recalls that the aircraft was mainly used for fighter patrols of 1-3 hours duration, a role which he had been used to when flying with 804 Squadron's Gladiators from Orkney and *Glorious* so, when the occasional dive-bombing task came along, the squadron's aircrew were not fully worked up in the role. At Dakar, when the fleet was ordered to support the Free French and attack 'The Cardinal', the Skuas' bombs all fell wide of the mark and this could be directly attributed to the lack of practice during the passage to the target and to the fact that they were only launched for fighter patrols. At Spartivento, it was the same story when the Skuas attacked an Italian cruiser, but afterwards the Admiralty woke up to the deficiency and ordered some practice—much to the relief of Dick Smeeton. 800 Squadron did, however, achieve notable success against Italian aircraft, particularly flying boats and other maritime reconnaissance types.

In order to increase the time available to the Skua patrols, several night flying tests were initiated so that a flight could return to the carrier after dusk. As CO, Smeeton elected to carry out much of this work which he concludes was rather daft 'because it always meant that I was the last to be recovered from the last patrol!'. The Skua only equipped three carrier-borne squadrons in two carriers, *Ark Royal* (800, 801 and 803 Squadrons) and *Furious* (801 Squadron), but it was a step in the right direction. Further in the right direction was the Fairey Fulmar, the first eight-gun fleet fighter to reach the RN. Although this type represented a leap-forward in technology for the Fleet Air Arm, the needs of a fleet fighter to have extended endurance and a second seat for an observer or TAG (depending on the mission) meant that the Fulmar's speed was considerably less than the corresponding RAF types like the Hurricane. However, the type in the hands of fighter aces like Charles Evans, succeeded in destroying 112 enemy aircraft in its two years of first line operational service (1940-42).

Initial trials were carried out aboard *Illustrious*, herself new to the RN, and the Fulmar was found to be a good deck-landing aircraft although, due to its weight, good use was made of the accelerator for launching. 806 Squadron took its newly delivered Fulmars (together with a few Skuas) to *Illustrious* for the carrier's work-up period in Bermuda and later, with an all-Fulmar Squadron, the carrier went to the Mediterranean. Other Fulmar Squadrons and their respective carriers were: 800 in *Furious/Indomitable*; 800X* in *Furious*; 800Y* in *Argus*; 800Z* in *Victorious/Indomitable*; 803 in *Formidable*; 804 in *Eagle/Argus/Furious*; 806 in *Illustrious/Formidable/Indomitable*; 806B in *Illustrious*; 807 in *Furious/Ark Royal/Argus/Eagle/Indomitable/Hunter/Battler*; 808 in *Ark Royal/Biter*; 809 in *Victorious*; 813 in *Campania/Nairana/Vindex*†; 884 in *Victorious*; 893 in *Formidable*; 784 in *Campania* (for training).

Fulmars were involved in many epic carrier operations, including the Malta convoys (where 800X-Z Flights led RAF Hurricanes to Malta), the hunt for the German pocket-battleship *Bismarck*, Norway, the 'Torch' landings, Taranto and later during the Russian convoys. The advent, later in the war, of the night fighter led to the conversion of several Fulmars to the nocturnal role. Three special flights were formed as part of 784 Squadron and the aircraft deployed to the British-built escort carriers *Campania, Nairana* and *Vindex*. The former used the Fulmar in 1944/45, as an element of 813 Squadron and it was on a Russian convoy sortie that the Fulmar flew its last operational sortie, in February 1945. The front-line day fighter tasks of the type had been taken over by the Seafire by the end of 1942.

Vice Admiral Sir Donald Gibson, KCB, DSC, JP, specialised as a pilot in the Royal Navy in 1938, and found himself as a Lieutenant and Senior Pilot of 803 Squadron (*Formidable*) in the Mediterranean during the hectic battles of 1941. Despite several near squeaks and a crash-on-deck after combat with Italian torpedo-bombers, whilst flying the Fulmar, he remembers it with a glow of affection. 'We were very fond of the aeroplane, even if it wasn't that fast. It certainly couldn't catch a 109‡ but was effective against Heinkel bombers and some of the Italian aircraft.' In the hands of pilots like Gibson and Charles Evans, the Fulmar did provide the fleet, especially in the Mediterranean theatre, with some form of air defence. In the hands of a good pilot, speed is not necessarily the major factor! The next Fairey naval fighter, the Firefly, showed the lineage of the Fulmar, and this was undoubtedly the manufacturers

---

* Formed to act as navigation leaders.
† In a night fighter role.
‡ The Messerschmitt Bf109 was the standard Luftwaffe day-fighter at this time.

Used mainly from cruisers as a fleet spotter and later as an air-sea rescue aircraft, the Supermarine Walrus amphibian was used with great gallantry from carriers to rescue downed aircrew. This particular example is the first to see service and is flown by Lieutenant Commander Caspar John (later Admiral of the Fleet and First Sea Lord) (Rear Admiral Cambell).

replacement ideal. In the event, several other types actually replaced the Fulmar in front-line service, before the Firefly I was ready for operations in 1944.

The last of the first generation of new types to equip the Fleet Air Arm in the late 1930s/early 1940s was the Supermarine Walrus amphibian. This single-engined biplane was mainly used on catapult duties from the RN's capital ships. It was possible, however, to land a Walrus on the deck of a carrier and, as early as April 1940, the type had been deployed in *Ark Royal* during the ill-fated Norwegian campaign. Several hundred pilots owe their lives to this rugged 95 mph (153 kph) aircraft, known to all and sundry as the 'Shagbat' especially during the operations against Japanese-held islands in the East Indies, when more than once a Walrus alighted on an inland lake to rescue downed carrier aviators.

*   *   *

With only a few months of war experience, it was apparent to the Admiralty that there was a high priority need for fighters to defend the fleet on equal terms with the attacker. The obvious answer was to adapt existing aeroplanes for carrier use. The Air Ministry initially made available some war-weary Hawker Hurricanes for adaptation. The first of the so-called Sea Hurricanes was delivered for service with 880 Squadron in January 1941. The squadron embarked in *Furious* six months later, making the Sea Hurricane the first single-seat monoplane fighter in the RN and, until 1942 when the Supermarine Seafire appeared on the scene, it was the fastest. Some immediately went to CAM-Ships (Catapult Armed Merchant Ships) and these were designated Sea Hurricane 1As (or 'Hurricats'). The Mark 1B was the first deck landing variant, it was followed by the 1C (with 20 mm cannon), the improved 11C and the Canadian-built

XIIA. Between January 1941 and August 1943, about 800 were delivered to the FAA and the aircraft achieved considerable fame in the defence of Atlantic and Russia-bound convoys.

During the defence of Convoy PQ18 (the one after the ill-fated PQ17 to Russia), Sea Hurricanes of 802 and 883 Squadrons destroyed five enemy aircraft and damaged 17 more, whilst losing four of their own number. So it can be seen that their impact was quite considerable, despite being superseded by more advanced types. In the Mediterranean, Sea Hurricanes flying from fleet carriers contributed to the relief of Malta. The 'Pedestal' operations (see Chapter 8) in 1942 was remarkable for many things, including the destruction, by Lieutenant R.J. Cork, DSO, DSC, RN, of three Junkers Ju88s and three Cant Z1007 aircraft—part of the total tally of 39 enemy aircraft downed by the fleet's fighters. Cork later became leader of the 15th Naval Fighter Wing (*Illustrious*) and was killed in April 1944. Later that year the Supermarine Seafire had ousted the Sea Hurricane from its place on the fleet carriers and, by late 1943, the aeroplane had left front line service.

Armoured fleet carriers with the Sea Hurricane embarked were: *Formidable* with 806 Squadron; *Illustrious* with 813 Squadron; *Indomitable* with 800 and 880 Squadrons; *Victorious* with 885 Squadron. Escort carriers with Sea Hurricanes embarked were: *Avenger* with 802 and 883 Squadrons, *Biter* with 800 Squadron; *Campania* with 813 Squadron; *Chaser* with 835 Squadron; *Dasher* with 804 and 891 Squadrons; *Nairana* with 835 Squadron; *Striker* with 824 Squadron; *Vindex* with 813 and 825 Squadrons, although it should be noted that several units were composite squadrons.

As good as the Sea Hurricane was, the Admiralty fought long and hard to have the Spitfire adapted for carrier work. Such a legend has grown up, quite rightly, around the beautiful design of Reginald Mitchell, that it sometimes overshadows the particularly bad sea legs of the earlier Seafire Marks. In his book *Wings on My Sleeve* (Airlife Publications 1961), the naval test pilot

The Sea Hurricane was first fleet fighter of World War 2 which allowed the FAA to meet their enemies on equal terms. Teamed with Martlets, they made up the defensive part of a fleet carrier's air group in the 1941–42 period, as in this photograph. Note the Albacores on the after end of the flight deck and the barrier erection gear set into the deck in the left foreground behind the group of ratings fallen in for divisions (Fleet Air Arm Museum).

The Seafire's relationship with the FAA and carriers was one of love and hate; love because it was a truly beautiful aeroplane in the air, but hate because it really should have stayed there and not tried to land back aboard a carrier! Despite the numerous flight deck accidents, the Seafire, like these LIIIs aboard Illustrious *(probably 894 Squadron), provided a more than adequate air defence/combat air patrol umbrella for fleet operations. The second Seafire from the bow has, incidentally, clipped wings, whilst the aircraft which has just left the accelerator is a Fairey Barracuda* (Fleet Air Arm Museum).

'Winkle' Brown says of the Seafire, 'The view for'ard from the cockpit . . . was even worse than from the Hurricane and called for a special technique of approach. The possibility of putting the machine down on a pitching, rolling flight deck had definitely not occurred to the designer and the . . . undercarriage was delicate.'

Initially, 48 former RAF Spitfire Vb fighters were transferred to the Royal Navy and converted to interim carrier standards at Eastleigh and Hamble, Hampshire. Some trials had already been undertaken by the late Commander Peter Bramwell, DSO, DSC, of the Service Trials Unit, with a 'hooked' Spitfire aboard *Illustrious*. The navalisation was very basic and did not even include wing folding. The Seafire 1b, as the RN called them, served with 801 and 807 Squadrons in *Furious* (October 1942-September 1944), although during the Salerno landings 842 Squadron was beefed up with a few from a central pool. In September 1942, the FAA received their first true Seafires—the Mark II and this was followed by the Mark III, which was not only faster but had folding wings. During the Torch landings in 1942, on the North African coastline, between Casablanca, Oran and Algiers, the territory was held by the Vichy-French. Several Seafires from *Furious* were in action and this was the aeroplane's first aerial victory in combat against the Vichy-French Air Force. By the end of that year, six Seafire squadrons had been formed—801, 807, 808, 880, 884 and 887 and they were to be followed in 1943 by 809, 886, 894, 895, 897 and 899 Squadrons.

Escort carriers also embarked Seafires, although with less than excellent results, but despite the deck landing problems, 833, 834, 842 and 879 Squadrons were equipped with the Supermarine type. During the Salerno landings, combat air cover was provided by *Attacker, Battler, Hunter* and *Stalker* and the Seafire was the principal fighter used until a beachhead airfield could be established. This meant frequent, almost continuous sorties, and one squadron's log records, not untypically, that 75 patrols were mounted in just four days! The story was the same in Southern France during Operation Anvil-Dragoon in August 1944 when *Attacker, Emperor, Khedive, Hunter, Pursuer, Searcher* and *Stalker* were deployed to the battle zone. Again high sortie rates were achieved including 201 sorties in 8 days.

Fighter cover for the attacks on the *Tirpitz* in her Norwegian lair was provided by Seafires, together with American-built Corsairs and Hellcats, and 894 Squadron succeeded in downing two 'bandits' during these inconclusive raids. In the Pacific too, the Seafire was active in the final months before VJ-day. Mainly operating with the British Pacific Fleet's (BPF) escort carriers—*Attacker, Chaser, Hunter* and *Stalker*, Seafires were also embarked in *Implacable* and *Indefatigable.* They joined in the raids on Burma and Malaya, as well as the famous attacks on the Japanese held island of Sumatra.

When VJ-day dawned, the Seafire was in service with a dozen front-line fighter squadrons and when the last Seafire powered by the Rolls-Royce Merlin engine left the FAA in 1946, it was the end of an era in which 1,699 Seafires had been delivered to the RN. The sea-going days of the Supermarine Seafire were far from over, and later, the Griffon engined variant* is discussed.

*   *   *

Although born in 1936, the Swordfish's replacement, the Fairey Albacore, was thought by many to be nothing more than a Swordfish with an enclosed cockpit and many observers preferred the latter's view. In fact, several advances in technology had been incorporated, including a windscreen wiper, an automatic dinghy launcher and a variable pitch propeller. Initially used as a land-based night intruder, the Albacore did not go to sea aboard a carrier until November 1940 when *Formidable* left for the South Atlantic with 826 and 829 Squadrons embarked. It was not until March of the following year that real action was experienced when the same squadrons attacked Italian capital ships with torpedoes and succeeded in damaging the battleship *Vittorio Veneto.* There followed operations in Arctic waters and the tropical blue of the Indian Ocean. By mid 1941, *Furious* and *Victorious* had also received the Albacore (817, 822 827 and 828 Squadrons) and eventually the aircraft also served in *Indomitable* (827 and 829), *Ark Royal* (828), *Argus* (828) and *Illustrious* (829). The aircraft contributed to the victories in Madagascar, North Africa and Sicily where *Formidable*'s 820 Squadron provided air cover over the beaches.

Michael Howe, now a Chartered Surveyor, spent several years of his youth sitting in the back of various Fairey Albacores and even surviving two crashes! 'I shall never forget my first experience of sitting in the back of an Albacore', he told the author, 'after being launched from the carrier. I have no idea now how high above the sea we started, but we seemed to drop straight down at least a hundred leagues and I'll swear I could feel the cold blue Med creeping up my legs before we started to pull away from that enormous monster towering miles above us—*Formidable.* However,' concluded Howe, who had spent his

---

* Several Griffon-engined Seafire FXV were in service with the BPF's 801 Squadron (*Implacable*) immediately after the cessation of hostilities.

Flying in its somewhat typical nose-high attitude is a 'Barra' from the light fleet carrier,
Vengeance, *which can be seen below with its attendant destroyer* (Fleet Air Arm
Museum).

Albacore time with 826 Squadron, 'I must report that we duly landed back on
the flight deck with dry undercarriage, in all respects'.

The designated replacement was yet another Fairey design—the Barracuda—
to its distinction the first metal monoplane torpedo-bomber for carrier
operations to have been built in the United Kingdom. Planned to fulfil a 1937
requirement, the 'Barra' had a most unenviable reputation which cannot be
blamed on the design, so much as the tasks it was asked to perform. Despite its
early beginnings on the Fairey Company's drawing board, it was not until
January 1943 that 827 Squadron received its first 'Barras'. There followed a
general re-equipping of the RN's carrier torpedo-bomber force from Albacores
and Swordfish; a year after 827 became operational, there were a dozen front
line squadrons.

Although committed to the battle zone at Salerno, the Barracuda had its most
famous exploits in Norwegian and Far Eastern waters. The former was the
attack on *Tirpitz* (see Chapter 6) and the latter represents its time with the BPF
which lasted until VJ-Day, but not much longer. The aeroplane naturally served
in the major fleet carriers of the *Illustrious* Class, especially *Formidable* and
Indefatigable, but several smaller carriers were also equipped, notably the light
fleets *Colossus* (827) *Vengeance* (812), *Unicorn** (817), as well as 815, 821 and
823 Squadrons embarked in different ships. In this latter role, that of
anti-submarine escort work, the 'Barra' had to be equipped with RATOG
(Rocket Assisted Take Off Gear) to become airborne from the 468 foot
(142.6 m) flight deck of an escort carrier. The Mark II and III variants were the

* *Unicorn* acted as a light fleet carrier for part of World War 2.

Barracudas to see service with the FAA during World War 2, 2,547 being built by Faireys and various sub-contractors such as Boulton Paul.

The Fleet Air Arm Song Book, which is quoted elsewhere in this book, includes no less than 17 songs featuring the Barracuda—such was its reputation. One of the more tuneful songs is entitled 'Fairey! Fairey!' and should be sung to the tune of 'Daisy! Daisy!', and it goes like this:

'Fairey! Fairey!
Give me your answer do;
What is wrong with my Barracuda Two?
Dive-bombing has strained my structure—
I've got a stressed skin rupture,
The rivets pop along the top
And one of them might hit you!'.

These satirical ditties should not let us detract from the many successful operations carried out by the 'Barra', nor did all the crews share the down-hearted feelings of their song-writer colleagues.

'An observer's dream' is how former Sub-Lieutenant Rob Roseveare (812 Squadron in Vengeance) recalls the Barracuda. He continues: 'because of the perspex blisters there were 360 degrees of vision up, down, forward and aft—almost as good as the open cockpit of a Swordfish and far better than the restricted Albacore'. 812 Squadron apparently did not suffer from the dreaded rivet popping, although several aircraft failed to return from exercise. Roseveare would be the first to say, however, that *Vengeance* did not see active service, apart from anti-pirate operations, so perhaps it is not a true reflection of front linc Barracuda Ops.

The third aeroplane designed and built by Fairey Aviation in this second

The early Firefly continued in service after the war and equipped many of the light fleet carriers then in service, as with Ocean *illustrated here. It also saw limited service in the early days of the Korean war* (Fleet Air Arm Museum).

generation of wartime carrier aircraft has already been mentioned in connection with its forerunner, the Fulmar. The Fairey Firefly was designed to 1940 requirements, but its seed had been sown during the 1920s when the Company offered the Air Ministry the Fleetwing as a rival to the eventually successful Hawker Osprey. The Firefly was faster and better armed than the Fulmar but it maintained the low-wing monoplane style which was so similar to its predecessor.

By July 1943, the aircraft was all ready to embark in a carrier, and three months later the first operational unit was formed—1770 Squadron at RNAS Yeovilton. The Firefly was equipped with airborne radar and photographic gear which proved such a useful asset on its operational debut against *Tirpitz* (from *Indefatigable*) when it was used in the fighter-reconnaissance role for which it was so eminently suited. It was to be in the Far East that the Firefly was to excel and it was here that its first aerial victory was scored—Lieutenant D. Levitt, flying a 1770 Squadron machine over Sumatra shot down an 'Oscar' of the Imperial Japanese Navy. 1770's sister squadron, 1772 *(Indefatigable)*, had the distinction a few weary months later of being the first squadron to fly over Tokyo.

One of the four BPF Firefly squadrons operational by VJ-Day was 1790 (*Implacable* and *Ruler*), a night fighter unit. Although in its infancy during World War 2, the experience gained led to an RN expertise in carrier night flying which was only lost with the demise of the fixed-wing carrier in 1978.

Carrier	*Squadrons*	*Carrier*	*Squadrons*
Implacable	1771, 1790	*Searcher*	882
Indefatigable	1770, 1772	*Theseus*	812, 816
Glory	837	*Triumph*	827
Nairana	816	*Vengeance*	814
Ocean	816, 1792	*Vindex*	882, 1790
Ruler	1772	*Warrior* (RCN)	825
Sydney	816		

Chapter 5

Find, fix and strike*

Britain and the Royal Navy were remarkably unfit for World War 2, especially in the way in which fleet tactics with aircraft carriers were concerned. During the inter-war period, as we have seen, not only was the Fleet Air Arm neglected and even ridiculed by the rest of the Navy, but no real fleet action experience had been gained.

The fleet distribution in December 1939—during the so-called Phoney War period—saw the following deployments of aircraft carriers: **East Indies** *Eagle* and *Glorious*—escorted by the old battleship *Ramilles* and the cruisers *Cornwall, Dorsetshire, Kent, Gloucester* and *Hobart* (RAN). **South Atlantic** *Ark Royal* and *Hermes* (together with the seaplane carrier, *Albatross*) were raider-hunting, escorted by the cruisers *Achilles* (RNZN), *Ajax, Cumberland, Exeter, Neptune, Shropshire* and *Sussex*. **Home Fleet** *Furious* was operating in a training role in the Clyde exercise area and also operating anti-U-Boat sweeps of the vulnerable East Coast of Scotland. It is remarkable to consider that the *Furious*, designed as a light battle cruiser in World War 1, was, following the sad demise of *Courageous*, the only carrier with the Home Fleet. In fact during this period she acted as the Senior Officer's ship during an east-bound convoy which brought the first 'Canucks' to Europe. **Mediterranean** Keeping the Royal Navy's presence alive in the Mediterranean was *Argus*, together with the old battleship *Malaya*, the 3rd Cruiser Squadron and an attached flotilla with *Galatea* as its flagship.

The first months of the war were, in reality, far from phoney. The Admiralty were well aware of the risk posed by the Kriegsmarine's U-Boat force and this led to the formation of the ill-fated anti-submarine hunting groups, centred on a carrier, as flagship. Therefore, instead of working with their relevant fleets, the carriers were rapidly transferred to that well-known patch of ocean known to many generations of seamen as the Western Approaches. The tactics were to use the Swordfish and Skua aircraft to assist convoy escorts and other anti-submarine warships in sweeping the seas of German submarines. Without doubt, the aircraft carrier at that time was not suited for such a task, because not only were the aircraft inadequately equipped to sink submarines, even if they were surfaced, but also the Royal Navy only possessed a few carriers to operate with the fleet against the much predicted fleet-to-fleet engagement in the North Sea and North Atlantic.

---

* The Fleet Air Arm motto is an apt title for a chapter about wartime carrier operations!

The war was less than a fortnight old when, on September 14, the Type XA U-Boat, *U-39*, sighted *Ark Royal* off the north-west coast of Scotland and managed, despite the escorts, to reach a firing position. Luckily the torpedoes misfired astern of the *Ark* and her escort destroyers, *Faulknor, Firedrake* and *Foxhound* immediately sank the submarine. *Ark Royal* had earlier received a distress call from a British Merchant ship, SS *Fanad Head*, which indicated that a German U-Boat (actually *U-30*) was in her vicinity. The carrier prepared a strike of torpedo-carrying Swordfish but, before they could be readied, a flight of three Skua from 803 Squadron, was launched, led by the CO, Lieutenant Commander Dennis Cambell, and his observer, Lieutenant Mike Hanson. These three were armed with four 20 lb (9 kg) Cooper bombs plus a single 100 lb (45 kg) depth delay anti-submarine bomb, besides the standard four 0.303 Browning guns.

The merchant ship had reported a position about 250 miles away from the *Ark* and Cambell's flight first made for Rockall and then split up to comb the target area in the hope of finding the submarine on the surface. By this time, the British merchant seamen had taken to their life-boats and one of Campbell's wing men found them and the U-Boat. He rapidly dived and dropped his bombs which exploded without damaging the submarine but blew the tail off the Skua and caused it, not surprisingly, to crash into the sea. The same thing happened to the other wingman! Having released his bombs a little higher, Cambell attacked the submarine with machine gun fire, expending all his ammunition, and then was forced to turn for home owing to lack of fuel. Of the aircrew who were shot down, the pilots, Lieutenant Thurston and Griffiths, were taken aboard the U-Boat which was not badly damaged but, alas, the TAGs were drowned. The two pilots became the first naval aircrew to be made prisoner in World War 2. The Swordfish were met by Dennis Cambell on his way back to 'mother' but they arrived only to find the debris of two wrecked aeroplanes and a sinking British merchant ship. They then directed a destroyer to the scene to rescue the lifeboats' occupants.

A great tactical lesson was learned during this episode, that the Cooper bombs may have been ideal for dropping on dissident tribesmen on the North West frontier, but they were certainly not anti-submarine weapons. A more important lesson was also brought home to the Admiralty by the lucky escape from *U-39*'s torpedoes—don't risk precious carriers hunting U-Boats! *Courageous* was not so lucky when she came up against a U-Boat on September 17 1939. She was already past her prime when the war began and certainly not suitable for independent anti-submarine sweeps in the favourite hunting ground off Southern Ireland. This area had already seen the sinking of the passenger liner *Athenia* on the first day of the war, an act which speeded the deployment of the anti-submarine hunting groups to prevent a recurrence of such a calamity, both by sinking submarines and by attracting their attention away from the merchant convoys.

With two Fairey Swordfish squadrons (Nos 811 and 820), but no fighters, *Courageous* left Plymouth on September 3. On September 17, the ship responded to a supposed SOS from the passenger liner *Kalvistan* and immediately launched a Swordfish strike together with two destroyers—half *Courageous'* escort screen, to search for the aggressor (which was believed to be a U-Boat), a totally ludicrous tactic but one which reflects the low standard of expertise of some non-aviator carrier captains at that time.

Some 500 miles west of the Scilly Isles, after a fruitless search, the Swordfish were recovered by the carrier, which was in the process of resuming its patrol course and turning out of wind, when three torpedoes hit her, dealing a death blow. *Courageous* was the first capital ship to be sunk in the war. The action of *U-29* led to the immediate withdrawal of carriers from the hunting group tactics.

Submarines were not the only German raiders at sea during the first year of the war. The pocket battleships *Admiral Graf Spee* and *Deutschland* (later *Lutzow*) were at large and later two of the eight hunting groups formed to search for them were based around carriers—Force I from Ceylon with *Eagle* and Force K from Pernambuco with *Ark Royal*. As has already been mentioned, *Furious* was training and operating with Canadian convoys, whilst *Glorious* was operating first in the Mediterranean and then the East Indies area. The latter did return to Malta in early 1940 but was destined for a much needed refit.

Argus had been taken in hand and modernised in 1939 to take up duties as a deck-landing training carrier. In November 1939, *Argus* steamed to the Mediterranean and operated from the French naval base of Toulon, but returned to the Clyde with the collapse of France and the declaration of war by Italy in the summer of 1940, being far too vulnerable and valuable to leave there. The more active role for *Argus* must have surprised many observers at the time, because she had been relegated to second line duties as an aircraft target carrier, having been converted as a tender for the Queen Bee drones—pilotless Tiger Moth aircraft.

After returning from the China Station in 1937, *Hermes* was used as a floating new-intake school at 'Yonderberry Trat', above Saltash Bridge at Plymouth until she was due to be paid off in 1939 after what would have been nearly 20 years of service. With the outbreak of war, she was hastily manned by 'pensioners, "wavy" navy men and other so-called flotsam and jetsam', recalls

Charles Stevens, a general service storekeeper attached to 814 Squadron at the time. With the outbreak of hostilities, however, the *Hermes* was to be found escorting the British Expeditionary Force to France, as part of the Channel Force.

Hermes was then temporarily 'loaned' to the French Navy, then operating against submarines and surface raiders from Dakar. After having seen the precise seamanship displayed by Captain Lord Mountbatten, then Captain (D) in *Kelly* in the Western Approaches, Charles Stevens recalls that the ratings aboard *Hermes* did not have a great opinion of French seamanship or fighting spirit, yet others felt that considering the difficulties this was not surprising. As Stevens puts it himself, 'French sailors (at this time) were obviously not very sure of themselves or their Government' but 'their ships were very smart and looked good with graceful lines'.

Now we must turn our attention to another great calamity in the history of the British aircraft carrier—the loss of *Glorious*. This sad event did not, however, take place before carriers had demonstrated that they could operate effectively in support of land operations, given the right tactical doctrine.

The Norwegian Campaign which followed the German Invasion—Operation Weserübung—in April 1940, was the first major operation in World War 2 which involved the RN's carriers in their projected roles of protecting forces ashore and the fleet offshore. The deficiencies in the Fleet Air Arm's fighter equipment procurement meant that only Skuas and Sea Gladiators with RAF Gladiators and Hurricanes, were available. The Axis forces invaded on April 9, but it was not until the next day that *Furious*, the only carrier available, was able to transport her Swordfish squadrons (816 and 818) to Norwegian waters. Although a very elderly ship by this time, she was commanded by Captain Tom Troubridge (later Vice Admiral Sir Tom Troubridge and Fifth Sea Lord 1945-46), one of the new breed of air-minded Senior Officers. *Furious'*

Left *After a long period with the Mediterranean Fleet,* Glorious *was deployed with* Eagle *in the East Indies when war broke out in 1939. Following the loss of* Courageous, *she returned to the Home Fleet and was committed to Norway where, as a result of bad luck and bad management, she was also lost. She is shown here in the Mediterranean* (RAF photo via Lieutenant Commander Richard Swift).

Right *A Swordfish of 814 Squadron over* Hermes *when she was raider-hunting in the southern hemisphere. Despite being scheduled for disposal,* Hermes *was returned to service in 1939 and she served the fleet well until sunk by the Japanese in 1942* (RN photo via Charles Stevens).

Swordfish immediately went on the offensive and, despite a lack of fleet fighter protection, several hits on German warships were claimed.

Ark Royal was in the Mediterranean at this time, but her Skua squadrons (800 and 803) were ashore at Wick and Hatston (Orkney). By an incredible feat of navigation, they flew across the North Sea to Bergen and sank the German cruiser *Königsberg* (8,130 tons/8,260 tonnes)—the first warship of the war to be sunk by aerial bombardment. An ironic ending to this notable episode was that the BBC reported that the RAF had carried out the strike! It was not until a fortnight later that *Ark Royal* and *Glorious* arrived, bringing badly needed fighter support in the shape of those remaining Skuas, plus 801 Squadron and Sea Gladiators* (802 and 804) respectively. By this time, *Furious* has only eight serviceable Swordfish left and was suffering the after-effects of the close attention of the *Luftwaffe*. She went home for some emergency repairs but returned in May to assist *Glorious* in the ferrying of RAF fighters to aid the defenders of Norway, whilst *Ark*'s air group put up a spirited fight.

By this time it was obvious that the Germans would be victorious and in early June it was decided to evacuate the RAF aircraft aboard *Glorious*. With great skill, daring and without deck-landing training, the young air force flyers put their machines down on the carrier's pitching deck. What happened next is the subject of controversy still, but the grim facts are that, for whatever reasons *Glorious*, escorted by only two destroyers (*Ardent* and *Acasta*) and without any search aircraft in the air, made a return voyage to the UK. She was unlucky enough to run into *Scharnorst* and *Gneisenau*, pride of the German Kriegsmarine and a formidable duo with 11 inch (27.9 cm) guns. All three British warships and most of their crews were lost, including the RAF pilots. *Glorious*, which had been such a happy ship in the Mediterranean, will long be remembered as the ship in which the Taranto plans were made.

The RN was itching to avenge the loss of *Glorious*, although the fact that one of the destroyers, *Acasta*, did manage to hit *Scharnhorst* with a torpedo brought a crumb of comfort to the mess decks of the fleet. Meanwhile, *Furious* had been detailed off, with half of 816 Squadron, to make a high speed dash to Halifax, Nova Scotia, with £18 million in gold bullion, while *Ark* was still operating off Norway against the invading Germans. The hazards of German air attack were very grave at this time but, despite this, her air group contributed to the defence of the remaining 'free' areas of Norway. The local commander, Vice Admiral Wells, a former Captain of *Eagle*, reported to the C-in-C Home Fleet: 'Our Fleet aircraft are outclassed in speed and manoeuvrability, and it is only the courage and determination of our pilots and crews that have prevented the enemy from inflicting far more serious damage'.

The carriers had run up against, not for the last time as it would turn out, the crack Fleigerkorps X, and their skill was too much for the handful of Skuas and Sea Gladiators still airworthy. This did not, however, prevent *Ark* from launching a Skua strike against German warships anchored off Trondheim five days after *Glorious* went down. Led by Lieutenant Commander John Casson, 803 Squadron dive-bombed the battlecruiser *Scharnhorst* from 3,000 feet (915 m) whilst 801 Squadron (Captain T.R. Partridge, DSO, RM), although exposed to intense anti-aircraft fire, scored several near misses from low level

---

* One of the Sea Gladiators involved has been salved from a Norwegian Fjord and is 'resting' in the FAA Museum.

bombing. Sadly, eight Skuas and their several aircrew were lost to the ships' gunnery and defending Messerschmitt fighters.

'It is like dropping apples into a bucket from the back of a galloping horse', was the comment made by many Skua aircrew, but luckily this was the last operation in the ill-fated Norwegian Campaign. Many lessons had been learned from what was achieved off Norway. The operation also saw the appearance of the FAA's first fighter ace, Lieutenant W.P. Lucy, DSO, RN, whose success against Heinkels was legendary, but which also cost him his life.

After operating off Norway, *Ark* rejoined Force H at Gibraltar and took part in what Prime Minister Winston Churchill called 'This Melancholy Action', against the French Fleet at Oran. *Ark*'s own Captain, C.S. Holland, RN, was selected as a negotiator to try and arrange either the demilitarisation of the fleet, or its handing over to the RN. At that stage in the war, it would have been disastrous if Vichy elements had allowed the powerful warships to fall into Axis hands. The French refused to discuss the matter and, very reluctantly, Vice Admiral Sir James Somerville opened fire on the anchored warships, whilst *Ark*'s Swordfish spotted for the guns. The batttleship *Strasbourg* with her destroyer screen managed to break out and six Swordfish were launched in pursuit, whilst others mined the harbour entrance to prevent further evasion. The first bombing strike was unsuccessful as was a later torpedo attack, but the latter did prove to the Admiralty that a moving capital ship could be attacked with torpedoes, even if the strike aircraft must be inside the destroyer screen. The July 4 attack on the stranded *Dunkerque* also proved that airborne torpedoes were more deadly against a heavily armoured ship than armour-piercing bombs. Only four months later *Illustrious* would drive the lesson home.

After Oran, there were 'antics' with the Italians and the Skuas of 800 Squadron, led by Lieutenant Richard Smeeton, succeeded in several actions against shadowing aircraft. Somerville signalled *Ark* before the operation that: 'The object of this operation is to test the quality of the ice-cream'. Dakar was the next venue in the Franco-British undeclared war and *Ark*'s aircraft provided cover for General Charles de Gaulle's forces. She was, however, due for refit and left the area in September.

In November, *Ark Royal* returned to the Mediterranean with her new Fulmar fighters embarked and they were soon in action with the Skuas and Swordfish against Italian targets including Genoa and Triso Dam in Sardinia. During the early part of 1941, the scene changed to the Sierra Leone convoy routes in the Eastern Atlantic and it was here that the ship's company worked up for the battles on the convoy passages to Malta. The strain was intense in the Western Mediterranean and several times pilots of the new Fulmars flew for four long sorties a day.

In May 1941 came the *Bismarck* episode which is dealt with in Chapter 6 and then it was business as usual with Force H. She was almost continuously at sea during the summer and autumn, carrying out air reconnaissance and covering vital supply convoys. The Fulmars were frequently in action and once were even mistaken by the enemy for Hurricanes, fighters which were over 100 mph (185 kph) faster!

On the afternoon of November 13 *Ark* was returning to Gibraltar with *Malaya, Argus, Hermione* and their destroyers. A training strike had been organised and a dozen Swordfish were flown off, whilst another 14 were in the circuit waiting for the 'affirmative' to land on. As the last recovering Swordfish

The career of Ark Royal *was to be very short even by the standards of an advancing weapons system like the aircraft carrier for, on November 13 1941, U-81 fired a torpedo into her hull off Gibraltar; early the next morning the Royal Navy's favourite warship had sunk* (RN).

approached the rounddown, a submarine torpedo hit the hull beneath the bridge—the time was 15.41 hours and the *Ark* was doomed. Much has been written about the cause of the final sinking and it is a matter of conjecture whether the carrier could have been saved. Despite titanic efforts by the ship's company, especially the engineering department, at 04.40 hours the remaining men aboard were taken off. Captain Maund watched his beautiful ship go down at 06.13 hours and drew a small crumb of comfort from the fact that only one of the 1,541 men aboard lost his life. The blow struck to the core of the Royal Navy was great indeed, following as it did the loss of the 'Mighty Hood' but as the Admiralty's official history says: '. . . they [the ship's company and FAA personnel] had created that indestructible fellowship which had become the spirit of the *Ark*'.

Besides the loss of the sister ships, *Courageous* and *Glorious*, the first three years of World War 2 saw the loss of *Eagle*, the world's only twin-funnelled fixed-wing carrier, and the destruction of the famous *Ark Royal*. So famous was the latter considered that the Admiralty saw fit to publish an account of her career in 1942 at 9d for 94 pages! The loss of these carriers was offset in terms of warship replacement by a new class of carrier. The year before *Ark Royal* was launched, the Admiralty's Naval Estimates for 1936 made provision for two new carriers. Of 23,000 tons (23,370 tonnes) each, these would be the first of a new generation of armoured fleet carriers. History has called them the *Illustrious* Class after the first ship to be completed, but in fact they were all slightly different.

The ships would have an armoured flight deck, itself the roof of the enclosed hangar and a very powerful anti-aircraft gun armament of 16 × 4.5 in (11.4 cm) dual-purpose guns, 6 × 8 barrelled pom-poms, plus 38 × 20 mm Oerlikon guns for close-in defence. In fact, an original idea seems to have been to use the guns alone to defend the carrier without the use of carrier-borne fighters, which would either not have been carried or else would have been struck down below, beneath the armoured deck.

Illustrious and *Victorious* were launched in 1939 and completed in May 1940 and May 1941 respectively, both built by Vickers Armstrong. Harland and Wolff at Belfast had meanwhile received an order for another, to be called *Formidable* and she was completed in November 1940, so becoming the second of the Class to enter service. *Indomitable* followed from Vickers' Barrow yard in August 1941 with an extra half-length hangar. Two further carriers were ordered after much re-design work and some soul-searching by the Admiralty. Best termed the *Implacable* Class, they were heavier and entered service much later—*Indefatigable* in May 1944 and *Implacable* three months later—almost too late to be of major significance to the war effort in Europe. All six of these beautifully designed carriers remained in service for a short period after World War 2, except *Victorious* which underwent a major modernisation between 1950-58 to equip her for the powerful jets then coming into service.

Their wartime service was in every theatre and their contribution to the war effort is immeasurable. Much has been written about the lead ship, *Illustrious*, and the late Norman Hanson, DSC, describes seeing her for the first time in the Clyde: '. . . that great beautiful ship, serene on a silver sea, a faint wisp of smoke above her island and only the suspicion of a feather of wake astern to belie her apparent immobility . . .'.*

Without doubt the ship's incredible career had become a legend in the Royal Navy, especially with the sad loss of *Ark Royal (III)* fresh in everyone's mind. *Illustrious'* wartime career had started in the Mediterranean as flagship of Rear Admiral Aircraft Carriers (Mediterranean), Rear Admiral Lumley Lyster. Attacks on Axis installations by 815 and 819 (Swordfish) Squadrons followed, culminating in the famous Taranto raid (see Chapter 6) of November 1940. In January 1941, the enemy got their own back and *Illustrious* was singled out for attack by a large force of Junkers Ju87 dive-bombers—the infamous Stukas— and, despite gallant counter-attacks by the ship's Fulmars, seven direct hits were scored together with five near misses. Severe but not fatal damage had been caused; another carrier design would have been sunk for certain but the armoured deck proved its worth that fateful day.

A short stop-over was made in Malta and, despite another direct bomb hit, *Illustrious* sailed for Alexandria, then on through the Suez Canal to Durban, where a full under-water inspection was made. Although not officially in the war, the United States offered facilities for a major refit at Norfolk, Virginia, which was gladly accepted by the RN. This was the first of three occasions that an armoured fleet carrier would be repaired at an American dockyard. In fact, when she left Norfolk in December 1941 she was accompanied by her sister-ship, *Formidable*, which had also been repaired following damage by enemy action in the Mediterranean. The long refit was an opportunity to improve the fittings of *Illustrious* and to catch up with developments in radar and accelerator technology. Once in British waters again, the extra 50 ft (15 m) of flight deck came in very useful for the hooked Spitfire trials, which enabled the forerunner of the not unrelated Seafire to be welcomed into RN service.

Madagascar was to be her next operation and her new air group was embarked in March 1942; Swordfish of 810 and 829 Squadrons plus Martlets and Fulmars of 881 and 882. Despite a serious hangar fire, *Illustrious* launched 173 successful strikes on the Vichy French forces on Madagascar—the first

---

* Taken from *Carrier Pilot* by Norman Hanson and published by Patrick Stephens Limited (1979).

successful amphibious invasion to be covered by the RN. One of her other sister-ships, *Indomitable*, was also engaged in the operation. She carried Fulmars (800 and 806 Squadrons), Sea Hurricanes (880) and Albacores (827 and 831) in support of her sister-ship and the South African Air Force. *Formidable* was also in the Indian Ocean, operating off the Indian sub-continent and her Martlets (888 Squadron) destroyed a Japanese 'Mavis' flying-boat in August 1942—the last fighter victory in the area until 1944.

Illustrious stayed in the Indian Ocean during the summer of 1942 and was again involved in operations near and over Madagascar in the autumn, but this was on a much smaller scale. After a refit at Durban and a cruise to Mombasa (the Eastern Fleet's temporary headquarters), the ship returned to the UK in early 1943. Under refit, her flight deck was lengthened again, and several trials were undertaken before she joined the Home Fleet for sorties off Norway. In August, *Indomitable* was mauled by German aircraft in the Mediterranean and had to be withdrawn to Liverpool, so *Illustrious* took her place with Force H. Her air group now totalled 50 aeroplanes: Martlets (878 and 890 Squadrons); Seafires (894) and Barracudas (810). Besides *Illustrious, Formidable* was in this theatre, at Malta, ready to provide heavy aerial cover for the forthcoming Salerno landings.

The *Illustrious* provided a combat air patrol for the escorts whilst the smaller escort carriers provided a combat air patrol for the beaches. Admiral Vian flew his flag in one of the escort carriers, which provided mainly Seafires as air defence until an airfield could be secured ashore. Controlling the CAP from *Illustrious* were fighter direction officers (FDOs), a new breed of 'whizz kid' specially trained to organise the fighters in their operations away from ship. Lieutenant Duncan Lewin, who later rose to the rank of Captain, was one such FDO and his calm instructions are remembered by many pilots engaged in the

Offsetting the tragic loss of Ark Royal (III), *the commissioning of* Illustrious *gave the fleet a modern and effective carrier with which to hit back at the enemy. After service in the Mediterranean, Indian Ocean and Pacific, the carrier went on to serve in the peace-time Navy. This photograph shows her, surrounded by torpedo nets at China Bay, Ceylon, during joint operations with the US Navy* (FAAM via Robert Taylor).

heat of the battle. *Illustrious* also had an RAF wireless on board to listen to the German wireless telegraphy 'chat' and the operators would deliver a running commentary from the 'chat' of the attacking German aircraft. On one particular, most memorable occasion commentary went something like this: 'There's the carrier we're going to bomb'. They obviously meant *Illustrious*, and as this boomed out on the tannoy there must have been a few hearts in a few mouths on board that great ship, having already suffered at the hands of the Luftwaffe, at sea and in Malta's Grand Harbour.

Whilst under refit at Birkenhead, *Illustrious'* flight deck was extended again to 740 feet (226 m)—an increase of 120 feet (37 m) over her original design. The extra take-off run again proved very useful for the new aircraft she was to embark later. The pattern of carrier air groups was gradually changing in 1943 with the introduction of American types and the need to make use of the vast production facilities was apparent to the Admiralty.

The new air groups were made up of a Torpedo-Bomber-Reconnaissance Wing and a Naval Fighter Wing. In *Illustrious'* case, No 21 TBR Wing (Barracudas of 810 and 847 Squadrons) and No 15 NF Wing (Corsairs of 1830 and 1833 Squadrons), made a total of 49 aircraft. In early 1944, the ship left Greenock for the Indian Ocean to join the USS *Saratoga* for the strikes against Japanese-held territory in what is now Indonesia—the Sabang and Soerabaya raids. Actually, the Barracudas were replaced by Grumman Avengers (832 and 851 Squadrons) for the Soerabaya attack, but the former aircraft returned in time for a small strike against Port Blair in the Andamon Islands.

By the end of June 1944, *Illustrious* had been joined by *Indomitable* and *Victorious* for a strike, with the Eastern Fleet, against Sabang, when four Japanese fighters were destroyed by 15 NFW, whilst other Corsairs acted as gunnery spotters for the 'battlewagons'. *Illustrious* made a swift passage to South Africa to refit and to permanently replace her Barracudas with Avengers

A typical flight deck scene during the first few years of World War 2, as Swordfish torpedo-bombers are prepared for launching aboard a British carrier (possibly Illustrious*). The after end of the range includes Skuas and Fulmars which lends more support to the possibility that the carrier is* Illustrious (Fleet Air Arm Museum).

(854 Squadron). The Corsairs of 1837 Squadron, which had been temporarily aboard, were absorbed into 1830 and 1833 Squadrons to give 36 Corsairs in all. Norman Hanson, who commanded 1833 Squadron at that time, commented that the ship wasn't sorry to lose the Barracudas but . . . 'Fanny Forde [the Barracuda Wing Leader] and his boys were as integral a part of the ship as her rivets . . .'.

The British Pacific Fleet (BPF) came into being in November 1944 and with *Indomitable* the flagship, the *Illustrious* with *Victorious* and *Indefatigable* made up a new striking force. The actions of the BPF and the further part played by *Illustrious* in the final victory is covered in Chapter 9. The penultimate armoured fleet carrier was *Indefatigable* with a career which began with the keel laying ceremony exactly two months after World War 2 began. Despite being launched on December 8 1942, she was not completed until May 3 1944. After two months with Western Approaches Command which effectively shook-down the ship, the air group and the ship's company, she joined the Home Fleet. The summer and autumn of 1944 was taken up with sweeps against enemy shipping in Norwegian waters, including the unsuccessful attack on *Tirpitz* in Alten Fjord known as Operation Mascot.

November 1944 saw a complete change of scene when *Indefatigable* left Portsmouth for service with the BPF where her first operation—code named Lentil—was against the refinery at Pangkalan Brandon, Sumatra with *Indomitable* (wearing Rear Admiral Sir Philip Vian's flag as RAA). The New Year also saw strikes at Palembang and Sungei Gerong. During service with the BPF, *Indefatigable* was attacked and hit by kamikaze aircraft. Such was the design of the ship, the fortitude and skill of the ship's company, that her Captain reported her 'reasonably operational' only a matter of hours later.

With the Japanese surrender, *Indefatigable* anchored in the approaches to Tokyo Bay and, following VJ-Day, she was engaged in repatriating POWs to Australia. On returning home to Portsmouth in December 1946, she was placed in reserve only to be refitted for service with the Training Squadron, 1950-54. In 1956 approval was given to scrap her and she was moved from Gareloch for disposal by the British Iron and Steel Corporation that November. *Indefatigable* was awarded three Battle Honours: Palembang (1945); Okinawa (1945) and Japan (1945).

*   *   *

In terms of comfort, perhaps the best carriers, certainly during World War 2, were the armoured fleets because their armour plating protected the cabins below from the heat of the sun. This was particularly relevant in the Mediterranean, Indian Ocean and Pacific theatres.

These large carriers could also have their divisions which were not conducive to a happy ship. For example, the Class split their officers into a senior and junior wardroom. This was rather divisive and although it did not affect morale to any great extent, it was nonetheless undesirable. In any case many people consider the large armoured deck carriers and their successors like *Eagle* and *Ark Royal* far too big and this led to overcrowded messes and wardroom cabin flats, when the ship was at sea. Yet when the Air Group was ashore the ship could be to a certain extent undermanned—it would certainly feel that way. In the 1950s and 60s many of the officers and men preferred to serve in the smaller carriers like *Albion, Bulwark* and *Centaur*, as these were 'happy' ships. Officers knew the men not only in their own division but in other divisions, and consequently the ratings knew, on a more personal level, the officers in the wardroom.

Of course having an Admiral's staff embarked in a carrier also had disadvantages, especially in regard to overcrowding, and this meant that the staff were not always popular. From the Captain down, in fact, the ship's officers took a slightly poor view of the fact that the Admiral's staff had some sway in matters of accommodation. Normally it can be said that a carrier consisted of two families—one is the ship's company, the men who make the ship tick, the engineers, the deck officers, the deck hands, cooks, stewards, and other essentials which any ship requires—and the second part of the family is the Air Group, from Commander (Air) downwards, through the squadrons, pilots, to the aircraft maintainers. It is a well-known fact, while most of these two groups in carriers mix, there were those who were by convention or by historical reasons opposed to each other. This goes back somewhat to the 1920s and 30s when the Navy proper considered the Fleet Air Arm to be something of a club organisation which did not really achieve anything.

During the war with a large number of ships and a large number of men at sea, a third faction came into the life of many of the larger aircraft carriers, for example, *Victorious*. These ships were used as flagships which resulted in an Admiral flying his flag in a carrier. Not only did this mean more people to feed, but it also meant more staff on board, who would bump out the existing ship's officers from their bunks and cabins. A typical Admiral's staff would consist of the Admiral himself, his secretary (perhaps a Captain) and his Assistant Secretary (a Lieutenant Commander), and perhaps another Assistant Secretary (depending on the rank of the Flag Officer), a Chief of Staff (usually the Captain of the ship concerned), a Staff Officer (Operations) and several other officers, depending upon the exact nature of the task involved. For example, there could be a Staff Communications Officer, in which case he would have Leading Writers aboard as well. These were usually the only rating members of an Admiral's staff at sea. The Admiral himself, of course, would have his own steward, probably a Chief Petty Officer, and a Petty Officer cook, the Coxswain of his barge who would also probably be a Chief Petty Officer. Other staff appointments would be carried out by officers of the ship. This doubling up of roles in situations like the Malta convoys or the Salerno landings, made for rather overworked ships' officers!

Chapter 6

Taranto and victories

'Taranto and the night of November 11th/12th should be remembered for ever as having shown once and for all that in the Fleet Air Arm the Navy has its most devastating weapon'.

Admiral of the Fleet Viscount Cunningham of Hyndhope

In the late 1930s the Fleet Air Arm had abandoned high level bombing of warship targets and specialised in the carrier-borne torpedo attack role. This change of policy was proved right during various operations in the early years of World War 2. The emphasis was still, however, on stopping an enemy ship so that the 'big guns' of the friendly fleet could finish her off. The RN's Swordfish crews had spent a good deal of time practising night time flying, attacks and deck landings; in this regard the FAA led the world at the outbreak of war.

In January 1938, Captain Lumley Lyster, CVO, DSO, RN, had been appointed to command *Glorious*, at that time serving with the Mediterranean Fleet. Although a gunnery specialist by training, Lyster was keen to develop his ship's main weapons system—her aircraft. Using a scheme originally drawn up during the Abyssinian Crisis, Lyster worked up 812, 823 and 825 Squadrons to perform a concentrated and coordinated torpedo attack, by day or night against the Italian Navy in harbour or at sea. It was a time of tension due to the Sudeten-German question when Britain nearly went to war with Germany—it would have been inevitable then for Italy to side with her Fascist friends and hence the plan to cripple her fleet in the Mediterranean (or 'Italian Lake' as Mussolini was wont to call it) was drawn up. In the end, Prime Minister Chamberlain signed, with Adolf Hitler, a piece of paper which was said to bring peace with honour to the world—the Munich Agreement.

In June 1940—Britain's darkest hour—Italy declared war and the Mediterranean Fleet suddenly faced a strong and modern Italian Fleet mainly based at the naval dockyard of Taranto on the heel of Italy. Despite the sad loss of *Glorious*, many of her aircrew had previously been posted to the new fleet carrier, *Illustrious*, under Captain Dennis Boyd, where Lumley Lyster, now a Rear Admiral, flew his flag as Rear Admiral Aircraft Carriers. Here then was the beginning of a winning team. Aboard *Illustrious* were two squadrons of Swordfish (815 and 819) plus a composite unit of Fulmar and Skua fighters (806) and, together with the old twin-funnelled *Eagle*, they made up the carrier force of the Mediterranean Fleet. Under the effective air umbrella of *Illustrious*, the fleet under Admiral Cunningham was able to play a more offensive role in that theatre. A thorn in the side of Cunningham was always the presence of battleships, cruisers and destroyers at Taranto. Yet again the plans for a torpedo attack on the Italian Fleet were dusted off and modified for two carriers to mount in the autumn of 1940.

Initially it was hoped to mount the operation with a strike force of Swordfish from *Illustrious* (815 and 819 Squadrons) and *Eagle* (813 and 824 Squadrons) on Trafalgar Night, 1940. Unfortunately a disaster almost struck when *Illustrious* had a hangar fire, the most dreaded evil aboard a carrier, caused by a faulty overload tank in a Swordfish. The *Eagle* was later damaged by a near-miss during a Malta convoy operation.

On November 5, five Swordfish from *Eagle*, together with their aircrews, were transferred to *Illustrious* and they sailed on a routine cover operation for a Malta-bound convoy. RAF reconnaissance from Malta had established that the whole Italian Battle Fleet, including six battleships, was anchored in Taranto's harbour and inner basins. The excitement and tension grew aboard *Illustrious*. By November 11 all was ready and the specially fitted Swordfish with their overload fuel tanks meant that no TAG would be carried because the observer needed his place in the rear cockpit. The extra fuel which increased the already long endurance of the Fairey biplane to five hours thus enabled the launch point to be far enough away from Italy so as to go undetected. The strike was organised with two pushes with flare-carrying aircraft led by Lieutenant Launcelot Kiggell with Lieutenant Richard Janvrin (now a Vice-Admiral) as his observer, preceding their torpedo-carrying and bomb-carrying squadron mates. The latter was used to create a diversion in the *Mare Piccolo* area.

More eminent sources have described the actual attack in detail and readers are

The twin-funnelled Eagle *was sent to the Mediterranean after the outbreak of war, to reinforce Admiral Cunningham's fleet which also included* Illustrious *in its ranks. Together these two carriers played a decisive role in the Mediterranean theatre, in an operation which made naval history—Taranto. This actual photograph shows* Eagle *as she was—on the China Station 1937–40* (H. Liddle).

Swordfish aircraft in formation. These were the aircraft which effectively crippled the Italian Fleet at Taranto (Charles Stevens).

urged to consult Commander Charles 'Pegleg' Lamb's account in *War in a Stringbag* or the excellent article in *Air Pictorial**. Suffice to say in this account that the Swordfish put up a very good show despite all that the Italians could throw at them. Incredibly only two Swordfish failed to return to *Illustrious* out of the 21 which had departed, on average, four and a half hours earlier. One. Swordfish was even to return with half a wing missing, after a nasty brush with a balloon cable!

What was the result of this attack and how did it contribute to carrier thinking? Three Italian battleships were disabled and considerable damage was inflicted upon other warships and dockyard installations; the projected invasion of Corfu had been thwarted; British morale picked up; but most important the Admiralty and the 'gunnery crowd' at last realised that the FAA operating from carriers provided an ideal mobile striking force and a medium for exercising maritime forces—contemporary politicians please note! On the other side of the world, the lesson of airstrike against a fleet in harbour was studied in great detail by the third, as yet undeclared, member of the Axis, Japan. A final result is the annual Taranto Dinner of the Fleet Air Arm Officers' Association!

Illustrious was replaced in the Mediterranean Fleet in February 1941 by her newly commissioned sister-ship, *Formidable*. The '*Formid*' had been laid down by Harland and Wolff at Belfast on June 17 1937, launched on August 17 1939, and completed in November 1940. *Formidable* voyaged down the West Coast of Africa, round the Cape, up the Indian Ocean, and on February 2 1941, she carried out Operation Breach, a raid against Italian forces at Mogadishu where mine-laying operations were carried out by nine Albacores from the carrier's embarked squadrons—826 and 829. Strikes against Massawa followed and the Suez Canal was temporarily closed to her by German mine-laying activities, so she remained 'east of Suez'.

Also in the Indian Ocean was *Hermes* and between February 10 and 25 she

* October 1967, pp 343-346, by Rear Admiral A.S. Bolt and Captain A.W.F. Sutton.

was operating against Italian Somaliland under Vice Admiral Leatham, when both German and Italian vessels were sunk. Eventually Anglo-Indian forces occupied Mogadishu supported by *Eagle*, which had come south through the cleared canal. Meanwhile, *Hermes* had departed south to hunt for the German raider Admiral Scheer. During the seemingly endless anti-raider and submarine patrols in the Indian Ocean, *Hermes'* 814 Squadron were particularly active and flew almost constant lateral and forward reconnaissance sweeps, whilst on deck a flight, usually led by the CO (Lieutenant Commander 'Lofty' Leward) and the SOBS (Lieutenant Commander Henry Rolfe), was at immediate readiness in case an unidentified vessel was sighted by the search aircraft. Italian vessels were periodically captured (whereas the Germans usually scuttled their ships) including one which kindly 'donated' its piano to the carrier's wardroom. This trophy was only to be lost in the same ocean a matter of months later when it went down with *Hermes*.

As the ship had only one squadron, it was decided to dispense with the *Hermes'* senior observer (the modern day equivalent would have been the Commander (Ops) and the Commander (Flying) whose roles were taken over by 814's senior observer and CO respectively). This was, of course, particularly relevant in the days of a drastic shortage of experienced naval aviators. The next notable naval victory after Taranto was the engagement in the Mediterranean known as the Battle of Cape Matapan. The general situation in the area was beginning to be against the British, the troop convoys were despatched from Egypt to reinforce the hard-pressed Greek forces. The Italians, under pressure from Germany, moved in to intercept one such convoy. On March 27 *Formidable* flew off a reconnaissance sortie which soon spotted the Italian Fleet. Albacores with torpedoes were launched and succeeded in surprising the Italians, but were unable, mainly due to inexperience, to press home their advantage. True to form the Italians made off at speed and Admiral Sir Andrew Cunningham needed to slow them up if he was to bring the reluctant enemy to action. The Fleet Air Arm was his only hope and the Albacores managed to hit

The briefing room scene which preceded every carrier strike operation in World War 2 is typified by this scene in Pursuer*'s ready-room (Fleet Air Arm Museum).*

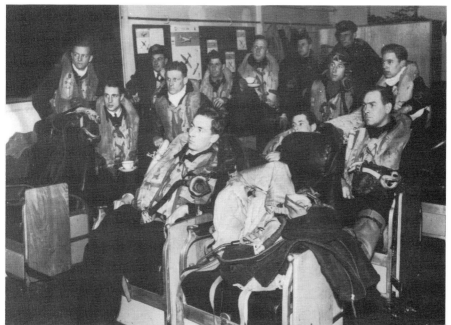

the new battleship *Vittario Veneto* in daylight. At dusk, the final strike launched hit the cruiser *Pola* which slowed and was left with *Zara* and *Fiume* to make a slow passage home. Next day, Cunningham caught and sank them together with two destroyers; there was no loss to the British forces.

Unfortunately, the tide was still turning and the German invasion of Crete meant that the Mediterranean Fleet was hard pressed to cope. A situation not helped by a Stuka dive bomber attack on *Formidable*, rendering her badly damaged. Again, as with *Illustrious* earlier in the year, she was saved by the armoured flight deck. The carrier proceeded to the United States for refit, leaving only *Ark Royal* to hold the fort in the Mediterranean. These operations were almost simultaneous with the famous North Atlantic incident known as the 'Hunt for the Bismarck' from the film of the same name. Here again the British fixed-wing carrier contributed to the destruction of an enemy capital ship. Two carriers were involved in the search and strike operation—the faithful *Ark Royal* and new Vickers-armstrong built carrier named *Victorious* under the command of Captain H.C. Bovell, RN.

Following the horrifying news that *Bismarck* and the heavy cruiser *Prinz Eugen* were at large in the Norwegian Sea and heading for the convoy routes of the North Atlantic, *Victorious* left Scapa Flow with the Home Fleet on May 22 1941. She had aboard an interesting composite air group made up of six Fulmars (800Z Flight) and nine Swordfish (825 Squadron) plus a number of crated Hurricanes destined for the Middle East, *Victorious*' original destination. Because she was not fully worked up, her own air group of Fulmars (809) and Albacores (827 and 828 Squadrons) were not aboard. This lack of air power rather hampered the operation but *Victorious*' Swordfish had an intelligent and keen leader in the shape of Lieutenant (A) Eugen Esmonde, who later went on to win a posthumous VC in the Channel Dash episode of 1942.

Bismarck, by now alone, having sent *Prinz Eugen* running for a French port, was shadowed by light cruisers until *Vic*'s Swordfish could mount a torpedo strike. The attack resulted in only one hit but it caused *Bismarck*'s No 2 boiler room to be abandoned and so reduced her speed. The same day, May 24, *Ark Royal* in company with Force H, left Gibraltar to join the hunt. This was particularly useful because *Victorious* was low on fuel and she had to make for the Clyde to replenish her bunkers.

On May 26 ten Swordfish were ranged for a reconnaissance of the area in which *Bismarck* was thought to be. The weather was particularly bad and it says a great deal for the tenacity of the aircrew and flight deck personnel that any aircraft were able to take off from *Ark*'s pitching at all, yet all were launched without mishap. Sub Lieutenant (A) J.V. Hartley, RN, and his observer, Sub Lieutenant (A) P.R. Elias, RNVR, sighted the *Bismarck* at 11.14 hours. Two Swordfish with long-range tanks were launched to relieve the shadowing aircraft and this pattern continued through the long daylight hours. One aircraft which temporarily lost touch with the quarry was reported to have signalled what was taken to be a British ship and asked 'where is the ruddy *Bismarck*?'. The answer left no doubt in the aircrew's minds—a salvo of anti-aircraft fire!

It was by now imperative that the German warship be slowed so that Vice Admiral Sir John Tovey, KCB, DSO, in *King George V* could bring the Home Fleet into contact. One returning search Swordfish managed to land on despite a pitch of 56 feet (17 m) at the rounddown and the last pair to be recovered had only ten minutes' fuel remaining in their tanks. Fifteen Swordfish were ranged for a torpedo strike immediately after the last of the recovered aircraft had been struck below. The strike was launched in the early afternoon and mistakenly attacked the shadowing cruiser *Sheffield* but fortunately the torpedoes dropped failed to detonate due to faulty pistols.

One aircrew flashed an apology to the cruiser: 'Sorry for the kipper'. Back aboard safely despite the worsening conditions, in which the DLCO had to be tied in position due to the gusty wind, the Swordfish were rearmed and a second strike launched, led by Lieutenant Commander T.P. Coode, RN, with his observer, Lieutenant E.S. Carver, RN. Visibility was still bad but the aircraft were able to locate their target after two hours in the air. Two hits were scored—one on the port amidships and the other on the starboard quarter. It was the latter hit which sealed the *Bismarck*'s fate for it put the rudder and steering gear out of action. Tovey later wrote that 'This was a result which the *Ark Royal* and her aircraft crews had well earned and which ensured my being able to bring *Bismarck* to action next morning'.

Ark's aircraft were up again to see the final action by *King George V* and *Rodney* and they were recovered despite a long-range German bomber's presence which could have been fatal for *Ark* but for the anti-aircraft fire of *Renown* and *Sheffield*. This episode can well be summed up by the words of the Admiralty spokesman: 'There can be no doubt that had it not been for the gallantry, skill and devotion to duty of the Fleet Air Arm in both *Victorious* and *Ark Royal* our object might not have been achieved'.

Mid-war operations

For some months, the Allies had been concerned that the Vichy French who occupied the island might invite Japanese or German submarines to use the base facilities at Diego Suarez to hinder the round-the-Cape convoy routes to the Middle East and Ceylon (now Sri Lanka). In May 1942 the RN provided two armoured fleet carriers, *Illustrious* fresh from repairs in the US and the newly commissioned *Indomitable.* The Air Groups were made up as follows:

Illustrious (41 aircraft)
Martlet   881 and 882
Fulmar   882 (as night fighters)
Swordfish   810 and 829
Indomitable (45 aircraft)
Sea Hurricane   880
Fulmar   800 and 806
Albacore   827 and 831.

For distant cover, the Mediterranean Fleet provided a sister-ship of the mainforce carriers, *Formidable.* The occupation, against some fierce resistance, was a model of what a carrier task force could do in a limited theatre operation. The torpedo bombers attacked potentially hostile warships whilst the fighters provided air defence and supported East African land forces to the south. Initially, there was only a partial occupation, but several months after the first landings, a full scale operation was mounted. It was by now mid-September and the only carrier available was *Illustrious* as *'Indom'* had been hit during Operation Pedestal in the Mediterranean and *'Formid'* had had to take her place. A slightly different air group of 45 aircraft in all was operational: Martlet—881; Fulmar—806; Swordfish—810 and 829.

The later operation was uneventful and, whereas 173 sorties had been flown in three days during the previous May, only 57 sorties were launched in the three days *Illustrious* stayed off-shore that September. For the FAA and the carrier force, this was the end of the single nation involvement in major operations against the Axis for, in November 1942, came the first of a long series of Anglo-American operations—the Torch landings in French North Africa.

Operation Torch was a full Allied landing at several places along what had been French North Africa. The Vichy were still in control of much of it and it was decided that all FAA aircraft would carry modified American markings as the population was still anti-British after the shelling of French warships at Oran. The operation saw the deployment of several British fixed-wing carriers in Force H, the Centre and Eastern Naval Task Forces, together with five American carriers to the west. The assault cover was given by Force H which included *Formidable* and *Victorious*, and it was one of the carrier's Martlets (Lieutenant S.M. Jeram* of 888 Squadron) which drew first blood when a Vichy Potez 63 flew over the assault convoy.

The carriers were equipped with 14 squadrons of Sea Hurricanes, Seafire and Fulmar fighters, besides the Martlets, plus Swordfish and Albacores: *Argus*—12 fighters; *Avenger*—12 fighters, 3 strike; *Biter*—15 fighters, 3 strike; *Dasher*—15 fighters; *Formidable*—30 fighters, 6 strike; *Furious*—28 fighters, 8 strike; *Victorious*—17 fighters, 30 strike. Whilst the fighters flew CAP and escorted the strike aircraft, the Swordfish and Albacores flew anti-submarine patrols against the U-Boat forces thought to be deployed in the area, as well as joining in the strikes ashore.

Furious' Scafires (801 and 807 Squadrons) were seeing their first action, despite its bad performance as a deck landing machine. As a fighter it was second to none at that time. Lieutenant Baldwin's combat with an opposing Vichy fighter has gone down in history as the first Seafire 'kill'. [The Naval History Section in London have now confirmed that, minutes earlier, Sub Lieutenant A.S. Long, RNZNVR, downed a Martin 167 over the sea.] George Baldwin does recall the event but not so much for the destruction of a fighter as for his own lucky escape. The attack on La Senia airfield had been carried out at dawn on November 8 by 807 Squadron which had been bounced by French fighters during the actual strike. Having 'got his De520' Baldwin turned for home almost out of ammunition. A comrade of the downed De520 saw Baldwin making his escape and attacked at 90 degrees, hitting the Seafire's fuselage with cannon fire immediately behind the cockpit and leaving a hole 'as big as the roundel'. Inside, the shell had almost severed the rudder controls and had destroyed the compressed air used for the flaps. Despite this damage, Baldwin regained *Furious* intact, a fact which says something for the skill of the pilot and the ruggedness of the Seafire.

It is not well known but, during the Torch operations, an Albacore pilot of 822 Squadron was almost awarded a Victoria Cross. During an attack on La Senia airfield, near Oran, by 822 Squadron, Lieutenant 'Jock' Hartley, RN, his observer, Lieutenant J.G.A. 'Owen' Nares, the Squadron CO, together with Leading Airman G. Dixon, were hit by ack-ack fire and their Albacore caught fire. Despite their predicament they pressed home their attack and were killed doing so. Strangely enough the only awards were Posthumous Mentions in

---

* Jeram was a Battle of Britain veteran.

Despatches. It will be recalled that only two VCs were awarded to the FAA in World War 2, and one of these—the only 'carrier' award—in similar circumstances in the Pacific only days before the war ended.

From November 7 until the capitulation of Oran three days later, there was much close-up air activity although the interference by surface units of the Italian Fleet which had been much vaunted never materialised. *Furious'* Albacores (822 Squadron) even managed to destroy 47 aircraft on the ground whilst protected by *Biter* and *Dasher's* Sea Hurricanes. The result was the capture of a foothold in North Africa which marked the end of Axis domination and it was remarkable because it was achieved with nominal loss. 'For this operation', recalls Vice Admiral Sir Conolly Abel Smith, then Captain of *Biter*, 'we carried Swordfish and Hurricanes; some of the latter were lashed up to the top of the hangar to be brought into service at the entrance to the Mediterranean when the Swordfish—up to then used on anti-submarine patrols and for recon-naissance—were flown off to Gibraltar. The operation was successful and a number of fights occurred between our aircraft and the French. (I cannot remember casualties but we lost no aircraft and there were certain claims by pilots of aircraft shot down). Operating Hurricanes was difficult due to lack of wind and limited speed of the ship: some Hurricanes dropped alarmingly on reaching the forward end of the flight deck!'

Next in line was Sicily, for so long the launching point of so many raids against Malta and the Mediterranean Fleet. The time was the summer of 1943 and Field Marshal Rommel and his crack Afrika Korps had been driven out of North Africa. It was now time to invade the 'soft underbelly' of Occupied Europe. *Indomitable* and *Formidable* with a combined Air Group of 97 aircraft were to lead the air operations which rapidly established control of the landing area. A rather gallant Italian torpedo bomber did make an attempt to sink the *Indomitable*, the flagship, and, in fact, his torpedo hit the ship aft. Luckily, the Captain disobeyed a fundamental order not to counter flood and managed to get the ship on an even keel and got it back to Malta and eventually Gibraltar for repairs. Rear Admiral Lumley Lyster, who had been flying his flag in *'Indom'*, transferred immediately to the *Illustrious.* It was during these landings in Sicily that the Seafire was confirmed to be a fairly unsuitable aircraft for deck operations, especially landings. It is rather interesting that six inches were taken off the length of the propeller blades locally, and this did not alter the aircraft's performance but allowed it that little extra clearance when making an arrested landing!

With Sicily under their belt, the Allied Commanders now moved towards the Italian mainland and the Salerno landings. The carrier forces would again include two fleet carriers, *Formidable* and *Illustrious* (which had replaced the damaged *'Indom'* in Force H). They would provide CAP for the actual invasion carrier forces made up of *Attacker, Battler, Hunter* and *Stalker*, together with a one-off design, *Unicorn.* The support carrier force was under the command of Rear Admiral Philip Vian of *Cossack* fame and after his experience here, he went on to command the BPF's carriers. His task was to keep 35 carrier-borne fighters over the fleet at all times—a difficult task considering that the Seafire was his main fighter. The Salerno landings were where its nasty habits really came to the fore and it is recorded that 55 damaged their propellers when landing on during the invasion. Nevertheless 265 sorties were flown and only ten machines lost, these mainly due to deck landing accidents.

The main invasion of Europe—D-Day as it is universally known—had very little carrier activity, but the landing operations* in the South of France led to seven escort carriers being deployed: *Attacker, Emperor, Khedive, Pursuer* and *Searcher* (under Rear Admiral Tom Troubridge) plus *Hunter* and *Stalker* with two American CVEs under Rear Admiral Durgin, USN. The Royal Navy's contingent consisted of Wildcats, Seafires and Hellcats, their main task being armed reconnaissance and spotting for the battleships.

*   *   *

The big bogey of the Home Fleet, following the destruction of the Bismarck in 1941, was her near sister-ship, *Tirpitz*, 42,900 tons (43,590 tonnes). Since January 1942 she had been a target for British forces in an attempt to neutralise the threat of her breaking out into the Atlantic and wreaking havoc in the convoy lanes on both ships on the North American and Russian 'runs'. At sea, *Tirpitz* was attacked by Albacores from *Victorious* on March 9 1942, but the enemy downed two of the attackers and was able to comb the tracks of the aerial torpedoes launched at her. The brave attack by midget submarines, when she was in Altenfjord, laid her up for six months until early 1944. Again there was a threat from her mere presence in Northern waters, so a carrier strike was planned and code-named Operation Tungsten.

Victorious and *Furious* with *Emperor, Fencer, Pursuer* and *Searcher* were to mount the attack using bomb-armed Barracudas covered by Corsairs, Hellcats and Wildcats. Anti-submarine patrols were also flown by *Fencer* and *Furious*. The attack, on April 3, lasted only one minute, but the damage caused by the Barras' armour piercing bombs killed or wounded nearly 500 of *Tirpitz*'s company. A further Barra strike scored five direct hits and the battleship was out of action for three months. The attacking forces' losses were slight and the action was one of the finest in carrier history.

Watching high above the assembled fleet was a young Wildcat pilot from *Fencer* which was providing the fleet umbrella to prevent German interference with the launch and form-up of the strike. Now Director of the Fleet Air Arm Museum, Dennis White, who retired as a Commander, recalls that 'it was a beautiful dawn with glorious weather and the departing strike, spread across the sky at different levels, was a magnificent sight, especially as one knew what they were going to do to the *Tirpitz*!'. Apparently one staff officer, in an effort to relieve the tension during the pre-op brief, told the assembled fighter pilots that the main aim of the strike was 'FUB—*F*** up Battleship*'. This thought certainly flashed across Dennis White's mind as he 'flagged around watching the squadrons and the various wings set off up the fjord'. Later in the month another attack was planned to finish off the *Tirpitz* but bad weather intervened. Another strike planned for May 14 actually neared the target before bad weather again made pursuing the operation fruitless. This sortie is noteworthy, however, because reconnaissance was provided by the Fairey Firefly fighter which had become operational by then; May 28's strike was also a non-starter.

The Home Fleet underwent a change of carrier constituents when *Indefatigable* replaced *Victorious*, and *Formidable* joined *Furious* in a new

* Operation Anvil-Dragoon.

A vivid action shot of an Avenger during a shipping strike in May 1945. Typical of escort carrier operations off Norway towards the end of the war in Europe, these aircraft from 846 Squadron are attacking a submarine depot ship. Their parent carrier was Trumpeter (R. Baillie via J. Bryant).

strike against the refitted and repaired *Tirpitz*. *Indefatigable* was on her first deployment having only been completed in May of that year, but she had the advantage of being able to embark many more aircraft than the previous four units of the *Illustrious* Class.

Operation Mascot entailed the launch of 44 bomb-armed Barracudas with an escort of 48 fighters—Corsairs, Hellcats and Fireflies. This time the attack was foiled by the 'bad weather' and wrecked in Kaa Fjord by German smoke generators used to obscure the target. By this time C-in-C Home Fleet, Admiral Sir Henry Moore was convinced that the Barra was not the tool for the job, but nevertheless, *Formidable, Furious* and *Indefatigable* gathered together for another series of strikes between August 22 and 24 1944. Together with *Nabob* and *Trumpeter*, a first strike was launched but fog hampered the operation and the 31 Barracudas were recalled leaving the 53 assorted Corsairs, Fireflies, Hellcats, and Seafires, to strafe the battleship. Two further actions were all but fruitless as was a further mission on August 29. In his book, *Aircraft Carriers**, Norman Polmar maintains 'this [the survival of *Tirpitz*] was perhaps the most striking failure of the FAA during World War 2 . . .'. Eventually, specially equipped Lancaster bombers completed the operation by sinking *Tirpitz* in her fjord with 12,000 lb (5,443 kg) bombs. Although strikes against enemy shipping in occupied Scandinavia continued, the Fleet Air Arm's carrier forces were now on the offensive in another theatre—the Pacific.

Flight deck routines

In this chapter, the air operations of the carriers involved in the various operations mounted in the early war years have been chronicled from the aircrews' point of view in most cases. It is time to take a look at the preparations

* Published by Doubleday in 1969.

for such operations. For reconnaissance operations, like raider hunting with Force K and in the 'Hunt for the Bismarck', the flight would be planned by the Commander Air Staff* who, in the Air Intelligence Office, would brief the observers on the task ahead. If it was to be a dawn launch then this briefing would be at an early hour indeed. The ground crews would also have to rise early and start preparing the aircraft at least an hour before launch time. Depending on the weather conditions at the time, this would either be done in the hangar or on the flight deck.

In the early war years, the FAA had divided up its maintainers into three main categories: Air Artificer (to deal with any airframe or engineering problem), plus the more junior Air Fitters and Air Mechanics. Four sub-specialities were also operated: Air-frames (A); Engines (E); Ordnance (O); and Electrical (L). Aboard *Ark Royal* each squadron had two Air Mechanics per aircraft with a Fitter looking after two and perhaps two Artificers reporting to the Air Engineering Officer.

If preparation work had been carried out in the hangar, the ground crew would bring each aircraft, its wings folded, to the flight deck via the lifts (operated by the engine room department) where the ranging party would take over. This was made up of seamen who would position (or range) the aircraft for the sortie. The pin party would then come forward to chock the aircraft and spread their wings. This could be a very unpleasant business wearing just overalls and gym shoes in a strong, rain-laced wind.

The aircraft ranged on deck were started and run up by the ground crew so that all the aircrew had to do was climb aboard, complete with bags, charts, and sometimes sandwiches. The lead aircraft would come to full power and signal the Fido that all was ready. In turn the Fido signalled the Commander (Flying) and, with the carrier into wind and the wireless masts down, the affirmative would be given. Chocks away and the first of the range was airborne then, until the strike had all flown off, the whole process was repeated. As technology improved and the catapult (or accelerator) was introduced, the procedures were tightened up and the safety of both ground crew, who, on removing the chocks, had to jump for the flight deck side nets, and the aircrew, was greatly improved.

Accidents still happened, and one of the most celebrated must surely be one aboard *Implacable* during a launch of Fireflies in the Pacific. It seems that the blade of a Firefly's propeller 'kissed' the flight deck during a hasty catapult launch and sent slivers speeding into the leg of the ship's 'Little F' (Lieutenant Commander (Flying)), Charles Lamb. Despite a 'peg leg' Lamb later continued in the Service but the incident does highlight the risks borne even by those who remain on the flight deck.

Landing on after a long sortie in the middle of the ocean could also be dicey. The procedure was for the carrier to turn into wind as the ground crew are piped to action with 'Stand by to receive aircraft'. In order to assist visibility the wind was usually left slightly to port—about 50 degrees—so that the ship's exhaust would keep clear of the airspace immediately aft of the flight deck. Unable to see much of the flight deck in the final stages of the recovery, the incoming pilot had to rely heavily on the DLCO for guidance on the way. Although this expert was dispensed with later in carrier evolution and replaced by the mirror landing sight, in the war years he was invaluable. Both pilot and

* Later Commander (Ops).

Not only did carrier aircraft have to contend with the risk of damage by enemy action, but they also had problems enough landing on their respective ships. Here is an Avenger from 820 Squadron (Indefatigable) *having problems with an arrester wire in July 1945. Both the pilot, Sub Lieutenant Leonard Baldwin and the TAG, P.O. Simpson, survived the plane going over the side and being dragged along by the carrier, riding the ship's wash* (J. Bryant/TAGS).

batsman had to be well trained, so much thought and practice went into the whole concept.

Once on the deck, and arrested, the pilot throttled back, then released the brakes to allow the aircraft to drift back with the wind. This eased the strain on the steel arrester wire which the incoming aircraft's hook had caught and allowed it to be disengaged by the ground crew. A director would then signal the pilot to proceed whilst either he power-folded the aircraft's wings or if the machine was of an earlier type, they were folded by the pin party. The aircraft would be directed over the lower barrier and either down the lift or to Fly One at the bow. At the end of the recovery, as the carrier resumed her original course, the aircraft would be ranged for the next sortie.

One or two of the ranging party carried out the role of duty fireman, clothed in asbestos garb, a necessity especially in wartime, during flying operations. Flying from carriers was dangerous at the best of times, but the strains of action resulted in some particularly bad incidents, not only from a crash on deck but from shell or bomb damage. Vice Admiral Sir Donald Gibson, a veteran of fighter operations in the Mediterranean, had a photograph of his original pilots' training course in 1938—only a mere handful of the men survived World War 2. Other pilots, like Captain Eric 'Winkle' Brown, tell a similar story, as do some observers and TAGs.

The awesome casualty figures for the number of Fleet Air Arm aircrew killed in flying accidents or action during World War 2, do not in reality give a true picture of the tremendous sacrifice paid mainly by volunteer pilots. Take, for example, Sub Lieutenant George Cathcart who failed to take off from the *Venerable* in February 1945 in an 1850 Squadron Corsair fighter. Everyone on board breathed a sigh of relief when Cathcart popped up in the wake of the carrier, to be fished out by a destroyer, apparently none the worse for a submarine pass under the ship's keel. Sadly, within four years, he had died of tuberculosis caused directly from his ditching.

As landing speeds increased, the use of the DLCO to bat the incoming aircraft to a safe recovery became an important technique aboard carriers. Experienced and specially trained pilots were used, as here aboard Vengeance *during her period with the BPF* (Captain Neame).

Norman Hanson, a wartime commander of 1833 Squadron, also a Corsair unit, recalls that, in his opinion, less lives were lost as a result of enemy action than of pilot error, and he continues, '. . . far too many young men were put into the game, who were temperamentally unsuited for it: square pegs in round holes. A lot of *too* young men who had no mental stability to fall back on and, as a result, panicked when something happened that they hadn't bargained for . . . . married men flying too carefully, thinking overmuch of their wives at home'.

Deck landing was hazardous enough anyway without the usual mechanical faults which could easily develop in an operational aircraft in wartime. Sub Lieutenant Peter George was bringing his Corsair in for his first deck landing aboard *Venerable* on February 12 1945, all set for a 'perfect' landing, because to his self-confessed amazement, his approach had been 'on the nail'. Suddenly his aeroplane thumped on to the deck, and literally bounced over the crash barrier. By sheer luck, there were no deck-parked aircraft at Fly One, and so George was able to go round again. Neither the 'batsman' nor his assistant, had noticed that the large arrester hook beneath the Corsair's rear fuselage was still locked in the 'up' position. The remarkable 'bounce' was later documented in the war diary of *Venerable* and Peter George says this was his greatest claim to fame!

'Winkle' Brown was not so lucky! Despite testing numerous aircraft on all types of wartime carrier, there comes a time when Lady Luck is not looking. The largest of the British-built and converted merchant escort carriers was *Pretoria Castle*, formerly a liner, then used as a deck landing trials ship. 'Winkle' Brown had the same problem as Peter George—hook down indicated in the cockpit but alas the appendage was still flush to the fuselage of, in this case, a Firefly prototype. Again, and this was really most unusual notwithstanding this account, the DLCO had not noticed the absence of the hook. The

Firefly attempted to jump the barrier and lost its undercarriage in the process, ending up almost over the bow! Fortunately Lieutenant Brown was not seriously hurt, and then perhaps only in pride. It was indeed fortunate for the Royal Navy that he was not incapacitated because he was later to become Chief Naval Test Pilot at Farnborough. Following the relative neglect of the inter-war years, the training of fixed-wing aircrew was put into top gear as it became clear that war with Germany was inevitable.

After learning the hard way during the 1930s, the RN realised that pilots needed as much sea time as possible. DLT, as it was known to several thousand naval carrier pilots, was carried out pre-war in *Furious*. These operations were mainly day-running with embarked squadrons, with a plane-guard destroyer on the port quarter. It was definitely one of the most vital tasks being carried out by carriers in the months leading to the outbreak of hostilities. *Furious* actually continued training new pilots, as well as carrying out anti-submarine sweeps, but all too soon the 'Phoney War' developed into a real shooting war, and *Furious* was detailed for more active service. In any case, trials of new types were becoming necessary and they were carried out in carriers, some in 'work- up', until the addition of *Pretoria Castle* to the fleet in 1943. It was envisaged that she would be replaced by *Illustrious* in that role in 1945/6 and the latter carrier was refitted to carry out the task.

The splendid work of the DLCO has been mentioned earlier in this chapter, but their contribution to pilot training hardly ever reached the 'headlines'. In January 1939, Neville Cambell, who retired as a Commander after the war, joined a training squadron at Donibristle in Scotland. His job was to complete the flying training of the fighter and TSR pilots, culminating in deck landing. He was a flight commander in 737 Squadron (Swordfish), when the era of the 'batsman' was dawning, and it did not take him long to realise how valuable they would be. The trainee pilots would spend hours practising ashore—being controlled all the time—and then they went to *Furious* in the Firth of Forth for their actual landings.

Commander Cambell continues' 'We gave them three runs in a Tiger Moth— the first the instructor did—the second both of us with ''hands and feet on'' and the third the trainee did by himself—that was the idea, but I am afraid after one or two terrible flights my instructions were ''Keep your hands and feet well away from the controls''! The trouble was that if one got too low in the Moth and into the ship's downdraught there was very little power available to pull out. The real value of the Moth was to let them look at the deck and get a rough idea of the approach; the actual handling of it bore no relation to the front line aircraft; I have seen a Moth land and the wheels never moved!

'As I say, I soon realised how invaluable the control officer could be in training pilots—but there were rumbles from the fleet—''No-one is going to tell me how to land my aircraft''—and one Captain, of *Ark Royal* I think, was reported as saying to his pilots that he knew what he'd do if his chauffeur stood on the pavement trying to tell him the best way to steer the car there. This may seem far fetched now but I well remember being called in to the Wing Commander's office at Donibristle—(we were still under the RAF then). It was Jackie Noakes (the inventor of crazy flying displays at Hendon) and he was concerned at the fleet rumours—did I think that this controlling of pilots was a good thing? I was emphatic that it was; I had by then seen numerous occasions on which we had helped a pilot who was doing a poor approach and furthermore we were in a position to wave off one who was clearly in a dangerous position. I had seen at least one fatal accident in *Courageous* which would not have occurred if the pilot had been controlled by a batsman. I was therefore never in any doubt whatsoever of the value of this revolutionary idea. Indeed, to the best of my knowledge, none of us in those squadrons was in any doubt.

'The proof of the pudding . . . when the Germans bombed the Firth of Forth on October 16 1939 it was decided to suspend deck landing training there and the actual work would be done in *Argus* off Toulon. I was one of four or five instructors in the ship. The trainee pilots still did most of their work at Donibristle and then came overland to Toulon for the deck landings, in Swordfish, Skuas or Sea Gladiators. I don't know how many came, but it must have been several dozen and *Argus* was hardly the largest carrier! We had one or two accidents but the only fatal one was a pilot in a Skua who spun in going downwind, not under the batman's control. I do not believe for one moment that this high standard could have been achieved in *Argus* without the deck landing control officer.'

Chapter 7

Trans-Atlantic assistance

The involvement of the United States in World War 2 led to a more rapid development of naval aircraft and their systems than would otherwise have been possible due to the limited facilities afforded to the Fleet Air Arm in Britain. A word or two here about the Anglo-American Lend-Lease Agreement would seem appropriate as so many of our carriers depended on US manufactured equipment during the latter years of the conflict. In March 1941, the US Government pushed through the Lend-Lease Act in the still isolationist-minded corridors of power at Washington. The Act set up an Aircraft Allocation Committee which issued war material to nations which seemed to them to be vital to America's defence. American designs were already being purchased by the United Kingdom as a separate arrangement to Lend-Lease.

The first American aircraft to come over to Britain was the Grumman Martlet (later called the Wildcat) which arrived in August 1940. This 310 mph (500 kph) monoplane was the first American fighter in British hands to shoot down an enemy aircraft and it also came to fame because 802 Squadron took them to sea in the British-converted merchant hull cum escort carrier called *Audacity*; here they soon proved their worth in the hands of pilots who were later to achieve

Abroad Victorious *from where 882, 896 and 898 Squadrons flew the Marlet and later the Wildcat, an unusual system of 'batting' had been developed to assist night landings. In this picture, the DLCO is giving the landing pilot the 'roger' as the aeroplane is nicely positioned for the arrester wires. Note the large gun turret to the right of the picture.*

more fame: Donald Gibson and 'Winkle' Brown. Their role was to protect convoys from prowling enemy aircraft such as the Focke-Wulf Condor and they continued this role throughout the war in several theatres. In 1942, Martlets were embarked in *Illustrious* and took part in the little-known Madagascar operations where this tough little fighter with a wing span of only 38 feet (12 m) gave a very good account of itself.

The Malta Convoys were the venue of Martlet operations. During Pedestal, *Indomitable* was at sea with 806 Squadron, whilst the third member of the *Illustrious* Class to be completed, *Victorious*, operated American-marked* Martlets of 882 Squadron over the Algerian beaches during the Torch landings. Later marks were called Wildcats and were supplied under Lend-Lease and again they proved to be dependable and rugged, serving with distinction aboard the small escort carriers and MAC-ships of the fleet, as well as aboard the largest fleet carrier. In the protection of convoys, dealt with more fully in the next chapter, they made their name in the annals of carrier history, especially during combined anti-submarine operations with Swordfish. The Wildcats provided the covering fire on several occasions, for example, the sinking of U-*U-288*, south-east of Bear Island on April 3 1944 during an infamous Russian convoy run. There seems little doubt then that the escort carrier was their true home and many operations were carried out from those small decks, including the destruction of the last German fighters by the FAA, when, during a strike on Stablenfjord in Norway, Wildcats led by Lieutenant Commander John Bird, were engaged by Messerschmitt 109s, four of which 882 Squadron promptly shot down. A pilot of that squadron during those Home Fleet operations was Lieutenant (now Captain) Keith Leppard and he vividly recalls the great affection with which the pilots of 882 spoke of their planes: 'I can't speak highly enough of the Wildcat', he told the author in conversation, 'it was so rugged and tough that you could tangle with the best the enemy had'.

The Wildcat was supposedly to be replaced by its larger brother, the Hellcat, but as is recorded above this did not actually happen, especially in the small carriers. Under Lend-Lease agreements, however, 1,182 Hellcats were delivered to the FAA during the last few years of the war.[†] It is interesting to note that like the Wildcat and later the Avenger, the British wanted to give the Hellcat another name—the Gannet. Just as, however, the Martlet became the Wildcat, the Tarpon—the Avenger, so the Gannet's nomenclature was standardised to Hellcat. To widen the scope of fighter operations, 74 Hellcats were refitted as night fighters with a radome on the starboard wing to house the search radar. 892 Squadron so formed in April 1945 and, although it did not see action, it embarked in the light fleet carrier *Ocean* for a short spell. True to tradition, however, it was 800 Squadron which first re-equipped with Hellcats in July 1943 and within a few months they were at sea in *Emperor*, a *Ruler* Class escort carrier. The ship operated with the Home Fleet for a while, before joining the BPF where most of the Navy's Hellcat operations were undertaken. The aircraft's maximum speed of 371 mph (597 kph) enabled it to carry out photo-recon-naissance sorties over Japanese-held territory with less risk than some other

* The so-called 'Torch Star'.

[†]Great efforts were made by the FAA's representatives in the US to obtain the best available for the fleet. Pilots of this era owe much to the skill, wit and charm of people like Richard Smeeton who reportedly was prepared to 'stick his neck out' in order to get the 'planes the RN needed.

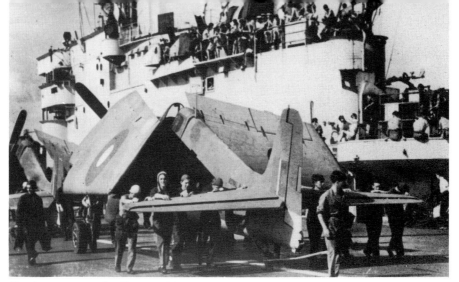

Bearing a strong family resemblance to the Marlet/Wildcat, was the Hellcat, which, although it did not see widespread service aboard British carriers, was nevertheless an outstanding carrier-borne fighter. These two Hellcats of 888 Squadron are being ranged prior to the strike against Pangkalan Brandan and the interest which this operation aroused can be judged by the crowded 'goofers' position on Indefatigable*'s island (Fleet Air Arm Museum).*

types, and 888 Squadron (in *Empress*) became past masters at the task. By late 1944, the BPF's Hellcat forces were as follows: *Emperor*—800 Squadron; *Empress*—838 Squadron; *Khedive*—808 Squadron; *Indefatigable*—1840 Squadron; and *Indomitable*—1839 and 1844 Squadrons.

The war in the Pacific ended before the Hellcat could be fully deployed in British hands against targets over the Japanese homeland, but several escort carriers were in the process of working up for this role when VJ-Day came. With the surrender, eight squadrons almost immediately disbanded and, by August 1946, the Hellcat had left FAA service completely. It should be noted though that one example was overlooked and it remained airworthy as late as 1963! It now rests in the Fleet Air Arm Museum at Yeovilton.

Without doubt, the most famous American-built fighter to enter service with the fleet was the Chance Vought Corsair—the 'bent-wing bastard'. As that name implies, it could be difficult to fly and it was certainly not a novice's aircraft. Yet many young RNVR pilots had their first fighter experience in the 'beast' during their training on the East Coast of the United States. One such young Sprog was Peter George, who as a Sub Lieutenant (A) flew the Corsair in America before joining *Vengeance*. For him 'the main features were the fact that it was a very stable gun platform, in all attitudes; it was versatile, being able to carry out dive-bombing missions and high altitude escorts in the same sortie. I seem to recall', he continues, 'that it was the fastest fleet fighter of the war—it had a wicked punch and was feared by its opponents, and once mastered by its pilots, it could run rings round anyone'.

Supplied under Lend-Lease arrangements, the 1,977 aircraft delivered equipped 19 squadrons, the first of which, 1834, was in action from *Victorious* in 1944 during the operations against the *Tirpitz* in her Norwegian fjord. Like the Hellcat, the Corsair was used operationally on a small scale with the Home Fleet as compared to its time with the BPF. Despite USN carrier-operating problems when deck landing the Corsair, the RN willingly took their allocation

The most numerous of the Lend-Lease aircraft from the factories of America was the Chance Vought Corsair. When it first entered service with the US Navy it was rated as unsuitable for carrier operations. Within months both the US Marine Corps and the Royal Navy had shown that given careful training, the Corsair could easily be deck landed. In fact, most of the FAA's Corsair squadrons were manned and even commanded by volunteers who had flown little else, proving this beyond the shadow of a doubt. Here are three of the 'bent winged birds' from Vengeance, *led by Lieutenant Commander Derek Empson in the Corsair coded 116. Empson retired as a full Admiral, one of only two RNVR flyers to be appointed to that rank* (Captain Neame).

as the USMC had already proved it could be a great success in shooting down the enemy. It was a 'a rugged machine which could take any amount of punishment on the flight deck and appear to make light of it', says Norman Hanson in *Carrier Pilot.* The former Commander of 1833 Squadron continues, 'somehow or other the Royal Navy would see to it that it could be deck landed'. Eventually, four marks were flown by the FAA and, the American Navy's original problems notwithstanding, they were adored by most of their pilots.

Squadrons allocated with the Corsair were all RNVR units which had trained in the United States, although, of course there were a few regular Navy and even Royal Marines pilots. An example of the latter was *Illustrious'* Air Co-ordinator, Major Ronnie Hay. Of the 19 squadrons equipped only 11 saw action—those that did not are marked*: 1830—*Illustrious*; 1831—*Slinger, Pursuer, Glory* and *Vengeance*; 1833—*Illustrious* (amalgamated with 1831); 1834—*Khedive* and *Victorious*; 1835—*Premier*; 1836—*Atheling* and *Victorious*; 1837—*Begum, Atheling* and *Illustrious*; 1838—*Begum* and *Atheling*; 1841—*Smiter, Formidable* and *Illustrious*; 1842—*Rajah, Formidable* and *Illustrious*; 1843—*Trouncer* and *Arbiter*; 1845*—*Puncher, Slinger, Formidable* and *Victorious*; 1846*—*Ranee* and *Colossus*; 1848*—*Ranee*; 1849*—*Reaper*; 1850—*Vengeance*; 1851*—*Thane, Venerable* and *Vengeance*; 1852*—*Patroller*; 1853*—*Rajah*.

Like so many Lend-Lease aircraft, the Corsair did not remain in service for long after VJ-Day, with only 1831, 1846, 1850 and 1851 still flying by Christmas 1945. The first and last mentioned units eventually disbanded in August 1946 and so passed the Corsair from the British carrier scene. The aircraft was, however, flying again from British-built carriers at Suez where 14F and 15F embarked in *Arromanches* (ex-*Colossus*) were in the thick of the air operations, and the Argentine Navy also flew them from *Independencia* (ex-*Warrior*) before the arrival of jets.

One of the most outstanding American-designed aircraft which saw service aboard British fixed-wing carriers was the Grumman Avenger. Originally designed as a torpedo bomber, the aircraft was deployed mainly in an 'iron' bombing role and it replaced both the Albacore and the later Barracuda aboard fleet and escort carriers. As with the Corsair, many young British aircrew went to the United States to carry out their basic training in the aircraft and this was where the first unit, 832 Squadron, was formed. This squadron went to sea in USS *Saratoga* during the Solomons campaign and was later embarked in *Victorious, Illustrious* and the smaller *Begum.* Initial escort carrier experience was afforded by the passage to the UK of many of the newly worked-up and equipped squadrons and, by January 1944, (when the Tarpon officially became the Avenger in FAA service), there were eight squadrons in Commission (832, 845, 846, 848, 850, 851, 852 and 854); by April a further four had been formed (853, 855, 856 and 857), followed by 820 (October) and 828 (February 1945).

Again it was the east of Suez theatre which saw the greatest use of the

Above *Sharing cramped quarters aboard the escort carrier* Atheling *are Corsairs and Hellcats, representing the two types of long range fighter aircraft available to the BPF during the Pacific campaign. This photograph was actually taken during anti-shipping operations off the Norwegian coast, prior to the formation of the BPF* (Fleet Air Arm Museum).

Right *Many fine Corsairs, and indeed several other types of Lend-Lease aircraft, went to a watery grave after VJ-Day. As an example here is a Corsair from 1846 Squadron after having been pushed off the rounddown of* Colossus *in the Indian Ocean* (Fleet Air Arm Museum).

A replacement for the Barracuda was found in the Grumman Avenger TBR, named the Tarpon by the RN for a few months until joint operations with the US Navy made standardisation desirable. Avengers operated from the largest to the smallest carrier and illustrated is Ravager *with one from 846 ranged on deck* (Fleet Air Arm Museum).

Avenger, whilst at home the aircraft was used from RNA Stations around the coast and with composite squadrons afloat on convoy protection work. With the BPF, the Avenger was particularly well-suited and loved, although it proved, at times, a difficult aircraft to exit in an emergency. Its activities were highly successful and it is worth mentioning here that Sourabaya was the first land bombing raid carried out by the aircraft (832 and 845 Squadrons) and that 828 and 848 Squadrons achieved fame by becoming the first units to bomb the Japanese homeland in July 1945. Again with the cessation of hostilities, the squadrons began to disband rapidly until finally only 828 was left in being; this unit closed shop on June 3 1946.

This was not the last to be heard of William Schwendler's beautiful design because at the height of the East-West Cold War, the RN needed a stop-gap replacement for the Wyvern/Firebrand aircraft and the Avenger AS4 seemed to fill the space until the Fairey Gannet entered service in 1955. Both British and Canadian squadrons were so equipped and one made the first deck landing aboard one of the new generation of light fleet carriers, *Bulwark*.

The end of hostilities in the Pacific theatre saw a number of strange happenings in the carrier world. Not only were the US-built escort carriers returned to the United States for conversion into mercantile vessels, but the very large number of naval aircraft of American design and manufacture were also surplus to requirements. More than that, in fact, because the Lend-Lease agreements drawn-up by Churchill and Roosevelt in the dark days before America entered the war, stipulated that the airframes must be destroyed. Unbelievably, carriers like *Colossus* deposited their aircraft into the briny. Rob Roseveare (then a young observer, RNVR, and now a senior executive in a British nationalised industry) was aboard the sister-ship, *Vengeance*, and remembers seeing even British-built aircraft, classified as unrepairable aboard, being committed to Davy Jones' locker. These aircraft, like the Corsairs aboard *Colossus*, had only weeks before been maintained and flown by willing hands, but were now destroyed almost without a moment's thought. A sad end to many an aircraft which had contributed towards the final victory.

Chapter 8

Escorts and convoys

'The value of carrier-borne aircraft in the protection of trade has been fully demonstrated'.

C-in-C, Western Approaches, 1944

The story of the escort aircraft carrier is bound together in a mosaic with several other facets of the British fixed-wing aircraft carrier story, including the life-giving convoys across the Atlantic and to Russia. To be included also are the merchant aircraft carriers (MAC-Ships) and the various assaults on Axis-held territory assisted by the escort carriers.

Let us firstly turn to the North Atlantic convoys between the United States and Europe. Following the fall of France in 1940, the Kriegsmarine's U-Boat forces were given the advantage of Atlantic ports from which to operate and this caused the Allied surface and airborne escort forces to be stretched to, and eventually past, their limits. The major problem was undoubtedly the mid-Atlantic Air Gap—the Black Hole—which German submarines could roam almost at will without fear of their refuelling and other 'domestic' operations being disturbed by an aircraft—the submarine's greatest enemy. As the toll of merchant ships increased, the Admiralty searched for a system which would eliminate the mid-Atlantic Air Gap, and this system had to be seaborne, travelling with the threatened convoys.

The initial reaction was to provide anti-aircraft ships for the convoys which suffered from the unwelcome attention of German long-range Focke-Wulf Condor bombers and reconnaissance aircraft. The menace of the Condor was two-fold because, not only were they bombers, but they also provided a command centre and search platform for marauding U-Boats. First, the Royal Navy provided catapult-armed merchantmen (CAM-Ships) equipped with Hawker Hurricane or Fairey Fulmar aircraft. These aircraft had a one-way trip because, unless there was land within range (perhaps Newfoundland or Northern Ireland), the pilot had to risk ditching or baling out in the hope that he would be rescued by other ships in the convoy or nearby. Most of these brave young men ended up in the 'drink' or 'oggin' (depending on the shade of blue of their uniforms!) and so this was obviously only a stop-gap measure.

In January 1941 the Admiralty ordered the conversion of the 6,000 ton (6,096 tonne) *Hannover*, a captured German blockade-running cargo ship. This conversion, carried out at Blyth, Northumberland, was to produce an auxiliary aircraft carrier from a merchant ship hull. On June 20 1941 the *Audacity* was commissioned initially as *Empire Audacity*, such was the confusion the merchant/warship combination generated in Whitehall. She was fitted with a simple flight deck and basic deck landing equipment—only four arrester wires and a flight deck half as long as *Ark Royal*'s. At first, the *Audacity* was destined to fulfil the anti-aircraft role of the CAM-Ships with Grumman Martlets (802 Squadron) led by Lieutenant Commander Wintour, a regular naval aviator. Later an anti-submarine role was envisaged and carried out.

Audacity left Scotland on her first convoy duty and the vigilant and efficient Martlet pilots were soon rewarded with the destruction of a Condor bomber. The carrier led the way for the escort and merchant aircraft carriers which were to follow and which were to play such a major part in the Russian convoys and in winning the battles of the Atlantics. Vice Admiral Sir Donald Gibson remembers the *Audacity* well, because he replaced Lieutenant Commander Wintour following the latter's untimely death at the hands of the Condor. 802 were not lucky with COs during World War 2, because, recalls Donald Gibson, one was killed in *Glorious*, and later another in *Avenger*. Sir Donald believes that he was the only wartime CO of 802 Squadron not to be killed whilst serving with the unit.

Audacity's luck ran out on her third tour of convoy duty (HG76), when she was torpedoed as she left the convoy to work up to speed in the hope of avoiding the attentions of lurking U-Boats. This was not to be and she was torpedoed in the engine room when the ship's company was at dinner. Luckily she did not sink immediately and most of the crew escaped but the Martlets went down with the ship. The auxiliary carrier was there to stay, however, for in the United States, merchant ships were being converted into small aircraft carriers for the Royal Navy. Their displacement of 8,200 tons (8,332 tonnes) made them larger than *Audacity* and the first, *Archer*, gave her name to the class of five and in command was a famous carrier personality—Commander J. Robertson, universally known as 'Streamline' because of the shape of his nose! These new ships had several new and useful additions to the ship's equipment including a hydraulic accelerator which was to prove so useful in later anti-submarine operations from escort carriers in the Atlantic. Unfortunately the Swordfish aircraft could not use them and they were then limited in offensive punch when the wind over the deck (WOD) slackened. Nevertheless the accelerators greatly assisted the Martlets.

Archer had a curious, almost see-through appearance with a small island to starboard. Despite a poor start to her warship career, including a collision while on trials, *Archer* survived the war and was not scrapped until March 1962. The second of these American-built vessels was not so lucky. *Avenger* was commissioned in March 1942 and she arrived in British waters during the following May and she was soon engaged in deck-landing trials for the Sea Hurricane. Sub-Lieutenant 'Winkle' Brown, DSC, was the pilot and in his book *Wings on my Sleeve* (Airline Publications, 1961) he recalls that 'the Navy simply stuck an arrester hook on them and played it by ear'. The successful Hawker design had already been operated at sea from the armoured fleet carriers and now Brown showed that they could be operated from these so-called 'Woolworth Carriers' as well.

The Fleet Air Arm pilots being posted to *Avenger* and her sister-ships certainly needed all the assistance they could have because they were about to go on the bitterly fought Russian convoys. Here the escort carriers not only

Keeping station on Formidable *are two of the first group of American-built escort carriers (or CVEs),* Biter *(centre) and the slightly larger* Avenger. *On deck in the foreground are cannon-armed Seafires and there is an Albacore in the after lift* (Fleet Air Arm Museum).

attacked 'snoopers' and enemy bombers, but also provided a replenishment service acting as oilers for escorts on long convoy routes or when operating in Support Groups. *Avenger* was the fifth British carrier to be lost to torpedo attack when *U-155* sank her on November 15 1942—not before much experience had been gained which would prove so useful as the war progressed.

By now, 1942-43, the United States was building a large number of escort carriers for the RN (CVEs, the Americans called them) and these were now being equipped with all American air groups of Wildcats and the larger Grumman Avenger torpedo-bomber-reconnaissance aircraft. *Biter,* another of this first group, was to become famous in the battle of the Atlantic (as the first escort carrier to sink a U-Boat), in the Torch landings, and as the venue for deck landing trials of the Supermarine Seafire, the naval version of the Spitfire, again carried out by 'Winkle' Brown. Brown went on to carry out deck land and launch trials aboard all British carriers as they came into service and his name will go down in the annals of carrier history as one of its leading figures. '*Biter*'s active service consisted mainly of operations in the Battle of the Atlantic when her complement of aircraft consisted mainly of Swordfish with, at times, Martlet single-seater fighters', writes Vice Admiral Sir Conolly Abel Smith. 'The latter proved not altogether satisfactory due to damage on landing on and lack of communication in the air which resulted in difficulty of navigation and finding the carrier.

'There were two methods of operating these carriers in the Battle of the Atlantic: (1) within the convoy; usually second in the centre column. For flying operations the carrier withdrew from her position in the convoy to steam into wind to fly off aircraft, returning to her position in the convoy on completion, but having to repeat the operation to recover the aircraft some two hours later—perhaps sooner for the fighters with less endurance. With the wind astern of the convoy's course this was inclined to cause the carrier to become some miles separated from the convoy and the convoy's A/S screen. Sometimes it was

necessary to withdraw two escorts to protect the carrier. This was, however, the method most favoured by C-in-C Western Approaches, whilst (2) operated in the vicinity of a convoy. A support group consisting of the carrier, or better still two carriers with 3 + destroyers as escort, would operate some distance from the convoy thus maintaining complete freedom of manoeuvre and availability for close support of the convoy if required when an attack occurred. This method was not favoured in the end by the C-in-C on account of shortage of escorts and believed vulnerability of the carrier. I think there can be little doubt that the introduction of these escort carriers made a considerable impact on the Battle of the Atlantic especially in the so-called GAP in which shore based aircraft could not operate.'

Dasher was a tragic ship which, after taking part in the Torch landings in North Africa and in operations off Iceland, was destroyed by an explosion below decks as 891 Squadron's Swordfish were being refuelled. She sank in the Clyde on March 27 1943, less than two years after she was launched. In true naval tradition, lessons were quickly learned and the fickle avgas (aviation gasoline) system, of American design, was immediately revamped. No other escort carrier was lost in this way despite the fact that although *Nabob* and *Thane*, of the later and longer *Ruler* Class, were both hit by torpedoes, neither had serious damage caused by an avgas explosion which was sure to have happened if the post-*Dasher* re-arrangements had not taken place. Other alterations included a lengthened flight deck mainly, it seems, for Swordfish operations, and revised diesel engines.

The combination of Fairey Swordfish and escort carrier was to prove a worthwhile operating tactic. The Swordfish had, by the end of 1942, almost vanished from the decks of the larger fleet carriers, but proved a valuable tool for the winning of the Battle of the Atlantic. In May 1943, a new weapon which was to prove deadly against U-Boats achieved its first success when one of 819 Squadron's Swordfish, flying from *Archer*, sank *U-752* in the eastern Atlantic by means of rocket projectiles. Swordfish frequently teamed up with the convoy's surface escorts and several more German submarines were destroyed by depth-charges, rocket attacks or a combination of the two. Over 1,000 hours of anti-submarine patrol time was logged by a handful of Swordfish from

Striker and *Vindex*, operating together in defence of an Atlantic convoy. The 'Stringbag' continued to operate from escort carriers and MAC-Ships until the former were returned to the Americans and the latter were returned to more peaceful work as mechantmen again. In fact, the last operational unit, 836 Squadron, was the parent unit for the MAC-Ships and it decommissioned in May 1945.

It is possible to divide the American-built escort carriers into three distinct groups, although some sources do use a different classification. For the purposes of this account, the warships can be divided as follows: *Archer* **Class** (BAVGs), 10,000 tons: *Archer, Avenger, Biter* (later Free French *Dixmude*), *Charger* and *Dasher*. *Attacker* **Class,** 11,000 tons: *Attacker, Battler, Chaser, Fencer, Hunter, Pursuer, Ravager, Searcher, Stalker, Striker* and *Tracker*. *Ruler* **Class,** 11,420 tons: *Ameer, Arbiter, Atheling, Begum, Emperor, Empress, Khedive, Nabob, Patroller, Premier, Puncher, Queen, Rajah, Ranee, Reaper, Ruler, Shah, Slinger, Smiter, Speaker, Thane, Trouncer* and *Trumpeter*. Life aboard these small carriers was at times rather cramped and often uncomfortable, especially in the Atlantic gales when an escort carrier's aircraft were being operated to their limit, and often beyond.

The CVEs were part of the large Anglo-American Lend-Lease arrangement and therefore the USN took an interest in their operation. In the middle of 1943, several escort carriers were converted to carry out a role as assault carriers off, for example, a newly established beachhead. These carriers included *Attacker, Stalker* and later *Thane* (a ship completed in Vancouver because Canada agreed to speed up carrier deliveries to the UK by completing the 'anglisation' of the warships). Other escort carriers were converted to become fully operational fighter bases—but afloat—the so-called fighter carriers. This was an Admiralty idea designed to provide air cover for the Invasion beaches of Italy and for Russian convoys.

These modifications caused a few heated exchanges between the American and British naval staffs, mainly because the former preferred the idea of an all

Above left *The familiar sight of an Atlantic convoy with its escort carrier* (Biter) *providing aircraft for air patrols and defence. As more carriers became available it was common for convoys to have two carriers providing round the clock air patrols* (Fleet Air Arm Museum).

Right *Four escort carriers were constructed from uncompleted merchantmen's hulls including the Swan Hunter built* Vindex, *named after a famous seaplane carrier of World War 1. Ranged at the after end of the flight deck is a strike of Swordfish used as anti-submarine patrol and strike aircraft* (Fleet Air Arm Museum).

The uncharacteristic 'E' on the flight deck of this escort carrier allows instant recognition as Emperor, *one of the* Ruler *Class, the third group of American-built Lend-Lease carriers for the RN. On the flight deck can be seen Hellcats of 800 Squadron, including one wearing D-Day invasion markings* (Fleet Air Arm Museum).

purpose escort carrier, to concentrate on the U-Boat menace in the Atlantic. The Admiralty on the other hand, wanted to keep their precious armoured fleet carriers away from the hazards of the beachhead area, as they intended a more active part was to be played by the RN in the Pacific. Such a beachhead was Salerno where *Attacker, Battler, Hunter* and *Stalker*, equipped with the Supermarine Seafire III, gave fighter air cover to the Allied landings, known as Operation Avalanche. Offshore was *Unicorn*, operating in the Mediterranean as a light fleet carrier. Further offshore still, the armoured fleet carriers *Illustrious* and *Formidable*, provided combat air patrols (CAPs) over Admiral Vian's escort carriers. The whole exercise was fraught with difficulty, because of the weather conditions, but much useful experience was gained, including the fact that the Seafire had a very frail undercarriage arrangement and that with a high approach speed due to calm conditions, the Seafire did not like landing on with only 13-15 knots WOD.

After Salerno, *Battler* went east of Suez to strengthen Admiral Sommerville's British East Indies Fleet, which had not seen a carrier since *Hermes* was lost to Japanese dive-bombers. In the Indian Ocean, *Battler's* Swordfish (834 Squadron) provided air cover for India-Aden convoys also seeking out German blockade runners and 'raiders'. Also after Salerno came Operation Anvil-Dragoon in the Gulf of Lyon, which Captain George Baldwin, CBE, DSC, RN (Rtd), then a Lieutenant (A) RNVR, recalls, went far more smoothly for the escort carriers as the weather had improved considerably thus enabling the Seafire to operate with plenty of WOD and in clear skies. Additionally German aerial resistance was light.

Rear Admiral David Torlesse, an observer by 'trade', captained one of the American-built escort carriers in World War 2, and this is its story as told by the Admiral: '*Hunter* was built on the Mississippi in 1943. She was a standard Liberty ship; as an escort carrier she was about 14,000 tons, with a single screw

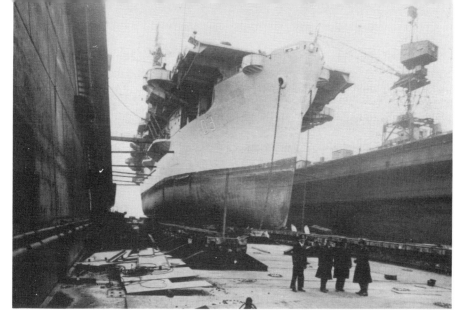

The slim lines and the top-heavy look of the flight deck on Ranee *is typical of all escort carriers. The design was, however, both utilitarian and economic, finding practical employment on Arctic convoys, in the Mediterranean and as part of the Fleet Train for the BPF. The CVEs' predominant user was from Greenock as part of the Atlantic escort groups which eventually defeated the U-Boat menace* (via J. Bryant).

and a speed of 18 knots. Her first Commanding Officer, Captain H.H. McWilliam, RN, told me that when he arrived to take her over he found the whole of her upperworks on the deckside, the ship had been nearly finished when it was decided to cut her down to the upperdeck for rebuilding as an escort carrier. She and her sister-ships were the first venture in shipbuilding of her builders, an iron pipe manufacturing concern, and a very good job they made of her. Anyone interested in the first year of her career will find some account of it in *Escort Carrier* by Kenneth Poolman*. Briefly she emerged from modification in the UK as an assault carrier, equipped to operate Seafire aircraft, and in this guise she joined the 21st ACS and helped to provide air cover for the landings at Salerno.

'My acquaintance with the ship began when I took command of her at Alexandria in September 1944. I found that besides 807 Squadron of 24 Seafire IIIs she carried the Wing Leader of No 4 Wing (a young RNVR officer of 24 [Acting Lieutenant Commander George Baldwin] with a command of 72 fighters), and his staff, the remainder of the fighter wing being carried in *Hunter*'s sister-ships *Stalker* and *Attacker*. The three ships formed part of the 21 Aircraft Carrier Squadron under Rear Admiral T.H. Troubridge with his flag in the cruiser, *Royalist*. Our first duty was to harry the German garrisons attempting to evacuate the Aegean Islands. There was no significant air or surface opposition and almost everything seaborne in the area was fair game for our Seafires. There was general satisfaction at being the means of paying off some old scores which had been festering since 1941.

'On completion of these operations, ships of the squadron gave seven days leave to each watch in the UK before refitting abroad prior to joining the East

---

* Published by Ian Allan.

Indies Fleet. *Hunter* refitted in Malta, being the first large ship to be refitted there after the 'blitz', her air squadron disembarking to RNAS Dekeila, near Alexandria, to work up and keep in flying practice. While the ship was at Malta, Churchill, Roosevelt and all arrived there for a 'Big Two' conference before meeting Stalin at Yalta. In late February *Hunter* proceeded to Alexandria to embark 807 Squadron (and one Walrus for ASR purposes) and carry out refresher training. At this time efforts were being made to interest Egypt in joining the Allies and, as a 'sweetener', *Hunter* hoisted the flag of the Admiral commanding, Eastern Mediterranean, and embarked HM King Farouk and his party for lunch onboard and to witness a day's flying by *Hunter* and *Stalker*'s two fighter squadrons. *Hunter* managed to provide her royal visitor with a thrill in the shape of an unrehearsed but spectacular deck-landing crash, and nothing would persuade Farouk that it had not been staged for his benefit!'

April 1944 saw the attempt to neutralise the risk posed by a battleship so close to the vital Russian convoys. The attack and subsequent operations have already been dealt with in the previous chapter but it is right to record some of the fringe operations here. Also in the Norwegian Sea area at the same time were the British-built *Activity* and *Ruler* Class, *Tracker*. These later escort carriers were providing air cover for the transfer from the USN to the Soviet Navy (Soviet Northern Fleet) of the cruiser *Milwaukee* (later called *Murmansk* by the Russians). Jolly successful they were too, in providing air cover as their Grumman Martlet (833 and 846 Squadrons) intercepted and destroyed Luftwaffe attempts to interfere with the task force. These two carriers also carried Swordfish aircraft which were also in action against U-Boats and sank *U-288* with rocket projectiles and depth charges.

Meanwhile, the escort carriers with the Home Fleet provided some 40 Martlets (Wildcats) to protect the main attack on *Tirpitz*. The attacks, although valiantly followed through, did not prove to be decisive but useful attacks were carried out against German convoy targets of opportunity along the long Norwegian coast. A classic example of how the big guns of the fleet, in this case a cruiser squadron under Rear Admiral McGrigor who was flying his flag in *Norfolk*, could work together with the escort carriers, was presented in mid January 1945 off the coast of Occupied Norway. McGrigor led *Bellona* and the screen of escorting destroyers to attack a German coastal convoy off Egersund. Despite a gallant defence by the overwhelmed escorts and an abortive attempt by a U-Boat to attack the squadron, they succeeded in sinking three ships. The escort carriers *Premier* and *Trumpeter* then provided air cover for the safe withdrawal of the surface forces preventing a revenge attack by Junkers Ju88 torpedo bombers of the Luftwaffe anti-shipping squadron. This close liaison could easily have worked in reverse if the target had required the attention of carrier-borne strike aircraft and if the carriers themselves had needed protection against a surface force which was in or near the launch position.

Escort carriers were, then, to see more widespread service than just Greenock-based sorties operating in the Atlantic. In 1943-44, four were with the Mediterranean Fleet, where, equipped with Seafires, they provided the air defence of the Italian beaches. In 1944, five were sent East of Suez to the then Eastern Fleet. 1945 saw six operating with Home Fleet, and 16 on the East Indies station operating against the Japanese, like their nine companions with the British Pacific Fleet (BPF). The Canadians operated *Nabob* between 1943 and 1944, giving them their first real carrier experience in the rough Atlantic before taking delivery of a series of light fleet carriers.

Although the CVE construction programme was concentrated in the United States, five more escort carriers were built in the UK, but not on the American mass-produced lines. The *Activity* (launched May 1942), *Campania* (June 1943), *Vindex* and her sister-ship *Nairana* (both launched May 1943) were adapted from merchant hulls. The largest of the escort carriers, *Pretoria Castle* (17,500 tons: 17,780 tonnes), was a converted Union-Castle Line vessel which, after giving stalwart service as a training carrier, was re-converted back to her former role after the cessation of hostilities.

Campania, *Vindex* and *Nairana* were named after World War 1 seaplane carriers and served well—especially in the Arctic. The latter became the first Dutch carrier—Royal Netherlands NS *Karel Doorman* in 1946. *Vindex* was purchased by the Port Line (who had originally ordered her as a refrigerated cargo ship). It is relevant here to compare the service lives of two escort carriers—one American-built—*Striker*; and one British-built—*Campania*.

	Campania (D48)	*Striker* (D12) (ex *Prince William* USN)
Launching	June 17 1943	May 7 1942
Builder	Harland & Wolff	Western Pipe & Steel Co
Displacement	12,450 tons (12,650 tonnes)	11,420 tons (11,603 tonnes)
Length (overall)	540 feet (164.4 m)	492 feet (150 m)
Beam	70 feet (21.3 m)	69.5 feet (21.2 m)
Draught	19 feet (5.8 m)	23.25 feet (7.1 m)
Machinery	Diesel motors	Geared turbine
Armament	2 × 4 inches (10.2 cm) AA	2 × 4 inches (10.2 cm) AA
	16 × 2 lb (0.9 kg)	8 × 40 mm AA
	16 × 20 mm AA	4 × 20 mm AA
Complement	700	646
Aircraft	15	18 (824 Squadron)
Speed (max)	17 knots (31.5 kph)	18 knots (33.3 kph)

Campania was actually a cargo liner which was taken over during construction and completed as an escort carrier by Harland and Wolff at Belfast. They completed her on March 7 1944, and on commissioning she was allocated to Western Approaches Command. She later transferred to the Russian/Arctic convoy runs and, on September 30 1944, one of her Swordfish (813 Squadron) destroyed the Type VIIC submarine, *U-921*, south west of Bear Island. Again on convoy escort duties in November, her aircraft downed two German flying boats of the Bu138 type on the Arctic Circle—this time it was Wildcats of 825 Squadron who were credited. The same composite squadron's Swordfish put down another U-Boat—*U-365*—in December 1944 before *Campania* became a flagship, first for Rear Admiral Rhoderick McGrigor* (1st Cruiser Squadron) and then, a month later, for Vice Admiral F.H.G. Dalrymple-Hamilton (10th Cruiser Squadron). *Campania*'s war ended with the entry of the Home Fleet into the Skagerrak and Kattegat.

Unlike the American-built escort carriers which returned home after

* Later Admiral of the Fleet and First Sea Lord.

hostilities ended, *Campania* continued under the White Ensign and, in 1949, she was lent to the Festival of Britain as a floating exhibition and during the actual Festival in 1951 she toured British and European ports with special displays. Her active service was not over, however, because in 1952 she went to the Monte Bello Islands (near Australia) as Rear Admiral David Torlesse's flagship for the atomic tests. *Campania*'s active days were over by now and in 1953 she entered Chatham to go into reserve; she was scrapped in November 1955.

One of a class of ten ships, *Striker* started her life at San Francisco and was a Lend-Lease escort carrier. On June 30 1943, after being suitably adapted for RN life, she sailed for Liverpool. More adaptations were made and she began convoy escort operations in the Atlantic and later, with Western Approaches Command. After taking part in the attacks against *Tirpitz* and other Norwegian targets, she moved to the west coast of France, but was unable to force any action there. During an Arctic convoy operation in August 1944, she recorded the highest individual carrier effort of her type, when 824 Squadron— Wildcats and Swordfish—flew 133 sorties which peaked at 27 sorties on one day and 26 on the next!

In November 1944, *Striker* changed her hunting ground to the Indian Ocean and, by January 1945, she was at Melbourne, Australia. In support of Operation Iceberg she joined the Fleet Train of the BPF and with her sister-ship, *Fencer*, and with *Slinger* she formed 30th Aircraft Carrier Squadron. *Striker* was now termed a replenishment carrier, and used to ferry air stores and aircraft to the front-line fleet carriers.

Various other operations were undertaken, including the transportation of the wounded from *Formidable* to Leyte after the latter had been hit by a kamikaze in May 1945. With the end of the war *Striker*, like many aircraft carriers, was engaged in transporting POWs who had been in Japanese hands. The end of the war also meant that *Striker* had to be returned to the United States so, following a passage home to Greenock, she was returned to the USN on February 12 1946 and scrapped later the same year. The preceeding carriers

Not exactly a large deck to operate from, especially in the teeth of an Atlantic gale! A TAG's eye view of an escort carrier (Fleet Air Arm Museum).

can be considered as typical of escort carriers. There is no doubt that they contributed considerably to the Allied Victory in 1945.

Another associated group of warships contributed to that victory. Their development and operation are classic examples of British ingenuity and the ability of the island-race to compromise. In 1941, both merchant ships and warships were in short supply, so the taking of merchant hulls to construct complete aircraft carriers was out of the question; however, an adaptation was proposed. The basic minima considered by the Admiralty for flying operations at sea in 1941 were 390 feet (118.9 m) of flat deck and 11 knots (20.4 kph) of speed through the water. This equated nicely to the 8,000 tons (8,129 tonnes) emergency war construction standard cargo hulls and accordingly two grain carriers were ordered with flight decks and off centre superstructures. So the merchant aircraft carrier was borne.

MAC-Ships were destined to fly the Red Ensign and be commanded by merchant navy officers, but they would have a small Fleet Air Arm contingent aboard. Following the adaptation of grainships, Anglo-Saxon Petroleum volunteered their larger (12,000 tons/12,193 tonnes) tankers for conversion. Despite Admiralty misgivings, the plan to commence tanker conversion began in 1942 and *MV Rapana* was converted in February 1943 with a 460 feet (140.2 m) flight deck. *Empire MacAlpine* was the first grain-carrying MAC-Ship with a 422 feet (128.6 m) flight deck and she was the venue for the first naval aircraft landing as a merchant ship when Lieutenant Commander R.W. Slater, OBE, DSC, RN, brought a Swordfish of 835 Squadron on to the deck. The merchant ship convoys now had a powerful ally, especially when two or more MAC-Ships were in attendance and flying operations could be alternated—one flying routine dawn-to-dusk patrols and the other available for a quick reaction search and kill mission.

On board were the normal carrier requisites—arrester wires, fuel supplies of avgas, fire fighting equipment and even a DLCO. The ground crew were under the command of the Air Staff Officer, but the ship was still in merchant navy hands—even some of the Swordfish carried the legend 'Merchant Navy' on their fuselages instead of 'Royal Navy'! Two Dutch merchant aircraft carriers (*Gadila* and *Macoma*) came on the scene later and they were provided with mini air-groups by 860 Squadron, also a Dutch unit. These ships were tankers but they flew the Dutch naval ensign.

The MAC-Ships' aircraft did not actually sink any U-Boats although many attacks were carried out which made U-Boats break off their own attacks on convoys. They were in their hour during the desperate days of 1943-44 when the Battle of the Atlantic was turning in the Allies' favour. Later as escort carriers arrived on the scene in strength their role was less vital, and so they all were returned to purely merchant service. MAC-Ships in service were as follows:

Grain ships: *Empire* Class, 8,000 tons (8,129 tonnes)—*Empire MacAlpine, Empire MacKendrick, Empire Macandrew, Empire Macdermott, Empire Macrae* and *Empire Maccallum.*

Tankers: *Empire* Class, 9,000 tons (9,145 tonnes)—*Empire Mackay, Empire Maccoll, Empire MacMahon* and *Empire MacCabe. Rapana* Class 8,000 tons (8,129 tonnes)—*Acavus, Adula, Alexia, Amastra, Ancylus, Gadila, Macoma, Miralda* and *Rapana.*

It is worth noting that British and Canadian scientists did consider using icebergs in the North Atlantic as mobile air bases! The scheme called for frozen water and sawdust to be stabilised and then propelled to the battle zone. Needless to say the idea did not materialise but Winston Churchill for one was most enthusiastic.

Convoys

The convoy runs to Malta have a special place in the history of the British fixed-wing aircraft carrier. The main need was to supply fighter aircraft for the badly depleted defenders of the island fortress. The old 'flat-iron' carrier *Argus* was the first to venture towards Malta with reinforcements—RAF Hurricanes which were launched from her deck towards the island, escorted by two-seat Skuas as navigation leaders. Force H acted as an escort and *Ark Royal* delivered a diversionary strike against Sardinia to keep the Italian Air Force pinned down whilst the 14 Hurricanes were en route; they all arrived safely, although *Ark* lost two of her Swordfish.

Illustrious' first sortie to see action was covering a Malta-bound convoy where she added not only her radar gear *radio direction finding* as it was still called) but also a squadron of Fulmars. Again Sardinia was attacked and *Illustrious* sailed on to join Admiral Cunningham's Eastern Mediterranean Fleet where until then *Eagle* had been the only carrier. She had been in action in a diversionary role as well, with her Swordfish attacking Rhodes.

The summer and autumn of 1940 were hectic times for the Mediterranean-based carriers, including the Taranto raid mentioned in Chapter 6, but by early 1941, the Mediterranean was becoming a dangerous place for an aircraft carrier, especially such an old one as *Argus*. It was therefore decided that *Argus* should continue to ferry spare aircraft for Malta as far as Gibraltar and for *Ark Royal* to take on to the launch-point for Malta. Later in the year, *Argus* took aircraft the other way, north to Russia during Operation Benedict, but this was a brief interlude before the runs to Gibraltar were resumed in October and November 1941.

Operation Perpetual in November 1941 was particularly noteworthy because, on the homeward leg, *Ark Royal* was sighted by the German submarine *U-81*, torpedoed and sunk almost within sight of Gibraltar, (see Chapter 5). This devastating blow to British naval pride meant that the little *Argus* had to be retained at Gibraltar together with *Eagle* to provide the badly needed fighter cover for Force H. So in the first half of 1942, she was again escorting convoys, but in late June returned to the UK as the deck landing training carrier until being placed in reserve in August 1944; she was eventually scrapped in 1947. *Eagle*, the RN's only two-funnelled fixed-wing aircraft carrier, was also briefly engaged on convoy escort duties in the Mediterranean and in the ferrying of aircraft—Operations Spotter and Picket—with Force H. She had on board by this time her own radar and carried ASV equipped Swordfish (813 Squadron). These ferry operations to Malta were particularly interesting, because for the first time the Supermarine Spitfire was operated outside the United Kingdom.

On June 12 1942 one convoy to Malta, code-named Operation Harpoon, saw *Eagle*'s fighters, Sea Hurricanes of 801 and 813 Squadrons, shoot down nine attacking Italian aircraft and damage nearly a dozen more. *Argus'* Fulmars were also active and shot down several more for the loss of two of their own number. Although these convoys did give temporary relief to the beleaguered island, there was need for a special effort. This special effort was Operation

Pedestal—perhaps the most famous Malta convoy of World War 2. It was the greatest concentration of carrier-power to have been then assembled—*Eagle, Furious, Indomitable* and *Victorious. Furious* was acting as ferry carrier with 38 badly needed Spitfires aboard, whilst the whole effort was to be escorted by two battleships, seven cruisers and two dozen destroyers. On August 11 1942, the convoy was nearing Malta when *U-73* managed to creep past the refuelling destroyers and fire four torpedoes at the *Eagle*. The old carrier went down in eight minutes, but 927 men were rescued by destroyers and a tug whilst four Sea Hurricanes of 801 Squadron were recovered aboard *Indomitable*.

Many people have been asked, over the years, what their thoughts were when they saw an aircraft carrier sink. Captain J.H. West, who as a staff officer aboard the flagship witnessed *Eagle*'s end, is no exception when he says that: 'We were far too busy thinking of other things, for example, our own survival, or the job in hand, to even consider the fact that one of the Navy's capital ships was going down!'

Those who witnessed the sinking of the *Ark Royal* a year earlier have a rather different story to tell as that famous carrier took somewhat longer to go to the bottom. Philip (Percy) Gick, then Senior Pilot of 825 Squadron and later a carrier captain, retiring with the rank of Rear Admiral, writes, not without some emotion one would believe: 'The old girl hung there for, I think, an hour and a half, but I could not watch and I think it was 6 o'clock when somebody told me that she had sunk'.

Another casualty on the Pedestal run was the armoured fleet carrier *Indomitable.* She was hit, on August 12 1942, by three aircraft bombs and near misses by three or four others. Luckily she was saved by her armoured deck and after extensive repairs, lasting four months, at Liverpool, she resumed service with the Home Fleet. *Victorious*, luckily, remained operational throughout the long drawn-out engagement and was able to take most of *Indomitable*'s aircraft

During the Malta convoy runs, Eagle, *very much the old timer in the Mediterranean was hit and sunk by* U-73. *She sank in just eight minutes, an inglorious end for a fine old lady* (via H. Liddle).

still in the air, aboard. It is worth noting here that no merchant ship was hit by enemy bombs whilst the carriers provided fighter cover, but when, in the Sicilian Narrows, *Victorious* and her consorts had turned westwards for Gibraltar, four merchant ships were lost to Axis bombers.

Pedestal was effective because, despite the loss of *Eagle*, two cruisers, a destroyer and nine merchant ships, the Axis could not achieve a blockade of Malta and the strikes against their supply lines to North Africa could continue. This convoy was the last of many because, in November 1942, Malta was effectively relieved following the defeat of Field Marshall Rommel in the desert. The valuable and gallant service by carriers during this period is especially remembered by the people of Malta to this day.

Aircraft carriers taking part in the aircraft ferrying convoys were *Argus, Ark Royal, Eagle, Furious* and *Victorious*. Between August 2 1940 and October 19 1942 they delivered 718 aircraft (Spitfires, Swordfish, Fulmars, Hurricanes, Albacores) to Malta in a total of 25 operations, two of which included participation by the US Navy's carrier *Wasp* (April and May 1942).

One Senior Officer recalls an interesting incident in *Argus* during Operation Harpoon which shows how luck can play a large part in such events. It concerns a mass attack by Italian torpedo bombers, three of which dropped torpedoes more or less together, aimed at the carrier. The normal avoiding action when torpedoes are seen approaching is for the ship to turn parallel to them and 'comb' the tracks. If they are coming from anywhere before the beam then the turn is towards, if from abaft the beam, the turn is away.

Now just before World War 2, the Admiralty changed the helm order system so that it took account of the way the rudder (and wheel) went and not the way of the helm, for example, pre-war the Captain would give an order 'Starboard 10' and the ship would turn to Port. This obsolete convention was finally reversed to avoid confusion. However, during this torpedo attack on the *Argus*, the Captain, on being told of tracks approaching the port bow, instinctively gave an immediate helm order of 'Starboard 30' when in actual fact he meant 'Port 30'. Unlike the movies a Captain never says 'hard-a-starboard' or 'hard-a-port' as this may only unnerve the helmsman, but on this occasion the helmsman on duty was so flustered anyway by the tone of what was obviously an emergency order that by mistake he put 30 of the port wheel on, and in doing so counteracted the mistake of the Captain and the ship safely combed the tracks of three incoming torpedoes. So *Argus* survived an attack which would otherwise have certainly sunk such an ageing and vulnerable hull.

Chapter 9

East of Suez—
The British Pacific Fleet

'They say that the Fleet came to Trincomalee,
Early in 'forty-four,
Heavily laden with men and with gen,
Bound for the Japanese war.
There's 'Vic' *and* 'Indom' *and* 'Illustrious' *too,*
The 'Indefat' *came for the ride.*
You get no promotion in the Indian Ocean,
We'd rather be back in the Clyde.'

FAA Song Book: (to tune of *Bless 'Em All*)

Since the days of Empire, the Royal Navy has had a presence overseas, particularly in the Far East. With the advent of the aircraft carrier, it was therefore logical that one of these units would be sent to the China Station from time to time. *Eagle* went there with 803 Squadron (Ospreys) and 824 Squadron (Fairey IIIFs) between 1933-35. Apart from showing the flag, her main function was the suppression of pirates in the sea lanes between Singapore and Hong Kong and this was effectively done using carrier-based aircraft. In 1935, *Eagle* was relieved by *Hermes* and the air group was transferred, although 824 Squadron had, by now, become 825 Squadron! During *Hermes* times in the Far East 1934-37 she sailed 42,099 nautical miles (77,967 km) and achieved 1,359 deck landings, sailing as far south as Bali (now part of Indonesia) and as far north as Chingwangtao. The fleet's summer anchorage was Wei-hai-Wei, 'opposite' Korea, in the Yellow Sea.

Eagle was again East of Suez in 1937, having brought 18 brand-new Swordfish Is for 813 and 824 Squadrons, leaving the Seals previously on station to depart for British waters with *Hermes*; the Seals were phased out of service in 1937-38 as the new Fairey biplane was introduced to the Fleet.

Once war had begun, *Eagle* went raider-hunting with other warships in the Indian Ocean as well as protecting trooping convoys from Australia. Despite an internal explosion in the bomb room, *Eagle* was the only operational aircraft carrier East of Suez in early 1940. The tide of war was moving in Europe and very soon *Eagle* had been recalled to the Mediterranean Fleet to replace *Glorious*, which had been sent to Norway.

It was not until the first months of 1941 that *Hermes* again returned to the Indian Ocean. Charles Stevens, a senior rate aboard, recalls that, '*Hermes* coped with warm and hot weather extremely well and [she] was well supplied

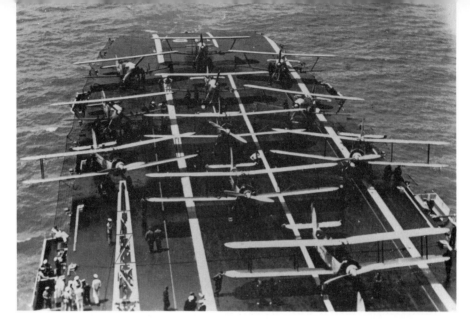

*Part of the RN's naval presence east of Suez between the wars was an aircraft carrier.
Either* Eagle *or* Hermes *(pictured here) were on station in a joint peace-keeping/flag-
showing role. The aeroplanes on the flight deck are Hawker Ospreys of 803 Squadron
(aft) and Fairey Seals of 824 Squadron. Shades of future aircraft carrier development can
be seen in the shape of the off-centred axial lines down the flight deck* (via H.J.
Bricknell).

with wind scoops for scuttles'. *Hermes* remained in the trade and convoy
protection role until joined by *Indomitable* in December, which was being used
as a ferry carrier.

In early 1942 the Royal Navy, under Admiral Sir James Somerville, had three
carriers and five battleships, plus attendant cruisers and destroyers in the Indian
ocean. In theory this was a force which could take on anything that the Japanese
could put in the area, but in practical terms the force was somewhat old and
antiquated. Of the carriers, only *Indomitable* was fully worked up and of
sufficient size to be of any use. The other two carriers were *Formidable*, although
a modern armoured fleet carrier, she was not sufficiently up to scratch to take
on the Japanese alone; and the third carrier was the small, and now somewhat
outdated, *Hermes.* The great advantage which the RN had, however, was that
Indomitable's air crew were capable of night operations, and under the flag of
Admiral D.W. Boyd, this was of considerable advantage. It had nine Sea
Hurricanes and 12 Fulmar fighters embarked, plus 25 Albacore torpedo
bombers. *Formidable*, on the other hand, had 12 Martlets, a fairly advanced
naval fighter for this time, plus 22 torpedo bombers. Poor little old *Hermes*
could only manage 12 Swordfish in her complement, but the total strike force
available to Boyd was 57 torpedo aircraft and 36 fighters. Set against them was
the Japanese fighting force of five large and one small carrier, plus four fast
battleships.

The other advantage which the RN had was the secret base some 500 miles
south west of Ceylon, at Addu Atoll in the Maldive Islands. Additionally quite a
number of the Albacore aircraft aboard both *Indomitable* and *Formidable* were
equipped with air surface vessel radar (ASV) and as the aircrew observers were
used to using such devices as well as flares to illuminate targets, Somerville (the

overall Commander) considered himself to be at an advantage if he remained away from the Japanese by day, but closed in at night, thereby making use of his superior operational skills. This then was the position in the spring of 1942. Unfortunately, when the Japanese strike, the ever expected strike on Ceylon, came, the two fleet carriers of the eastern fleet were still away at Addu Atoll leaving only *Hermes*, three cruisers and two destroyers there to counter the Japanese thrust.

On Easter Day 1942 the Japanese struck at Columbo sinking the destroyer *Tendos* and the auxiliary warship, *Hector*, causing substantial damage to the shore port facilities as well. Later in the day the Navy's only heavy cruisers in the eastern fleet, *Cornwall* and *Dorsetshire*, were sunk. Somerville's fleet had put to sea from Addu to look for the Japanese striking force, but although several carrier-borne aircraft came within range they were shot down. So it was that British Eastern Fleet was unaware of the exact position of the attacking Japanese, and shipping at Ceylon was ordered to disperse to sea. By chance a Japanese float plane sighted *Hermes* and her two escorts at sea, devoid of any aircraft. The Japanese attack on her resulted in the destruction of a colourful ship, which had served so long on the China station, and which, although outdated, had survived early anti-U-boat and anti-raider operations. Not a glorious end to such a 'wonderful' ship.

The victory claimed by the Japanese in the Indian Ocean was to be relatively short-lived, but it would be some while before the Royal Navy took to the offensive again with its aircraft carrier force, then slowly building up after tragic losses in other theatres. It was not until early 1944 that operations in the Eastern Indian Ocean were again resumed with aircraft carriers. The tide of the war in Europe and the North Atlantic had swung sufficiently in the Allies' favour to permit renewed opposition to Japanese expansionist plans in the Far East. Added to this, of course, was the availability of new American carrier aircraft and the aircrew to fly them—again with an American connection in that most were trained at such places as Pensacola Naval Air Station in Florida.

In the spring, *Illustrious*, under Captain R.L.B. Cunliffe, CBE, RN, arrived at Trincomalee to join the temporarily-lent 33,000 tonne USN aircraft carrier, *Saratoga*, for a series of operations designed to break in *Illustrious'* new air group—15 Naval Fighter Wing (NFW) and 21 Torpedo-Bomber-Reconnaissance Wing (TBRW)— and to cause a bit of havoc in Japanese-held Sumatra. The first operation was against Sabang on April 19 1944. A month later both carriers attacked Soerabaya oil refinery in Java—54 aircraft from *Saratoga* and 32 from *Illustrious*. Despite the accidental loss of two Avengers before the attack started, the strike was mildly successful and it marked the beginning of effective support by the RN for the hard pressed ground forces.

The necessity for a 'spare deck' in these waters was becoming apparent, especially if *Illustrious* was going to operate for a while away from land alone, until the arrival of *Victorious* and *Indomitable*. In early June, the escort carrier *Atheling* was used in trials for such a role, but her lack of speed made it impossible to contemplate such operations 'for real'. The need for the two extra armoured fleet carriers in this theatre was even more apparent.

The Eastern Fleet's next sortie was to the Andaman Islands but no worthwhile targets were found in the Port Blair area for *Illustrious'* Avengers and Corsairs. The operation was noteworthy, however, for the fact that over 89 per cent of the air group were airborne together—the first time such a high number had been launched by the ship. It is worth recording here, that air-sea rescue services were beginning to be organised in the Eastern Fleet in a very professional way. The need was great because the choice between falling into the hands of the Japanese or into the mouths of sharks had little to choose between them. Initially operational submarines were deployed at pre-arranged locations to pick up the crews of damaged aircraft which could not make it back to the carrier. Later Sea Otter and Walrus amphibians were used to good effect, and some truly gallant pilots managed to land and pick up aircrew from inland lakes in enemy-held territory. In his autobiography, *Action this Day*, published by Muller (1960), Admiral of the Fleet Sir Philip Vian records his own feelings towards these rescue operations mounted by the amphibian aircraft: 'They were invaluable in smooth water, and, at great risk, made rescues of pilots and observers ditched close inshore'.

It is perhaps a little known fact that squadron COs rarely flew as 'themselves'—the rest of the squadron were given the name of a fictitious officer to quote if captured and if the CO did fly he was known by yet another name. For example, Lieutenant Commander Norman Hanson, CO of 1833 Squadron, flew several missions as a Sub-Lieutenant. The reason for this deception was based on the methods used by Japanese if the CO was unlucky enough to be shot down and captured. Many pilots did, however, fear more falling into the hands of Bedouin in what was then Trans-Jordan, than into those of the Japanese. In reality, of course, being captured was pretty awful whoever the captors.

The arrival of *Victorious* and later *Indomitable* was not the only change in the Eastern Fleet's carrier force, for *Illustrious* had a change of command in the

After the initial operations, the BPF was formed in November 1944 and was centred on four fleet carriers of the Illustrious *Class. One of those which served in the Pacific was* Indomitable, *which survived several attacks by Japanese kamikaze aircraft. She is pictured here at Grand Harbour, Malta, a few months after her return to the western hemisphere* (RN via Captain Button).

With the coming of victory against Japan (VJ-Day), the 'Forgotten Fleet' was able to celebrate and here is Vengeance *fully illuminated* (RN via E.P. George).

summer of 1944. Captain Cunliffe was relieved by Captain Charles Lambe (later Admiral of the Fleet Sir Charles Lambe, GCB, CVO). So the first joint work-up of *Illustrious* and *Victorious* was as much for *Illustrious*' benefit as for the newcomers. Sabang was again the target for the new carrier force on July 25 1944, but the operation was mainly to use the big guns of the battleships and the Corsairs would provide forward spotting for the ships off-shore. The airfields ashore were attacked to suppress enemy fighters and for the first time the carriers' fighters were engaged by the enemy in aerial combat, but without casualties to the British. Operation Crimson had been a success and it was cordially received by SEAC's Supremo, Lord Mountbatten, with the words: 'The results will hearten all forces in South-East Asia'.

With *Illustrious* away under refit in South Africa, strikes against the Japanese were kept up by *Victorious* and the newly arrived *Indomitable*: August 24 Padang, Sumatra, Operation Banquet; September 18 Sigli, Sumatra, Operation Light; and October 17 and 19 Nicobar Islands, Operation Millet. During these operations, no counter attacks were mounted against the strike force until October 19 when Corsairs from *Victorious* (1834 Squadron) and Hellcats from *Indomitable* downed eight defending enemy aircraft without loss.

Despite the professional (and to some extent purely personal) misgivings of Admiral Ernest King, Commander-in-Chief of the US Navy, the Allies agreed that Britain should again play a major role in the Far East. Like the armies in Burma, however, the British Pacific Fleet (BPF) was destined to become a forgotten force and it is only almost 40 years later that the public are becoming aware of the effort and success of the BPF. The reasons why the BPF should, in the words of John Winton's classic book, become the *Forgotten Fleet*, are complex and no doubt reflect the distance from the UK of the operations, the somewhat reluctant way in which the USN gave the BPF credit, and the fact that a good proportion of the action took place within months of, and following the end of, the War in Europe (VE-Day).

Captain Duncan Lewin feels that the lack of publicity could have also been due to the fact that there were very few reporters embarked with the BPF. During his time with Force H, he recalls 'the warships didn't move without at least half a dozen reporters on board', but in the Pacific the USN provided billets for the press and so the media attention was focused on them and directed at the American public. The BPF was strategic in operational working, rather than being tactical as in the other theatres of the war, so in the latter there were more opportunities to report individual actions.

Columbo was the venue for the disbandment of the Eastern Fleet and for the creation of the British Pacific Fleet. On November 22 1944 Admiral Sir Bruce Fraser (of Battle of North Cape fame) assumed command of the powerful, if small by American standards, fleet. The BPF was centred on *Illustrious, Indefatigable, Indomitable* and *Victorious*, plus attendant battleships, cruisers and destroyers. At the same time as the BPF was created, a smaller fleet was established to fill the vacuum in the Indian Ocean—the East Indies Fleet centred on the escort carriers *Ameer, Atheling, Battler, Begum* and *Shah*. Rear Admiral Vian was the centre pin of the fleet as the Flag Officer of the Carrier Force (wearing his flag in *Indefatigable*)—later known as the 1st Aircraft Carrier Squadron (1ACS).

Although their main operational area would be Okinawa, the BPF had its base at Sydney, Australia, from where the air groups would depart to Nowra Naval Air Station. Because of seniority problems, Admiral Fraser was destined not to command at sea and, therefore, an able second-in-command had to be chosen. This was Vice Admiral Sir Bernard Rawlings, and he led *Task Force 57** (alternating with *TF37* for administrative reasons every three months or so) to sea.

The armoured fleet carriers had to spend a period working up together and so several 'operational training' strikes were planned. On December 20 1944 *Illustrious* and *Indomitable* struck at the Sumatran oil refinery of Pangkalan Bandan. Bad weather let the Allies down but Belawan Deli docks were attacked instead. *Illustrious, Indomitable* and *Victorious* had been joined ten days earlier by *Indefatigable*, with her extra hangar of aircraft which were to prove so useful in the strikes planned for the New Year. Considerable damage was inflicted on Belawan Deli on January 4 1945 by the latter three carriers, but it was Palembang, Sumatra which really started the ball rolling.

The largest British carrier strike operation of the war so far was a total commitment raid involving 126 aircraft (January 24) and 123 aircraft (January 29) from four carriers. It achieved the total destruction of the vital oil refinery of Sumatra—a heavy blow to the Japanese in the East Indies—and included the destruction of 37 Japanese aircraft in aerial combat. The raid is famous in FAA history not only because of its success but because of the planning which went into it—from Rear Admiral Vian in *Victorious* downwards. There was not only a friendly submarine laid on to collect any aircrew who were forced to bail out, but each flier was also given a 'blood chit' promising in several languages a reward to the person who assisted allied aircrew; as well as 50 gold sovereigns apiece to bribe one's way out of trouble. After a replenishment exercise on the way home to Australia, the BPF was considered ready and able to take on the Japs.

* The USN was divided into Task forces, which were made up of Task Groups; the BPF was smaller than a number of USN TGs, but it was accorded TF status by the Pentagon. This was an honour which flattered the BPF.

Under the flag of Vice Admiral Moody, there were 15 escort carriers operating with the East Indies Fleet on VJ-Day and a further eight in the BPF. One such carrier was Ameer, *part of the EIF and seen here with the Hellcats of 896 Squadron embarked* (Fleet Air Arm Museum).

Six escort carriers had now joined the BPF—*Chaser, Fencer, Ruler, Slinger, Speaker* and *Striker.* It was now into the Pacific Ocean proper, but whilst at Sydney, *Illustrious* was docked to have her centre propeller removed—after it had been damaged in the Mediterranean some years before. Although this loss reduced her speed to 24 knots (44.4 kph), she was still an effective fighting machine. In early 1945, she rejoined the fleet for a work-up with the USN—this was very necessary because, although the latter were very proficient in long-range daylight operations, there were considerable differences in the 'modus operandi' of the fleets which needed to be standardised if joint operations were to be achieved safely. One was the marking of British aircraft in a similar pattern to their American counterparts. Several British officers were seconded to the USN during this time, notably the observer who turned pilot, Frank Hopkins (now Admiral Sir Frank Hopkins, KCB, DSO, DSC).

Despite attempts to standardise on the same aircraft types, British Corsairs often differed from their American (usually Marine Corps) counterparts and so the commonality of supply which should have been possible was not achieved. Rather similar, in fact, to the way, 30 years later, that RN Phantoms with Spey engines and British avionics were not compatible with the outwardly similar USN Phantoms. It was also necessary for British carriers to practise replenishment at sea and soon destroyers, for example, were well experienced in coming alongside carriers to take on fuel in most weathers.

By March 1945 the BPF was ready to put to sea to join its American cousins. The air groups now consisted of four types of fighters; 36 Corsairs, 40 Seafires, 9 Fireflies and 66 Hellcats, but gone were the Barracudas, and in their place were 66 Avengers. Based at Manus in the Admiralty Islands, the BPF were ready for Okinawa—only a stone's throw from Japan! On March 26 strikes were made against airfields on a rota basis—two days on and two days off—

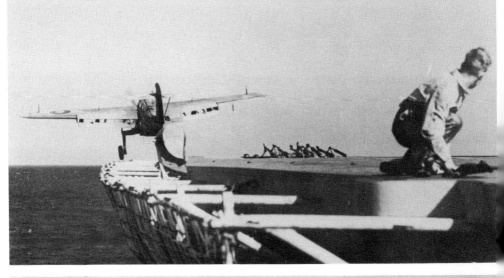

and refuelling was in Leyte Gulf. On April 1 the BPF was attacked by kamikaze aircraft, but no significant damage was caused despite a direct hit at the base of *Indefatigable*'s island. Due to the armoured deck and efficient damage control routines, the carrier was only out of operation for a short time, being 'reasonably operational' by the afternoon.

As a general rule, the suicide planes would turn back if intercepted at more than 25 nautical miles from the carrier, but any closer and nothing would stop them pressing on. Five days after *Indefatigable*'s light skirmish, it was the turn of *Illustrious* which was near missed, however, the resultant underwater explosion did cause hull damage. This was repaired later at Sydney but not before she had flown 643 sorties during her nine days off Okinawa; losing only a dozen aircraft, of which seven were operational accidents. One of these statistics was almost a 1833 Squadron Corsair, which was rapidly abandoned by its pilot on the flight deck when the kamikaze attacked! A cool-headed rating ran over, climbed in and stopped the 'bird' only inches from the deck edge!

Formidable had recently joined the BPF and she was sent to relieve *Illustrious* off Okinawa. *Indomitable* was also hit by a kamikaze—on May 4 1945, but again luckily the armoured deck protected the carrier from any major damage,

Top left *Although not as successful as its forerunner, the Swordfish, the Barracuda was embarked in several light fleet carriers, such as* Vengeance, *as signified by the 'A' on the tail. This photograph is also an extremely good illustration of a carrier arrested landing* (via R.W. Roseveare).

Left *At the other end of the flight deck, an unladen 'Barra' is launched into the air by means of the hydraulic accelerator which can be seen in its launch position between the departing aeroplane and the deck rating* (RN via Captain Neame).

Below left *Bedecked in the navy blue and white markings of the BPF, these two Barracudas of 827 Squadron demonstrate the vivid markings carried in the Pacific war. Any hint of red in the traditional British roundel would only have invited a deluge of 'friendly' anti-aircraft fire from the fleet and this could be particularly unpleasant for aircraft returning from a strenuous raid. In this case mis-identification was not a problem because the parent carrier,* Colossus, *did not see wartime action* (via C.H. Vines).

Below *Probably the most popular fleet fighter of the Pacific campaign was the American-built Corsair. Illustrated here during a wheels down fly-past is an example from 1850 Squadron* (RN via Captain Neame).

although she was effectively put out of the war. With *Illustrious* back in Sydney for repairs, it was the turn of *Victorious*, which had been operating against enemy airfields in the Sakishima Group—Operation Iceberg—to be hit this time by two kamikazes on May 9 1945 and, although able to resume air operations within an hour, Captain M. Denny also had to take her back to Sydney for repairs. *Formidable* was also picked out as a target by the fanatically brave Japanese and she too was hit—twice! (May 4 and 9). Despite 11 aircraft being destroyed on the flight deck and eight fatal casualties during the first raid, the ship, at reduced speed, resumed flying again next day—a glorious tribute to her designers, builders and most of all, the ship's company. The second raid reduced her to 15 operational aircraft and she had to withdraw to restock.

These early strikes represented an interesting piece of history in that they had remained at sea for 32 days—a feat of arms not parallelled since Nelson's day. They were also away from their main bases at Sydney for more than 90 days. It was during one of these suicide aircraft attacks that one of those famous exchanges of naval signals for which the RN is renowned took place: *Formidable* (hit by kamikaze): 'Little Yellow Bastard'. Admiral Vian (in *Indomitable*): 'Are you referring to me?'.

Whilst the BPF was operating off Okinawa, *Implacable* had arrived in the Pacific in May 1945 with 21 Avengers (828 Squadron), 48 Seafires (801 and 880 Squadrons) and 12 Fireflies (1771 Squadron). The carrier moved up to Manus at the beginning of June and she was deployed with *Ruler* to Truk, for what was termed 'live training' against Japanese positions, where she launched 216 sorties in two days. It is significant to note that 828 Squadron was worked up to fly night interdiction sorties—the only BPF carrier so trained with Avenger aircraft. In July it was *Formidable, Implacable* and *Victorious* who returned to Manus to prepare for the air attacks on the Japanese mainland island of Honshu.

In his classic work on the aircraft carrier, Norman Polmar records that: 'The British carriers had contributed significantly to the Okinawa campaign . . . [they] proved the value of armoured flight decks . . . when similar damage [from kamikazes] would have knocked out a US carrier'.*

The large scale operations mounted in the Pacific Ocean during 1945 were classical examples of combined carrier power. The magnitude of the operations can be grasped by imagining that once an hour about 500 aircraft took off and 500 landed in the combined US and British Fleets! Just how was this vast aerial *Armada* controlled? 'I have', says Captain Duncan Lewin, CB, CBE, DSO, DSC [+], a wartime FAA pilot and later Captain of *Eagle* 'to express the view that the Pacific carrier was centred on the Fighter Director Officers (FDOs). The incidence of radar, however primitive, of improved R/T ship-to-ship, and ship-to-air communication, all of which was centred in the Fighter Direction Office, conspired to lead to the Command being nearly entirely reliant on the FDO for the information upon which decisions had to be made. The Command was superlative but would have been as vulnerable as Jellicoe at Jutland but for the FDO.'

When asked the nature of the FDO's job during those days, Captain Lewin, the senior British FDO on Vian's staff, had this to say: 'The Pacific was the first and, incidentally, the last occasion when strategic air power was exercised on a

* *Aircraft Carriers*, (Doubleday), 1969.

massive scale from ships. Although these operations were predominantly conducted by the USN, the BPF played a significant part in the closing stages. The control of operations on this scale and the air defence of the fleets from which they were mounted, posed problems which would have been insoluble even a few years earlier. Without radar, however rudimentary, and a fairly elaborate system of voice communication, they would have remained insoluble. Additionally, a range of skilled officers and men capable of maintaining and operating this new material, which was only just becoming available, had to be recruited and trained from scratch. The requisite skills did not exist until the material which called for them had been developed and deployed.

'The end product of a great deal of strenuous and imaginative work ashore was an Aircraft Direction Room (ADR) in every major warship but predominantly in aircraft carriers. Supported by a devoted and competent body of ratings, without whom the thing would have been impossible, the Fighter Direction Officers (FDOs) became the interface between airborne pilots, the Command and operational planners. Because the war was almost exclusively an air war, nearly everything of operational, and certainly tactical, consequence was routed through the ADR. Perforce tne FDOs, most of whom had been actors, hop merchants, lawyers, school boys or a host of other occupations a few months earlier, had to learn on the job. Because of the imperfections of the available equipment, including IFF (Identification, Friend or Foe), the air defence of the fleet smacked much more of an art than a science. There is no doubt that being dedicated to an activity 24 hours a day for months on end engenders a sixth sense which no amount of formal training can impart. This, together with the youth, enthusiasm and stamina of those concerned resulted in the BPF's FDOs putting up a performance of which they could be justly proud'.

On the offensive side, the BPF was concentrating on the Tokyo Plain and *Implacable*'s aircraft flew just under 1,000 sorties during eight days when flying was possible. Operations included attacks against airfields, shipyards, factories and railway installations, the province of the Avengers and Fireflies, whilst the Seafires flew armed sweeps attacking targets of opportunity. *Implacable*, together with *Formidable* and *Victorious*, were then withdrawn from the operational area and, although they did not know it, their war ended on August 11 1945. Two days before, one of *Formidable*'s Corsair pilots, from 1841 Squadron, Lieutenant Robert Gray, RCNVR, a British Columbian who already held the DSC, led a formation against Japanese warships in Onagawa Wan Bay and sank a destroyer. Gray, oblivious to the enemy's ack-ack, pressed home a most determined attack and sank the warship. He was, however, unable to recover the aircraft and lost his life as the Corsair plunged into the Bay. This gallant act was recognised by the award of a posthumous Victoria Cross—the British Empire's highest gallantry award—and the only *one* awarded to an FAA aircrew member operating from a carrier! [Perhaps a reflection of the problems the FAA still faced in the higher echelons of the service?]

Illustrious had already returned home and *Indomitable* was still at Sydney, leaving only *Indefatigable* to operate alongside the Americans until VJ-Day. She carried 40 Seafires, 12 Fireflies and 18 Avengers into the final stages of World War 2, and anchored in Tokyo Bay with the *Victoria* fleet on August 27 1945.

In the event, the light fleet carriers despatched to the Pacific—*Venerable, Vengeance, Glory* and *Colossus*—were not deployed in action. There was,

*Four of the new light fleet carriers were destined to have joined the BPF for the projected long struggle against the Japanese. This rather unique shot shows those four carriers lying together in Australian waters—*Colossus, Glory, Venerable *and* Vengeance *(RN via C.H. Vines).*

however, tremendous work for them to do with the coming of peace—POWs and internees to be repatriated, pirates to suppress and general transportation duties. *Glory* was, however, the venue for the Japanese surrender of the South West Pacific whilst escort carriers, such as *Archer* and *Hunter* (21 ACS) were busy in the Indian Ocean.

Rear Admiral A.D. Torlesse, Captain of *Hunter*, takes up the story. 'Early in February 1945, *Royalist, Hunter* and *Stalker* sailed for Trincomalee to join the East Indies fleet. During the summer *Hunter* took part in various operations against the Japanese in the general area of the Andaman and Nicobar Islands and the north end of Sumatra, and in support of the army in its operations ending in the capture of Rangoon. During one operation her aircraft found the Japanese cruiser *Haguro* in the Malacca Straits, and she was sunk in a brilliant destroyer operation during the following night (May 16 1945). On this occasion a Japanese aircraft attempted to bomb *Hunter*, the unlucky destroyer she was refuelling at the time received the bomb intended for the carrier.

'With other units of the fleet, *Hunter* took part in the surrender and occupation of Penang. Then, as Senior Officer of a division of four escort carriers, she provided fighter cover for Operation Zipper, the assault landing at Port Dickson which was unopposed, thence she proceeded to Singapore to take part in the surrender ceremony. In October, *Hunter* sailed for the UK where, after discharging aircraft and stores, she and *Stalker* sailed for the USA to be handed over to the US Navy.' So ended an interesting but so far poorly documented interval in the carrier story.

Indomitable, Vengeance, Venerable and *Colossus* under Rear Admiral

Harcourt carried out the occupation of Hong Kong and adjacent mainland Chinese ports. Later, the escort carrier, *Slinger*, arrived with RAF personnel. On September 16 1945 the Japanese forces at Hong Kong formally surrendered to Harcourt. It was only then that the British realised just how bad conditions had been in the Colony under the Japanese. Peter George, then a young Sub-Lieutenant with 1850 Squadron (*Vengeance*) recalls that his ship's navigator's wife had been interned in 1942 and that on liberation by an FAA party, her husband did not recognise her because she had aged so much.

The BPF continued to exist for some months after the war had ended, involved in all the problems that the aftermath of a bloody war brings. Air Groups were changed as Lend-Lease aircraft were withdrawn from service and carrier personnel were withdrawn to be de-mobbed. In the light fleets, the Barracudas were replaced by Fireflies. In early 1946, *Implacable*, still on duty, had embarked 18 Seafires (801 Squadron), 12 Avengers (828) and 12 Firefly night fighters (1790). The night fighter concept was now beginning to take shape and it was soon found that a two-man crew (Fireflies) were far more effective than single pilot (Hellcat) operations, especially in bad weather.

So what did the BPF achieve and what were the results in the carrier navy? After the respect earned from the Americans by the FAA, the most important achievement was the ability to train up aircrew and flight deck personnel rapidly—in three months. They were ready to operate side by side with the better equipped Americans in less time than it had taken ever before. The need for a twin-engined aircraft had been demonstrated and plans were in hand at home to provide an effective carrier fighter of that configuration. The armoured deck concept was sound but the actual size of the carrier had to be increased because the increasing size of late-generation aircraft like the Avenger and the forthcoming Firebrand would necessitate more room even if the same number of aircraft were going to be accommodated.

It is hardly conceivable that the RN had *52* carriers in service and 18 under construction in 1945, but three years later, only *Implacable, Triumph* and *Ocean* remained active. The ambitious carrier programmes which, with the light of experience from the Pacific, had led to the superior design of the *Audacious* and *Hermes* Classes were deferred. The *Gibraltar* super-carrier Class was abandoned. As we shall see in Chapter 11, not all was doom and despondency though.

Chapter 10

The light fleets

'805 flew from Nowra
To embark for a tropical cruise
We were greeted in Vengeance *the right way*
The Fish-heads bought plenty of booze
Oh land us on, Hughie land us on'.

From 'Hughie' (tune: *Frankie & Johnny*), *FAA Song Book*

The disastrous turn of events which led Britain to have only seven aircraft carriers available to the fleet in 1941 (*Illustrious* and *Formidable* were both undergoing repairs in the USA) led to the Admiralty looking for ways of quickly producing fleet carriers on a smaller scale. They were not, however, scaled down versions of the *Illustrious* Class armoured fleet carriers but differed in several respects, most notably in having a mercantile hull and no armour. Sixteen ships were planned in two classes, but only ten were to see service in the RN: **Colossus Class** (13,190-13,350 tons)—*Colossus, Glory, Ocean, Perseus, Pioneer. Theseus, Triumph, Venerable, Vengeance* and *Warrior*; and **Majestic Class** (14,000 tons)—*Hercules, Leviathan, Magnificent, Majestic, Powerful* and *Terrible*.

Despite the good intentions of the Board, only six units of the *Colossus* were commissioned and operational by VJ-Day; these were the light fleet carriers, *Colossus, Glory, Venerable* and *Vengeance*, plus the aircraft maintenance carriers *Perseus* and *Pioneer*—a new breed. The aircraft maintenance carrier concept had been planned in 1938 to provide the fleet's carrier squadrons with world-wide back-up, and one ship, the 4,750 ton *Unicorn*, had been laid down a few months prior to the outbreak of war. When completed in 1943, she was used as an operational carrier at Salerno (with Seafires) and later on convoy duties with the Home and Mediterranean Fleets, before going East of Suez in 1944 and ending up in the Pacific from whence she returned to Britain in 1946. After three years of reserve, she again sailed to the Far East in the role of a ferry and spares carrier, a duty which she performed admirably during the Korean conflict 1950-53. She also doubled as troopship on several occasions. After a further six years in reserve, she was finally scrapped at Dalmuir in 1959. Often mistaken for a light fleet, *Unicorn* was a rather ungainly looking warship with a high-free board and tall island superstructure. *Pioneer* and *Perseus* also carried out valuable service in maintenance roles until they too went to the breaker's yard in 1954 and 1958 respectively. In 1951, however, *Perseus* was used for steam catapult trials—another revolutionary British invention, which is dealt with later in the book.

In World War 2, then, the light fleets did not see action, except in the shape of the anti-piracy operations carried out by *Vengeance* off Malta, where Barbary Coast pirates were again active after the Axis had been driven out of North Africa. At Hong Kong, after VJ-Day, *Vengeance*'s air group was in action against Chinese pirates in the 'islands'. These operations mainly consisted of flare dropping by the Barracudas to aid surface forces at night, and machine gun attacks by the Corsairs.

In the BPF, all four operational light fleets were equipped with Corsairs and Barracudas, eg, *Colossus* with 1846 and 827 Squadrons, respectively. In home waters, *Ocean*, the fifth unit to be commissioned, had been equipped with Hellcat NFII (892 Squadron) and Firefly NF1 (816 Squadron) night fighters, to develop a new role for carrier-borne fighter aircraft. The name ship of the first group was *Colossus*, yet another Tyne-built ship, laid down in June 1942 and launched in September 1943. In 1945, she joined the BPF's 11th ACS just in time for the end of hostilities. Part of Rear Admiral Harcourt's Hong Kong relief force, *Colossus* spent the next few months ferrying medical teams and food to help relieve the suffering of those who had been in Japanese hands during World War 2.

Only two weeks after returning to Britain (July 1946), *Colossus* was transferred on loan to the French Navy and renamed *Arromanches*. She spent two spells in the South China Seas, operating off Indo-China in 1949 and 1953-54, having been purchased by France in 1951. *Arromanches* was again in action off Suez in 1956, flying Chance Vought Corsairs and, after a refit in 1957, she emerged as an angled-deck carrier flying Breguet Alize ASW aircraft until another refit in 1968. After this, she was dubbed a *Porte Helicoptérès*—a Helicopter Carrier—and operated 24 ASW helicopters, with the occasional fixed-wing deployments until 1972. She was paid off in 1974. '

At Belfast, *Glory* was commissioned in April 1945 and, after a brief work up, left to join the 11th ACS in the Pacific. In September, she received the surrender

This photograph was originally captioned in Lieutenant Commander Vines' personal album as: 'That's what we called a deck park!'. What more can be said about the rows of Barracudas and Corsairs aboard Colossus *during a transit through the Suez Canal* (RN).

Crossing the line is an important part of the tradition of the British seaman and naturally aircraft carriers were no exception. In fact, the large area offered by the flight deck provided an ample setting for King Neptune's Court. Here the Court Photographer is attempting to capture a victim's image on film. Note the large notice on the island super-structure warning the flight deck party to take heed of propellers (Captain Neame).

of Japanese Forces in New Guinea and, like her sister-ships, assisted with the evacuation of POWs. *Glory* stayed in the Pacific area until 1947 when she was due for refit. This was completed in 1949 and the carrier was assigned to the Mediterranean before becoming involved in the Korean conflict, first during its worst period in 1951, again in 1952, and finally in 1953. During this time she also contributed a naval air presence over Malaya during the successful anti-communist operations. Periods with the 1 and 2 ACS followed before she began ferry operations to the Far East. *Glory* then took on another role in January 1955, that of a snow relief base in Scotland, during a particularly bad winter. The plan to convert her into a troopship was abandoned in 1958 and in August 1961 she was towed away to be broken up at Inverkeithing.

Her sister-ship, *Ocean*, led a similar life after commissioning in August 1945. In December she was the venue for the first jet landing* and later she served with 2 ACS in the Mediterranean. There, she was engaged in supply operations to Palestine and later she went to the Far East trooping. Korea was *Ocean*'s first taste of action before Cyprus took her attention in 1955. Again in action, at Suez, *Ocean*'s helicopters lifted 500 officers and men of 45 RM Commando into Port Said, so opening the way for an entirely new type of British warship—the commando carrier.

In 1957, she was placed in extended reserve and was put up for disposal in 1958, being scrapped in 1962. Meanwhile *Triumph* and *Theseus* were completed in early 1946. With no active role to play following peace, *Triumph* was refitted as a training and trials carrier, and was engaged in twin-engined aircraft trials. In 1949, she was deployed to the Far East and her aircraft were in action over Korea following the outbreak of hostilities there. Called home in 1950, she acted

---

* By Lieutenant Commander E.M. Brown in a Vampire—see Chapter 11.

as a troop transport before taking on another training role—that of Cadet Training Ship. Following a period in reserve, she was converted to the role of Heavy Repair Ship and was transferred to the Far East. In 1972 she was refitted and placed in reserve in 1975; she is still alongside at Chatham, at the time of writing.

Theseus, on the other hand, had a slightly more active flying life. Initially deployed to the Far East for 1st ACS BPF, she was refitted to become flagship of 3rd ACS Home Fleet, where she stayed between 1948 and 1950, during which time the first carrier landings at night by jet were undertaken on June 19 1950. *Theseus* relieved her sister-ship, *Triumph*, off Korea with 17th Carrier Air Group where she stayed until rejoining the Home Fleet in 1951. She went twice to the Mediterranean Fleet during the Korean conflict in order to relieve *Ocean* and *Glory* for service there. In 1954, replacing *Implacable* as the flagship, she joined the Home Fleet Training Squadron where she stayed until 1956 and Suez. At the end of that year she was placed in reserve prior to being 'made into razor blades' in March 1958.

The Commonwealth Navies were also destined to receive light fleets of their own and, following *Ocean* from the yards, were *Warrior* and *Magnificent* for Canada, *Sydney* (ex-*Terrible*) and *Melbourne* (ex-*Majestic*) for Australia. *Warrior* was laid down in 1942, launched two years later and completed in January 1946. She was commissioned as HMCS *Warrior* on January 24 and left Portsmouth for Halifax, Nova Scotia, two months later. During her Canadian duty she operated Seafires (803 Squadron), Fireflies (825 Squadron) and Barracudas, building on the RCN's experience during their operations with the escort carrier, *Nabob*. The Canadians had the expertise and manpower available to buy an escort carrier in 1943, but were prohibited from doing so by political problems associated with Lend-Lease, nevertheless a Canadian took command of *Nabob* in September of that year with a predominantly Canadian crew—the largest ship in the RCN at that time. *Nabob* saw service with the Home Fleet until August 1944, when she was torpedoed off Norway. Although, with great skill and courage, she was navigated home, the Admiralty pronounced her beyond economic repair as a warship and she was eventually sold to the Dutch for mercantile use after the war.

*Warrior was replaced by the larger (*Majestic *Class) light fleet* Magnificent *which served with the RCN until 1957. In 1957, cruising off Canada's Atlantic Provinces, she carried a mixed air group of Sea Furies and Avengers* (Public Archives Canada/DND).

The experience of operating the Avengers and Wildcats (of 852 Squadron) allowed the RCN to use *Warrior* until such time as their larger *Majestic* Class carrier, *Magnificent*, was completed by Harland and Wolff at Belfast. On returning to the RN, *Warrior* was taken in hand for special flight deck trials and these are described in the next chapter because they are part of the great revolution in carrier design after World War 2.

Following the trials *Warrior* went into reserve, before returning to active service as an aircraft transport for the operational carriers off Korea. Further service for Korea followed before, in 1954-56, she underwent an expensive refit to equip her with an angled deck* and new arrester gear. The refit was necessary because she was due to go to Christmas Island, wearing the pennant of Commodore R.B.N. Hicks, DSO, RN, for Operation Grapple—the British nuclear tests in the Pacific Ocean. After this unusual interlude, she was put up for sale and in 1958 was purchased by the Armada Republica Argentina and renamed *Independencia*. She was withdrawn from Argentine service in 1971, after many years of operating Corsairs and North American Harvards from her decks.

Magnificent was completed in 1948 and served with the RCN until 1957/58 with Fairey Fireflies and Hawker Sea Furies (871 Squadron) embarked. In 1950, the decision was made to replace the Fireflies with Avengers and these continued until the ship was withdrawn in 1957. A sole remaining Avenger is preserved at CFB Shearwater, Nova Scotia, where the ship's bell also rests, bearing witness to Canada's role in the development of the carrier.

The Commonwealth connection was also followed by *Vengeance* which, after service on the BPF with Corsairs (1850) and Barracudas (812) under Captain Mortimer Neame DSO+, RN, relieved *Theseus* as Home Fleet training carrier. There her original Arctic warfare fittings proved most useful during the cold weather exercise Operation Rusty in 1948-49. Then followed a spell as a ferry carrier to Singapore, after which *Vengeance* went to Devonport to be converted for service with Royal Australian Navy and the 5th Aircraft Carrier Squadron. In Australian waters she trained aircrew and flight deck personnel for active service in Korea, but did not see service, this being left to the larger *Sydney*.

The 20th CAG (Carrier Air Group) was embarked in *Vengeance* in the summer of 1953 with Sea Furies and Fireflies (805 and 816 Squadrons). Later that year and periodically in 1954, the 21st CAG was embarked with 808 and 817 Squadrons, again Sea Furies and Fireflies respectively, but no squadrons were embarked in the ship after May 6 1954. Again back at Devonport, *Vengeance* was put into reserve until December 1956 when she was sold to the other airminded South American Navy—Brazil. After a refit in the Netherlands, to provide her with an angled deck, mirror-sight deck landing aid and new radar, the *Minas Gerais*, as she became known, commissioned on December 6 1960. At the time of writing she continues to be deployed in the anti-submarine warfare role, with Grumman Trackers and Sikorsky S61 helicopters.

Vengeance's sister-ship, *Venerable*, was also originally equipped with Corsairs (1851) and Barracudas (814), but in 1948 she was commissioned in the Royal Netherlands Navy as *Karel Doorman* (her predecessor of the same name

---

* See Chapter 11 for a description of this major achievement by Captain Dennis Cambell and Lewis Boddington.

One facet of seamanship developed during World War 2, particularly during the Pacific campaign, was underway replenishment, as demonstrated here by Vengeance *and an attendant destroyer. The carrier is portraying the role of tanker and making use of her heavy deck crane (formerly known as a seaplane crane) for passing a fuel line to the escort* (RN via Captain Neame).

was the Clydebank-built escort carrier, *Nairana*) and she operated a mixed bag of Sea Furies and Fireflies (later replaced by Avengers) until her major refit in 1954. This operation provided a steam catapult and an angled deck suitable for Hawker Sea Hawk and Grumman Tracker operations, although the former jets were replaced by Sikorsky H-34 helicopters before she was withdrawn from service in 1968. A major fire had caused this withdrawal, but Argentina, impressed by the 8 degree angled deck and needing to obtain a jet-capable carrier to operate their A-4 Skyhawks from, bought her. Using the incomplete *Majestic* Class carrier *Leviathan*'s boilers, she was refitted and commissioned as *Veinticinco de Mayo*. She is still in service although her silhouette has changed so drastically that she can hardly be recognised as a light fleet. None of the *Majestic* Class actually entered service with the Royal Navy, although *Leviathan* did languish in Portsmouth Harbour for many years after her construction was suspended in May 1946.

Harland and Wolff built and completed the third light fleet to sail under the Canadian flag—the angled deck *Bonaventure*. She was sold to the RCN in 1952 and completed in January 1957. She featured all the then current aids, including a steam catapult system and deck-landing mirror sight. Initially equipped with the McDonnell F2H-3 Banshee single seat jet fighter and the Canadian-built Grumman CS-2F Tracker ASW aircraft, she operated in the strike role until 1961. *Bonaventure* then became an ASW fixed-wing carrier when the Banshees were phased out, but Trackers remained aboard and Sikorsky Sea King helicopters were embarked. Despite completing a half-life refit and modernisation in 1967, *Bonaventure* was destined to be one of the shortest serving *Majestic* Class, when the Liberal Government of Pierre Trudeau paid her off on July 3 1970. She was later sold for scrap and ended her days at Taiwan.

The last light fleet to be commissioned and certainly the last one to see action, was the *Vikrant*. Laid down by Vickers Armstrong in 1943, this Tyne-built ship

Top left *The fourth unit of the BPF's light fleet carrier squadron was* Venerable, *which became the Dutch carrier* Karel Doorman *in 1948 and later the Argentine's* 25 de Mayo *(1969) where it continues to serve* (RN via D. Barrett).

Centre left Venerable *in her guise of* Karel Doorman *with a Grumman Tracker parked for'ard. Note the typically Dutch radar fit which is also characteristic of* 25 de Mayo (RN via Admiral Griffin).

Left *Originally laid down at Harland & Wolff's yard at Belfast as* Powerful, *the Canadian light fleet* Bonaventure *served the Maple Leaf from 1952 until defence cuts forced her out of service in the late 1960s. That was when this photograph was taken showing her anti-submarine air group comprising Trackers and Sea King helicopters, with an S-55 plane-guard helicopter aft* (Canadian Forces photo).

Above *Illustrating several facets of modern carrier activity, this photograph of a Skyhawk of 805 Squadron (which flew Sea Furies in Korea from* Sydney) *after recovery is worthy of study. The aircraft has been halted by the arrester wire and the short distance of the landing run is adequately illustrated. Note also the Landing Signals Officer's position aft, by the first wire and the low-level projector sight* (RAN).

Left *The underwater lines of a light fleet, designed mainly, it is said, to protect the flight deck in heavy seas. This view can be compared with* Hermes *(page 29) and* Ranee *(page 93)* (RN via Peter George).

Below *Probably* Melbourne's *last visit to British waters was in June 1977 when she took part in the Silver Jubilee Review at Spithead to mark the HM The Queen's 25 years on the throne. Ranged on the angled deck are Skyhawks and Trackers.*

Above *After serving with the Royal Navy,* Vengeance *moved south and was attached to the Royal Australian Navy for several years. She is seen here with Barracudas and Corsairs embarked in January 1946, before transfer. Compare the superstructure with its limited radar and radio antennae with the photograph* **below** *which shows the island of* Melbourne *(ex-*Majestic*) during flying operations in November 1970. The aircraft on deck are a Douglas Skyhawk (hardly visible), a pair of Grumman Trackers and another pair—Westland Wessex helicopters* (Australian War Memorial Negs 125127 & M787(9)).

was completed by Harland and Wolff for the Indian Navy in 1961. Since then she has been Asia's only aircraft carrier and, in 1972, played a part in the Indo-Pakistan War. Her air group today consists of Sea Hawk fighters and Breguet Alize anti-submarine aircraft—just as it did in 1961. There is, however, now every indication that a new fighter, in the shape of the British Aerospace Sea Harrier, will enter service with the Indian Navy to replace the venerable Sea Hawk, whilst the Alizes will continue to operate as before. It will be noted, however, that all the other light fleet operators have reverted to America to provide their air groups, with the twin-engined Tracker aircraft predominant.

The first *Majestic* Class to be laid down was *Terrible*, and in 1948 she was purchased by the RAN, being accepted for service in 1949 as *Sydney*. As an operational fixed-wing carrier, she operated 37 Sea Fury and Firefly (815 and 816) piston-engined aircraft. In April 1950 the 21st CAG formed and was embarked in *Sydney* with Sea Furies and Fireflies (808 and 817 Squadrons respectively). They saw service in Korea, relieving *Glory* in September 1951. In 1957, *Sydney* was destined to become a flying training carrier to provide work-up and deck landing practice facilities for the newly commissioned *Melbourne*. Her conversion, however, was actually carried out to fit her out as a fast transport, mainly for the Australian involvement in Malaya. She was recommissioned in 1962, but kept her helicopter facilities which proved most useful in Vietnam during the next decade, and *Sydney* was nicknamed *Vung Tau Ferry,* her last trip being in March 1972. *Sydney* was decommissioned in 1973 and put up for sale, being sold for scrap in October 1975.

Laid down only five months later, but not completed until 1955, *Melbourne* (ex-*Majestic*) arrived in Australia on May 10 1956 with an air complement of Sea Venom and Gannet aircraft. During the next 11 years *Melbourne*, as flagship of the RAN, played a most active role, representing Australia at sea, especially with SEATO (South East Asia Treaty Organisation). In 1967-69 came her half-life refit and a new air group made up of American-designed and built fixed-wing aircraft—McDonnel Douglas A-4G Skyhawks and Grumman Trackers—together with British-built Westland Wessex 31 helicopters (later replaced by Sea Kings from the same stable). Another refit followed in 1975-76 before *Melbourne* visited the UK for the Queen's Silver Jubilee Review at Spithead. Although due for replacement by *Invincible* in 1982 (until the Falklands conflict intervened), the decision to scrap *Melbourne* was confirmed in 1983, after the carrier had been paid off in June 1982. *Melbourne* was broken up in South Korea in August 1984 and as *Invincible* was not transferred to the Royal Australian Navy, which today relies on the limited maritime strike capability of the Royal Australian Air Force, its surface escorts and submarines for sea control. The RAN's Fleet Air Arm suffered a major blow to moral when the fixed wing element was finally disbanded when it also became clear that *Hermes* (the Falkland's flagship) would also not be transferred from the Royal Navy; many aircrew left the service or joined the Royal Navy.

Chapter 11

The post war revolution

The rapid run down of the RN's carrier force after VJ-Day is understandable but, in the long term, it was almost disastrous for the development of the carrier. Following the success of Japanese operations in the Pacific, the Admiralty had, in 1942, drawn up plans to produce a class of aircraft carriers. At 36,800 tons (37,392 tonnes) and with over 800 feet (244 m) of flight deck, the ships would be uprated *Implacable* Class designs which could carry 100 of the large American-designed naval aircraft. The four major warship yards were contracted to build *Audacious* (Harland and Wolff), *Africa* (Fairfield), *Eagle* (Vickers Armstrong) and *Irresistible* (Cammell Laird). A further super-carrier class was also envisaged, to be called the *Gibraltar* Class, its units would be of 45,000 tons (45,723 tonnes). The termination of hostilities effectively put an end to the plans and the *Gibraltar* Class plus *Africa* and *Eagle* were cancelled; *Audacious* became *Eagle* and *Irresistible* became *Ark Royal.*

The 1942-43 building programme would have provided the RN with three super-carriers, four large fleet carriers, ten *Colossus* Class, six *Majestic* Class and eight slightly larger *Hermes* Class. The latter Class were planned at 18,300 tons (18,594 tonnes) with 736 feet (224 m) flight decks and an air complement of 50 aircraft. Again the shipyards were contracted but, in the event, only four were proceeded with: *Albion* (Swan Hunter), *Bulwark* and *Centaur* (Harland and Wolff), while at Vickers Armstrong, *Elephant* was re-named *Hermes*—the last British fixed-wing carrier to be launched. In the late 1940s, the RN would have possessed 38 fleet and light fleet carriers, plus 1,300 front-line aircraft. As events turned out, the changing industrial and political scene meant that aircraft carriers had a very low priority in terms of hulls, but thankfully the imaginative and world-beating flight deck and other systems under development in the latter half of the war were continued.

Despite the experience built up during the war years, the flight deck accident rates in the late 1940s were appallingly high, around 200 accidents per 10,000 deck landings—1 in 50! Despite an increase in landing speeds with the introduction of jet-powered aircraft, there was a gradual improvement from December 1949 onwards. By 1951, a rate of 100 accidents per 10,000 deck landings had been achieved. The Admiralty Adviser on Aircraft Accidents (AAA) concluded that the worst period for accidents, the second half of 1949, was caused by inexperience in operation of the standard deck landing technique introduced in July of that year.

For some years, although operating the same aircraft types, the RN and the

USN had adopted two different types of deck landing technique. In the RN the system was basically a 500 feet (152 m) circuit with a base leg approach on the curve (because of the invisibility caused to the pilot by the big propeller and engine) just above the stalling speed. This is the speed at which the aircraft is only just staying in the air, and by way of comparison the following table may be useful:

Aircraft	Date	Stalling speed
Fairey Flycatcher	1924	44 knots (81.5 kph)
Blackburn Skua	1938	63 knots (116.7 kph)
Hawker Sea Fury	1948	85 knots (157.4 kph)

Higher stalling speeds meant higher approach and deck landing speeds, making it more difficult for the DLCO to give the 'cut' when the aircraft was exactly the right place over the rounddown—'in the groove' as it has been called.

During 1948/49, an interim deck landing technique was introduced using the RN's approach with USN flight deck signals. Despite a series of training courses, the first of which began in February 1948, to convert DLCOs to the new system, the result was in the words of a pilot at that time: 'utter confusion!' Carrier trials were carried out in *Implacable* so that DLCOs had a chance to use the signals themselves and to be also on the receiving end. In a nutshell, the signals were completely reversed so that whereas previously pilots had been used to up-stretched arms meaning 'go-up, you're low' they now had to remember that the same signal meant 'you're high'; in the tense moments of an emergency landing it was not really known how the old hands would react. In practice, the so-called standard technique was adopted which allowed for a 150 feet (46 m) circuit flying an imaginary box and the pilot being given the 'chop' as the aircraft 'flared' 30 feet (9.1 m) above the deck, catching the wire. In such aircraft as the Sea Fury, the point of flare was absolutely critical, but in the Firefly it was a little less so. Both Regular and RNVR pilots had to contend with a complete reversal in batting signs nonetheless.

When in 1955/56, the revolutionary angled deck/mirror landing sight combination was introduced, a new approach and a 500/600 feet (150/185 m) circuit were introduced. Pilot error was still a major contributor to landing accidents, especially those where the undercarriage was not locked down or where it was inadvertently retracted whilst the aircraft was on deck. AAA established in 1951 that 70 per cent of fatal accidents were caused by pilot error, including loss of control during aerobatics and, in poor visibility, crashing into the sea.

Although the evidence suggests that increased aircraft performance was more than compensated for by technological developments, there was a critical period in the late 1940s when aircraft were large and fast enough to render operations on the small axial flight decks very hazardous. The main problem seems to have been a very high percentage of barrier crashes, the result of skipping or floating over the arrester wires or even losing a hook there. Longer stroke oleos, which had the effect of dampening the 'bounce' on the deck and dampers in the arrester hook mechanism helped a great deal.

The advent of jet aircraft with tricycle undercarriage improved the pilot's view for deck landing and this certainly compensated to a considerable extent for the higher approach and deck landing speeds. The tricycle arrangement made aircraft much easier to bring on board a carrier as the pilot could see the

Once the undercarriage 'bounce' problem had been sorted out, the Firefly was considered to be a good deck landing aircraft and, together with Sea Furies in Theseus *and other light fleets off Korea, they achieved several periods of over 1,000 accident free landings. This particular Firefly is about to take an arrester wire (seen raised above the flight deck in the bottom of the photograph) with its 'A-frame' hook, suspended below the fuselage* (RN via R.B. Wigg).

deck throughout the approach, something not possible with tail wheel aeroplanes like the Seafire, Firefly and Sea Fury.

A firm believer that the problems of deck landing would be made easier by jet aircraft with tricycle undercarriage was Lieutenant Commander J.S. 'Bill' Bailey, OBE, who had completed 2,000 deck landings by 1950*. During this time, only two minor deck accidents had been recorded against Bailey, both of which had taken place in Wildcat operations from *Argus* during World War 2. The problem of landing propeller-driven carrier aircraft was still there. Despite this, however, the RNVR Firefly and Seafire Squadrons managed to complete their deck-landing training without great mishap.

The recently introduced Firefly—Marks 4, 5 and 6—had a higher accident rate than its hangar-companion, the Sea Fury, for a time until the larger stroke oleos and improved arrester hook dampers could be introduced.

A major limiting factor in the safe operation of carrier-borne aircraft is the degree of movement on the parent carrier. Although this factor was shown to be a contributor to deck landing accidents, the official policy, as exemplified by the AAA Monthly Summary, October 1951, was that 'a really well worked-up squadron can deck land in unfavourable sea conditions'. This was proved correct many times but, as the AAA concluded, 'a higher degree of skill is required'. During *Ark Royal IV*'s first shake down to Gibraltar, her newly embarked air group of Seahawks (800 and 898 Squadrons), Gannets (824) and Skyraiders (849B Flight) operated safely in bad Biscayan weather and also at night! Experienced pilots can land almost anything anywhere, as Seafire and

* One witness of this feat in *Illustrious* was Lieutenant 'Paddy' McKeown, who recalls that Bailey was flying a Seafire and had joined the 'Clockwork Mice' training DLCOs. In all he made some 60 full stop landings that day.

Swordfish pilots found on escort carriers bobbing about like corks in the mid-Atlantic during World War 2.

The problem of steadying down a carrier in a seaway was given considerable thought by interested parties in the Admiralty and at the test establishment at Haslar. At the office of Director, Naval Air Warfare, Captain (now Rear Admiral) A.S. Bolt was like other aviators, convinced that the bow-shape of contemporary British aircraft carriers was wrong. The carrier should make a fine entry in the water, this meant that the bows should be narrow. British carriers had a very wide 'V' stem which gave buoyancy forward in a bad seaway. Despite the fears of Director General Ships that the sea would wash over the 'front end', ship movement trials were carried out. DG Ships' worries were, of course, somewhat spurious because in a sea that produced such a mighty wash, flying would be impossible in any case!

Whilst ships roll, it is the pitch—the forward and aft movement—which caused most concern in the fixed-wing carrier. The period of pitch is dependent on the ship's speed and the distance between waves, rather than as a function of length. On the other hand, the amplitude of pitch is a relationship between ship's length and wave length, together with the ship's draught. Thus a fleet carrier of 30,000 tons (30,482 tonnes), 750 feet (228.6 m) long, such as *Indomitable* was a steadier platform than a light fleet carrier, such as *Glory* or *Theseus*, at 18,000 tons (18,290 tonnes) and 690 feet (210.3 m) in length. Anti-pitch fins were tested in America but the related equipment and machinery weighed so much and anti-pitch flight deck gear added so much top weight that the Navy had, in the end, to rely on the skill and experience of pilots to overcome the difficulties of a moving flight deck.

The Admiralty devised a 'rough weather procedure': (1) Pilots to be informed that ship was pitching and therefore periodical waves-off on this account must be accepted. (2) The ship would be subject to steady periods and pitching periods in cycles, best judged from the bridge. The Commander (Air) or his deputy should warn the DLCO accordingly if motion was momentarily too severe.

The light fleet carriers involved in operations off Korea (1950-53) were fortunate because the Yellow Sea, being almost land-locked, did not suffer from swell and scend common in the open ocean. *Theseus* certainly found this to be true during her operational period there, October 1950-April 1951, when the Yellow Sea, in Captain Bolt's own words 'rarely became sufficiently disturbed to prevent flying operation from a light fleet carrier. *Theseus* achieved a sequence of 1,236 accident-free deck landings in the winter of 1950 and this was just as well as replacement aircraft had to be transported 2,500 miles (4,630 km) from Singapore! In late 1951, *Glory* was off Korea and she achieved a period of 1,115 accident-free landings. AAA concluded that such a 'magnificent effort . . . once more confirms that an increased carrier flying intensity results in a reduced accident rate'.

After leaving Korean waters, *Theseus* went to Hong Kong to engage in a realistic exercise with the Colony's forces. During the operation, the North East monsoon was blowing, causing the carrier to move, particularly to pitch. Such action could easily cause an aircraft to miss the arrester wires and to float into the 'dreaded' barrier. Three such accidents occurred in one day.

*   *   *

'Barrier! Barrier!
It's the biggest bugbear in a carrier,
Batsmen, crazy,
You feel helpless as you float,
And the goofers stand and gloat.'

The Barrier Song Chorus, *FAA Songbook*

The barrier was a dreaded device which, although it protected the parked aircraft for'ard, it usually severely damaged the aircraft which had haplessly engaged it. In single-engined propeller aircraft, the aircrew were reasonably well protected but, with the advent of jets and twin-engined aircraft like the Sea Hornet, something had to be done. Most Captains and all pilots were not keen on the steel barrier!

Donald Gibson, whose association with aircraft carriers spans 29 years (1939-68), feels that the immediate post-war period, especially the time of the Sea Fury and Firefly, was 'the most perilous time for the FAA, even though it was during peacetime. We were flying the most advanced propeller-driven aeroplanes', he continued, 'and of course, one was faced with the dreadful barrier. It was, however, a most vigorous period in carrier development. I can remember that one morning', he recalls, 'there was five barrier crashes, and that was not particularly unusual'.

Aircraft would apparently 'happily' bounce over the barrier and Gibson remembers to this day, seeing his two ground crew, (who moments before had been marshalling his Fury), leap over the carrier's side as another Fury jumped the barrier and 'landed' in the forward deck park. Seven aircraft were destroyed but miraculously no one was seriously hurt and the two ground crew were

The barrier was 'the biggest bugbear in a carrier' the song says, and even experienced pilots could fall foul of it when deck landing. In this case, a Sea Fury has engaged one of Indomitable*'s wires which has 'come adrift' causing the aircraft to make an emergency entry into the barrier. Damage is minimal to the aircraft, but the deck would have remained blocked for several minutes whilst the aircraft was removed, causing other aircraft in the circuit to hold, before commencing their own recoveries* (RN via Captain McKeown).

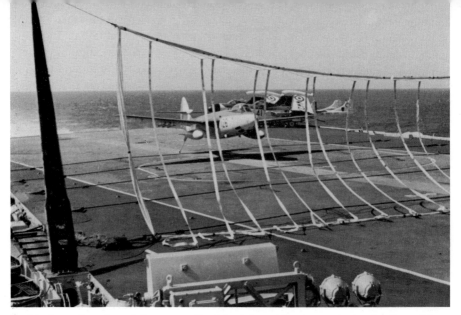

In this shot taken aboard Centaur, *a Sea Hawk is making an emergency landing without wheels, due to an undercarriage fault. In the foreground the emergency nylon barrier has been rigged even though the carrier was equipped with an angled deck* (RN via Captain McKeown).

collected by the planeguard. On another occasion, a fellow pilot 'borrowed' Donald Gibson's Fury, coded 113, and bent it in a barrier jump—not really the thing to do to the Air Group Commander's own mount!

With the operational debut of the Supermarine Attacker—the RN's first operational jet fighter—a new design of barrier had been introduced. Earlier jet operations during the Autumn Exercises of 1949 had seen Sea Vampire F20s embarked in *Implacable*. Despite rough weather conditions a number of successful deck landings on the moving flight deck were made. The steel barrier, however, had not been rigged because of the risk to the pilot, sitting as he did, so close to the aircraft's nose. This meant a slow down of the aircraft recovery interval and hence operational efficiency. When 800 Squadron took their Attackers to sea in *Eagle* in September 1952, a new nylon webbing crash barrier, designed by British Ropes Ltd, was fitted. Unfortunately, it was rigged on the last arrester wire motor, with a second, almost taut wire behind. During an exercise in Northern Waters, 800's Attacker FB1s were returning to the ship, when the CO, Lieutenant Commander (later Captain) George Baldwin, lost his hook on landing and entered the first nylon barrier. It worked perfectly—for 30 yards (27.4 m) anyway—until the Attacker reached the second barrier. This engagement stripped the wings and other appendages from the Attacker which ended up on the forward lift, having been stopped by the steel supporting wire of the second barrier which had cut into the fin. The date was September 21 1952, and the aircraft was WA498, one of the first production batch. Just as a reminder, Baldwin has been plagued with a bad back ever since!

The greatest invention in terms of aircraft carrier safety was the angled deck, which dispensed with the barrier altogether (except for emergency landings), thus allowing free landings again, the first time since 1931! Added to this was the simultaneously-invented mirror landing sight which not only made a pilot's approach that much easier but also helped to reduce the number of arrester

The angled-deck of Centaur, *a partial angle contrived on what would have otherwise been an axial layout, shows up well in this aerial view. During normal flying operations, the parked ten Sea Hawks forward would have been safe because any 'bolting' aircraft could use the angled deck from the lift for'ard to take-off again. The three aircraft with their wings folded (right) are Sea Furies* (RN via Rear Admiral Rolfe).

wires necessary on the flight deck. Rear Admiral (now Vice Admiral Sir Conolly) Abel Smith, as Chief of Naval Air Equipment, was concerned at the problems which the jet age had brought to carrier flying. He set up a high-powered committee, including Captain (now Rear Admiral) Bolt, Captain (now Vice Admiral Sir Richard) Smeeton, Captain (now Rear Admiral) Dennis Cambell and Mr Lewis Boddington, who spent many years on carrier research and development at RAE Farnborough.

Initially the Admiralty had been looking at another idea to improve the performance of carrier aircraft—the flexible deck. This concept was first born in 1944, when the need to increase the range and endurance of the jet aircraft then appearing on the horizon was studied in great detail. In early 1945, RAE Farnborough proposed that undercarriageless naval aircraft were possible. In all, nine schemes were put forward and all were rejected. A tenth scheme was proposed by Major F.M. Green, a retired Royal Flying Corps officer who was known for his inventive genius. He proposed a large flexible rubber carpet suspended along the sides and at one end by shock absorbers. Arrester wires would be positioned at one end of the flight deck and once the landing momentum had been arrested, the wire would pull the aircraft backwards on to a flap which would tilt down and put the machine on to a trolley on the hangar deck below. Take-off would be by means of a trolley-mounted catapult, perhaps not on the same level as the flight deck. So the 'rubber' deck or 'flexible' deck concept was born.

After a great deal of debate, a team led by Lewis Boddington produced models and then full scale tests. Initially a concrete-filled Hotspur glider was dropped on to a practice deck at Farnborough. Lieutenant Commander (A) Eric Brown was selected to carry out the tests, first with the Hotspur and then on a full scale flexible deck mock-up. A Bell Airacobra was selected for an initial

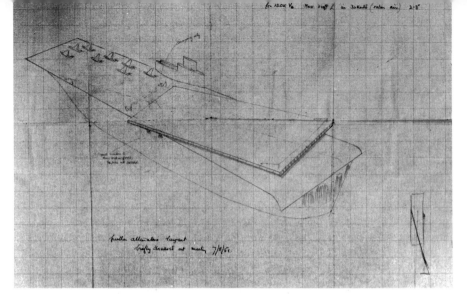

Above *A previously unpublished photograph of Captain Cambell's original sketch for the flexible deck, dated August 7 1951* (Bob Downey). **Below** *RAE scientist Lewis Boddington's original design for* Ark Royal's *angled flight deck, dated August 28 1951. The design was tried in* Triumph *that year (but for touch-and-go only), painted on* Centaur's *flight deck in 1953 and incorporated in* Ark *(then building) for her commissioning in 1955* (Bob Downey).

flying test because its tricycle undercarriage arrangement was the closest approximate to the jet aircraft available. The type of approach to the deck was important and Brown used a Hellcat on the trials carrier *Pretoria Castle* to cross-check his ideas.

The de Havilland Sea Vampire F21 jet was chosen for the trials and was modified to make a belly landing, including the provision of a hook to catch the only arrester wire. After more tests, a first landing on the flexible deck dummy at Farnborough was attempted on December 29 1947. A successful series of trials followed, although the first landing had been a little 'hairy'. At the end of October 1948, it was decided to fit the light fleet carrier, *Warrior*, with a flexible deck up to the after end of the island, with a steel plated dummy deck to finish off the arrangement to the ship's bow.

On November 3 1948 the first trial landing was made at sea and the testing continued until May 1949. It is noteworthy that the Sea Vampire used for the trials was the first British jet to be catapulted from a carrier and the first tricycle

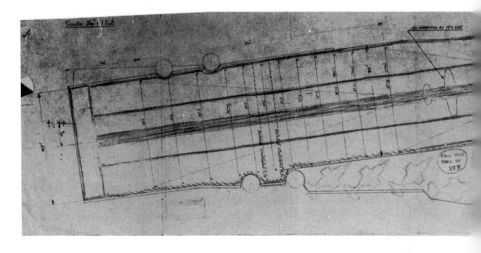

undercarriage aircraft to use this form of launch. Despite a series of successful trials, the system was not adopted for operational service. The reasons were two-fold and it is relevant to quote Eric Brown: 'Firstly, it arrived at the wrong point in time after the war was over and the impetus to military matters was waning rapidly. Secondly, the idea was a little too radical in that it meant a widespread requirement for flexible deck installations ashore and afloat for what was a comparatively small performance gain. In other words, it was not cost-effective'.

It did lead, however, to the most radical idea since the flat-top itself. On August 7 1951, a Conference, chaired by Captain Cambell (as Assistant Chief Naval Representative to the Ministry of Aviation) met at the Ministry to discuss ways and means of operating undercarriageless aircraft from carriers. The discussion centred primarily on the various possible ways in which the flexible deck could be set up for operational, as opposed to trial, conditions. The elimination of the barrier but the retention of the deck park was agreed to be a desirable target. Cambell produced several pencil sketches of possible alternatives and the largest of these showed the flexible deck angled 10 degrees to port.

The idea produced no noticeable reaction at the time, but Lewis Boddington, having pondered on the various schemes, came to the conclusion that the angled principle could also be applied forthwith to *Ark Royal*, then just nearing completion. This would then enable 30,000 lb (13,608 kg) swept wing aircraft to be accepted. Boddington accordingly wrote to Cambell and the Director of Naval Construction (DNC) enclosing a plan view design of such a deck; this was only three weeks after the initial meeting. Since both Cambell and Boddington were also ex-officio responsible for the occasional carrier trial in *Triumph*, it was not long before the angled deck principle was tried out on a touch-and-go basis: the flight deck's landing line being re-painted at 10 degrees, but the arrester wires not being altered (or used) thus necessitating the touch-and-go mode of operations.

Although the trials were outstandingly successful, the Admiralty decided to postpone adoption of the invention until the next generation of carriers. These in the event did not come to be built following the Defence White Paper decision of 1966. It is interesting and somewhat worrying to reflect that this truly revolutionary idea, which had taken only a matter of weeks in the summer and early autumn of 1951 to originate, develop and test, could have been lost to the Royal Navy for ever. As has happened so often in the carrier story, the US Navy

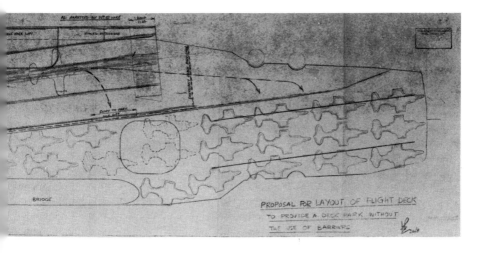

PROPOSAL FOR LAYOUT OF FLIGHT DECK TO PROVIDE A DECK PARK WITHOUT THE USE OF BARRIERS

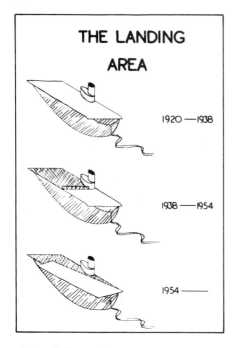

THE LANDING
AREA

1920 —1938

1938 —1954

1954 ———

Left *This illustration, taken from a slide prepared by Rear Admiral Cambell, shows the landing area available to recovering aircraft during the evolution of the fixed-wing carrier. At the top, there is the free deck period; in the middle the barrier blocking off half the deck and finally, the angled deck. The hatched area represents deck parking* (Rear Admiral Cambell).

Right *The new era of carrier design and operations was personified by the 'new' Ark Royal, seen here during her first commission under the guidance of Captain Dennis Cambell, DSC, the co-inventor of the angled-deck which was designed into Ark during her building. Other features, at that time unique, included steam catapults, mirror sight landing aid, DAX, and CC tv. Note, though, a heavy gun armament was still carried* (RN via Rear Admiral Cambell).

(being informed on an exchange basis of our developments) had quickly taken the idea up. Rear Admiral Cambell still recalls the significant looks exchanged between some USN visitors to the Farnborough Air Show in September 1951, when they were first informed of the idea. In May 1953, the US Navy Department suggested as a quid pro quo that USS *Antietam*, fully angled, might give demonstrations in the Channel: this proposal was gladly accepted and the Service Trials Unit, based at Ford on the Sussex coast, carried out the trials. Cambell and Boddington were invited on board as honoured guests and some years later were each awarded the US Legion of Merit.

Meanwhile the impact of *Antietam*'s demonstrations managed to convince the Admiralty that all carriers should be similarly converted as soon as possible. The first such conversion was carried out aboard *Centaur* in 1953, although *Ark Royal* has the distinction of being the world's first carrier to enter service already equipped with an angled deck. It is perhaps significant to record that Dennis Cambell was the *Ark*'s first Captain.

Captains Bolt and Smeeton had proposed a port side extension for *Ark Royal* to give an angle more like the 10 degrees initially suggested by Cambell and Boddington; however the Admiralty was not persuaded and so *Ark* was left with a partially angled deck until her final modernisation some years later. Now that there was no need to use barriers, the tension had gone from carrier landings. There was, however, now a need to update the arrester gear and catapults to keep pace with developments. First, however, we must turn our attention to the invention of Cambell's assistant, Lieutenant Commander (E) (now Rear Admiral) Nick Goodhart—the mirror sight deck landing aid.

Since the early post-war period many pilots had been concerned at the high deck landing accident rate of the comparatively slow aeroplanes on the old axial deck. The standard approach technique helped, but the incoming aircraft, being

tail-wheeled, still tended to bounce even in a tail-down attitude. These piston-engined types were also destined to leave service in the near future and the high rate of approach of the new jets meant that the DLCO would probably be unable to react to any faults in approach attitude in time. Obviously the best way for a pilot to correct his attitude was to judge the situation himself, but here the standard approach lacked the necessary path which would allow him to do that.

Nick Goodhart, an engineering officer and test pilot, considered a steadily descending approach at 3 degrees or so which would allow for the pitch of the carrier's deck. The aircraft could, however, smack into the rounddown or drive into the deck, and although not necessarily fatal in themselves, the aircraft's undercarriage would be wrecked. So the problem was two-fold—give the pilot the opportunity of correcting his approach path himself and have stronger undercarriages fitted to naval aircraft. The latter was a matter for the airframe equipment designs, but the former had to be solved more radically.

'When I was a young sprog, the Goofers I'd enthrall,
Hermes, Vic and Centaur, I guess I've played them all,
But never did one good DL—at least that I recall,
That deaf dumb and blind kid—sure flies a low meatball.'
FAA Songbook, (Tune: *Pinball Wizard*)

The difficulties inherent in deck landing an aircraft on a moving deck became increasingly difficult. We have seen how, just before the outbreak of war, the DLCO was introduced and was equipped with 'bats' to control the approach attitude of an aircraft to be recovered. In *Victorious*, a small semaphore was installed to relieve the 'batsmen' of the necessity of standing up with his back

Top left *Aboard* Eagle, *the 'badgers' attach a* Wyvern *to the last of the hydraulic accelerators. Note the hold-back ramps. The rollers are positioned behind* (Fleet Air Arm Museum).

Left *A remarkable illustration of the mirror deck landing aid in operation aboard a fixed-wing carrier, probably* Bulwark *in the mid-1950s. The angled lights and the mirror's concave shape can be clearly seen. The recovering aircraft is a Sea Venom of 809 Squadron* (RN via R.B. Wigg).

Below left *In the late 1940s, there were a number of accidents which could be attributed to a combination of poor deck landing characteristics in the Firefly and the continued use of the steel crash barrier. This photograph illustrates such a combination. The damage caused to the aircraft is self-evident, but the aircrew are unscathed* (RN).

Above *Older carriers like* Indomitable *were prone to deck accidents for the simple reason that their flight decks were still of the axial type as can be seen by the white line running down the centre of the flight deck. Incidentally, the aircraft ranged at Fly One are a mixture of Firebrands and Fireflies* (RN via Captain Button).

against a howling gale of WOD. It was evident, however, that something better had to be developed or invented. So the mirror landing aid was born. It was made up of a gyro-controlled mirror, facing aft on the port side of the flight deck (with a spare on the starboard side).

In this mirror, the incoming pilot could pick a line and blob of white light (for which the term 'meatball' was conned) and a datum line of green lights allowed the pilot to see whether he was high or low by glancing at the 'meatball' relative to the datum line. The mirror was horizontally concave so that it could be seen as the pilot turned in towards the angled deck. He would watch himself approach monitoring only the air speed—about 115 knots (213 kph)—which was later indicated by sound pulses heard in his headphones, lined up for the deck centre line, and with speed and altitude correct, he would arrive at the rounddown ready to pick up a wire. If the plane shuddered to a stop, the throttle(s) would be closed, if not the fact that the engines were still running at high revs, would allow the aircraft to 'bolt' if the hook did not engage. The pilot could then circuit the ship—go round again—and repeat the approach process.

The mirror sight, allied to the angled deck, led to a figure of 50 accidents per 10,000 landings—a considerable improvement over that 1949 figure. Over the years, the mirror sight developed (by John Curran Ltd of Cardiff and RAE

Bedford) into the projector sight, giving better results in bad weather. The idea was the same but the equipment had been improved, using only graduated bars of light and dispensing with the mirror. *Ark Royal* had the 'sight' fitted during her 1958/9 refit.

The mirror landing sight also meant rather more accurate landings were possible and this, coupled with the added safety of the new clear deck, enabled the number of wires to be reduced from over a dozen in the early fleet carriers to as few as four. This reduction led to a considerable easing of the problems associated with 'wire pulling'—the need to deck land aircraft and test each and every wire—before a carrier's air group could embark at the beginning of a new commission. Although the DLCO was phased out with the introduction of the mirror sight deck landing aid, and later the projector sight, there was still, in the minds of many naval aviators, the need to provide some form of verbal talk-down during the final stages of approach when it was possible for a carrier-borne observer to watch the tell-tale movement of the approaching aircraft by means of the aircraft's own reference lights.

In the early 1960s Rear Admiral 'Percy' Gick and his staff chief, Commander Keith Leppard, visited the USN 'at home' and one of the outcomes was a paper discussing this need for a verbal talk-down despite the excellent assistance of the projector sight. So was born the Landing Safety Officers (sometimes called the Mirror Control Officer) who was positioned on the flight deck adjacent to the sight and who was able to bring the aircraft in. He was also responsible for some of the continuity and initial deck landing training and such was the good effect that this system had that the LSO remained aboard the fixed-wing carrier until the last days of *Ark*.

*   *   *

The need to be able to pull up a fast flying and heavy jet aircraft led to the development, by the Scottish firm of MacTaggart Scott, of a direct acting arrester gear. This development was one of the milestones in carrier design and it replaced the hydraulic or pneumatic-type which created considerable inertia. To overcome this problem two tubes were fitted under the flight deck and the arrester wires were attached to pistons. The system could also take higher landing speeds and therefore allowed for the problems which could arise in jet operations at sea.

A well-worked up squadron of second generation naval aircraft could produce a landing cycle of less than 30 seconds interval from one recovery to the next. This meant that, during exercises especially, the pressure on the flight systems, particularly the arrester gear, could be tremendous. It is not surprising to learn, therefore, that flight decks were continually being strengthened and their equipment re-vamped during every available opportunity, such as refits. Both *Ark* and *Eagle* (the latter only partially so) had specially up-graded decks to contend with the reflected power of the Spey-engined Phantoms during launch and in the event of a 'bolter'.

Launch by artificial means has been part of the British carrier scene since *Courageous* and *Glorious* were fitted with catapults in the early 1930s. Since then the system was continually being improved until the invention by the late Commander C.C. Mitchell, OBE, RNVR, of the steam catapult in the early post war period, a system which is still in use today, albeit with other navies! The free and rocket-assisted (RATOG) take-off was still employed for those aircraft capable of becoming airborne after a relatively short run—the Skyraider AEW1 was one of the last major users of the former system while the latter was still used with great effect during the Korean operations.

In the days of *Ark (III)* it was necessary to launch aeroplanes weighing 8,000 lb (3,629 kg) into the air at a speed of 60 knots (111 kph) relative to the deck. By the end of World War 2, the weights and speeds had increased to 30,000 lb (13,600 kg) and 83 knots (154 kph) respectively. By the last decade of the fixed-wing carrier, aircraft weights had risen to about 60,000 lb (27,200 kg) and the terminal velocity at the end of the catapult run was over 100 knots (185 kph); the actual figures still being secret. In the early days, the hydraulic accelerators were easily capable of launching an aircraft from the deck where there was insufficient wind over the deck (WOD), but with the increase in weapons load and fuel carrying, a more positive system which could cope with varying conditions and types of aircraft was necessary. In 1940, the air hydraulic type was introduced into service in the *Illustrious* Class which had then entered commission. This enabled speeds of 66-75 knots (122-139 kph) to be obtained. Later carriers of the *Colossus* and *Majestic* Classes were also fitted with this system.

The introduction of the jet carrier aircraft radically altered the whole 'ball game' because it was found that such were the flight characteristics of the first generation jets, that they could not become airborne without some artificial assistance. Without doubt, the British invention of the slotted cylinder catapult saved the day, but the old energy storage medium of air could no longer be used. Experiments had taken place directly after the war using the system pioneered by the Germans to launch their 'doodlebugs'.

The modern steam catapult was located in pairs at the bow and/or the waist of the angled deck in such a way that only the tracking and later, the blast deflector plates, were visible on the flight deck itself. Beneath deck level were the workings of the system, including the steam reservoir and the various valves used to control the pressure for the different aircraft types and loads. On deck, in the track, is a shuttle which, together with various bridles and stropes, is attached to the aircraft to be launched. In order to obtain the correct attitude for flight, the aircraft's arrester hook was sometimes used to hold back the aircraft; the Phantom went a stage further by introducing an extendable nose wheel to give the correct attitude. A typical launch cycle would take about 40 seconds; with twin 'cats' this could be a launch every 20 seconds.

Experiments were carried out aboard the converted light fleet maintenance carrier, *Perseus*, in 1950 and much of the development work of Commander Mitchell's invention was carried out at Belfast. Mitchell had by now retired from the RN and had taken up a post with Brown Brothers of Edinburgh, the main manufacturers of steam catapults. At Belfast, the carrier was tied alongside at RNAS Sydenham where the procedure was to launch a Seafire (or similar) from the berthed carrier and, after the circuit, the aircraft would land on at Sydenham airfield, taxi to the quayside and be hoisted back aboard *Perseus*. The launch trials would then be continued. These trials found that aircraft weighing between 15,000-30,000 lb (6,804-13,608 kg) could be launched with a speed of over 90 knots (166.7 kph). The air hydraulic systems being fitted to the new carriers *Albion, Bulwark* and *Eagle* could cope with the same weight of aircraft but had a less reliable performance, especially during the constant use which launching a full strike would often bring them. In 1955, the new *Ark Royal,* followed by *Centaur, Hermes* and *Victorious* were fitted with a steam catapult system which would become standard through the navies of the western world.

Steam catapult installation*

Ship	Type of catapult	Number	In service	Removed
Ark Royal	Cantilevered track	2	1955	1980
Bonaventure	Cantilevered track	1	1957	1970
Centaur	Cantilevered track	2	1959	1970
Eagle	Centre track	2	1965	1978
Hermes	Cantilevered track	2	1960	1971
Karl Doorman	Cantilevered track	1	1958	1969
Melbourne	Cantilevered track	1	1955	In service
Victorious	Cantilevered track	2	1959	1969
Vikrant	Cantilevered track	1	1961	In service

During the *Perseus* trials, several test launches using the new steam experimental catapults were carried out using stub-winged Seafires on a one-way flight. A particularly amusing anecdote is recalled by Alex Brown (then a Lieutenant Commander) who was Flight Deck Officer (FDO) during the Steam Catapult trials (1950-1952) in *Perseus* and this is his account: 'After the trials for many months with ''floating deadloads'' in the basin of Rosyth Dockyard, we went to sea for the second stage of the trials and shot off ''concrete deadloads''. During the summer of 1951 we loaded on six Seafire 47s for the third stage of the trials. The Seafires were in quite good condition having been ''mothballed'' and their wing tips had been removed at the folding point. We proceeded to sea for trials off May Island. Each Seafire was fuelled with about 20 gallons (90 litres) of 100 octane and then in turn loaded on to the catapult. The catapult had been built as a superstructure on the forward end of the flight deck.

'As there were no pilots in the cockpits, after the engine was started, I had to pull a couple of cords which had been threaded through the side of the cockpit—one to pull the throttle fully open and the other to close the ''throttle damper''. To the onlookers amusement, the first three aircraft took off beautifully and, although the flight was slightly wobbly, flew ahead of the carrier until the fuel ran out. However, the fourth Seafire took off and did a climbing turn to starboard to a height of about 500 feet (152.4 m) still doing a slow turn. Then to the dismay and astonishment of all it started to do a kamikaze attack on the *Perseus*. Fortunately, it ran out of fuel and dived into the sea a few hundred yards short of the carrier. The two remaining Seafires had their tailplanes and rudders mutilated with blows from axes—also a single ''flap'' was lowered and still the Seafires tried to fly ahead of the ship. Naturally the ''Fishheads'' and ''Plumbers'' were heard to remark—''Are pilots really necessary?''.'

Steam catapults produced a much more comfortable launch sensation than the previous accelerators, but the whole sequence needed some getting used to. Later deck improvements included blast deflector screens and wheel rollers to

* Data kindly supplied by Brown Brothers & Company Limited, the world's principal catapult engineers.

decrease the time taken to line up the aircraft on the catapult tracks. Initially, the launching bridle, 6 feet (1.8 m) of steel cable, which dragged the aircraft from the deck and away over the bow, was lost. This was expensive and also meant that a large number had to be carried aboard a carrier. Eventually, but not until *Ark*'s 1966-69 refit, a bridle catcher—known as a Van Galm bridle-catcher—was developed, giving the carrier that characteristic snoop, and saving the Navy a small fortune in lost steel.

*　　　*　　　*

The needs of all flying at sea are most demanding and, in 1951, the decision was taken to provide a modern radar capable of dealing with 'modern' high-speed piston-engined and jet carrier aircraft. At the end of a flying exercise, or in the event of war, it would be necessary to marshal aircraft and have the carrier ready to receive them with due reference to their fuel state. Normally aircraft would be picked up at 15 miles (27.8 km) from the carrier and guided (through the gun defence zone—later the missile engagement zone) to the deck for a touch-down with a system known as the Carrier Controlled Approach. CCA is a very skilled job and, like its cousin fighter director, it requires tremendous concentration by the operators (who, incidentally, were known as 8-9-10 squadron aboard *Ark*). The aircraft was under positive control in the 'stream' until it reached the mirror sight beam for a visual touch-down.

*　　　*　　　*

There had been uniforms other than navy blue aboard carriers even since *Argus* landed on her first aircraft. In the early days it was the light blue of the 'crabs' with a large number of RAF officers making up the air complement. During and after the war, the khaki of the Army was also be found aboard. In Korea, the Carrier Borne Air Liaison Section (CBALS or *C-balls*) was a vital part of the precision close support given by carrier aircraft to UN ground forces. The terminology was later changed to Carrier Borne Ground Liaison Sections (CBGLS), and each carrier had such an outfit. Their task, apart from the talk down, by radio, of the strike aircraft on to a target ashore was to train pilots and other aircrew in recognition and to brief the Command on 'pongo' matters in general. Usually called 'tame pongos', the CBGLS usually came from well-known regiments such as the Royal Warwickshires (RWR) or the Royal Welsh Fusiliers (RWF) and were often trained in the art and science of air photograph interpretation or even forward air control. The normal complement can be exemplified by those in the air group aboard *Ark* during her second commission under Captain Frank Hopkins. The CBGLO was a Major from the RWR, with a Captain from the Royal Artillery (who was also an Army pilot) plus a Sergeant Clerk, a Clerk and a driver in the Section which boasted its own Land Rover, used on one memorable occasion as the personal transport for HM The Queen. The cadre of CBGLOs very rarely returned to run-of-the-mill Army life, because as a naval aviator once put it 'they had been "couthed" by their contact with the RN'.

Chapter 12

The advent of the jet

When World War 2 ended, the Fleet Air Arm was in the process of receiving improved versions of existing airframes and some totally new designs for carrier work, for the naval jet age had begun in 1945. One type in particular stands out—the Supermarine Seafire XV to 47*. These aircraft were powered by the Rolls-Royce Griffon engine and, despite its availability to replace the Merlin-engined Seafire III, the first model, the Seafire XV, did not go to sea until September 1945 when the following squadrons were equipped: 801—*Implacable*; 802—*Premier* and *Vengeance*; 803—*Warrior* (RCN); 805—*Ocean*; and 806—*Glory*. It was not very successful as a carrier fighter and was even banned from carrier operations from June 1946 until January 1947. It was replaced by the Seafire XVII which flew with the RN and RNVR from 1946 until 1954 with 800, 802, 803, 805, 807 and 883 (RCN) Squadrons.

Problems with the engine supercharger, which had prohibited XVs from deck flying, were still apparent in the Seafire 45, which did not enter front-line service. The Seafire FR46, a fighter reconnaissance variant, was developed with contra-rotating propellers, but did not enter service either, although it paved the way for the final Seafire, the FR47. This was the ultimate version of the Spitfire/Seafire series with a performance close to that of the early naval jets. The Seafire 47 went to sea in *Glory* (804 Squadron) and *Triumph* (800 Squadron). In later October 1949 until February 1950, Triumph provided air support for strikes against Malayan bandits, four months later sailing north to Korea where 360 Seafire sorties were flown in support of the United Nations forces until relieved by the Sea Fury equipped *Theseus* in October 1950. When the Sea Fury arrived, the Seafire was displaced, thereby closing a fascinating chapter in carrier aviation history.

Rear Admiral Torlesse, who commanded *Triumph* in Korea, recalls the Seafire with some affection although he was 'well aware of their shortcomings as it was not really sufficiently robust for a deck-landing role—in other respects it was a beautiful aircraft; intensive flying operations showed it up only too plainly, and we quickly ran through all there were!'.

Another Supermarine aircraft which appeared at the end of the war but which continued to serve until the early 1950s, was the Sea Otter. Quite a change from the sleek lines of the Seafire, the Sea Otter was a carrier-borne amphibian used

---

* In 1946 the method of denoting aircraft mark numbers changed from Roman to Arabic type.

Ungainly, yet well loved, the Supermarine Sea Otter, successor to the equally beloved Walrus (or 'shagbat'), was the air-sea rescue tool of the RN's carriers until the beginning of the Korean War, when the helicopter took over as the plane-guard. Tales of the heroism of these aeroplanes and their aircrew are legion but an example would be the US Navy pilot rescued after ditching 80 miles (148 km) from the UN Fleet off Korea; the pilot of the Otter subsequently received a US decoration for a rescue 'in very exacting sea conditions' (Fleet Air Arm Museum).

for air-sea rescue and communications duties. 1700 Squadron was equipped with them in November 1944, followed by 1701 and 1702 which all took them to sea in escort carriers such as *Khedive, Begum* and *Trouncer.* When *Theseus* arrived off Korea in October 1950, her ship's flight consisted of a Sea Otter and, until replaced by an American-loaned Sikorsky S51 helicopter, the Otters provided a valuable life saving role.

There were also four particular designs which, although flown (and two were actually used in second-line service) did not embark in carriers. Their existence, however, is relevant because they represent a continued development of the piston-engined aircraft. This story really begins in the Pacific in the second half of World War 2, when the inherent safety and extra range of twin-engined aircraft was shown to be necessary in the vast tracts of ocean where the carrier-to-carrier engagements took place.

On March 25 1944, Lieutenant Commander Eric Brown, the deck landing expert, brought a specially adapted de Havilland Mosquito on to the deck of *Indefatigable,* steaming down the Irish Sea. Concurrent with the plans to make the world's first twin-engine deck landing, were plans to develop a nylon crash barrier for *Indefatigable* as the aircrew of two engined aircraft would be too vulnerable in a steel engagement. Ably assisted by Lieutenant Commander Bob Everett, the CO of DLCO Training School, 'Winkle' Brown brought a specially adapted Mosquito on to *Indefatigable*'s deck for a perfect landing. Although there were plans—Operation High Ball—to sink Japanese capital ships in harbour using RAF Mosquitoes operating from escort carriers, the Mosquito did not enter front-line service with the RN's carrier force. As 'Winkle' Brown is quick to point out, however, 'the Mosquito made an invaluable contribution in pointing the way to what was required in the next generation of twin-engined naval aircraft'.

In 1945 two piston-engined aircraft designed to replace existing carrier types were first flown—the Fairey Spearfish, as a replacement for the Barracuda, and

With remarkable skill by both DLCO and pilot (Lieutenant Commander Eric Brown) a Sea Mosquito was landed aboard Indefatigable *in May 1944. Commander Brown was awarded a well-deserved MBE for this achievement as it was the first carrier landing undertaken by a high performance twin-engined aircraft. Although the Mosquito did not enter regular service aboard carriers, its successor, the Sea Hornet, did and this early operation did much to assist* (RAE via Captain Brown).

the Supermarine Seafang to replace the Seafire. The end of the war, and the development of jets, saw to it that they did not progress further, although the Spearfish was used by the Carrier Trials Unit at Ford. This unit existed to investigate carrier deck landing techniques and to evaluate new developments in deck landing facilities such as the rubber/flexible deck described in the preceding chapter. One other task of the CTU was known as 'wire pulling' and this meant checking the settings of arrester gear after overhaul and refit. To do this several types of aircraft, for example Seafires, Spearfish, Barracudas and Avengers were loaded to a range of specific weights, and landings were then carried out on each and every wire, checking the run out of the wire against the design standard. Dennis Bourne, who spent some time with the unit during the post-war period, says that these operations 'called for accurate "batting" and flying, since on the straight (axial) deck there were ten wires in most cases'.

A sister unit was the Service Trials Unit (STU) which was also at Ford for some time where it evaluated new service aircraft, their supporting equipment and their armament. It was what one may describe as the forerunner to the Intensive Flying Trials Units which were set up for each new aircraft, such as 700Z for the Buccaneer and 700A for the Sea Harrier.

Finally, when dealing with the propeller-driven aircraft which did not quite make it, mention must be made of the only twin-engined aircraft specifically designed for naval use, the Short Sturgeon. Despite not being used in her intended role as a reconnaissance bomber in the *Audacious* and *Hermes* Classes, the Sturgeon, which first flew on September 1 1949, did become a successful second-line type, mainly based on Malta for target towing jobs.

'Winkle' Brown said: 'for getting everything together in near perfection I have found nothing to excel the superb Sea Hornet'. There is no doubt, then, that this twin-engined aircraft really caught the imagination of its pilots. It first flew on July 28 1944, and was originally destined to be a land fighter. However the success of Mosquito trials mentioned earlier led to a naval specification being prepared. Undoubtedly a beautiful aeroplane, de Havilland produced two

Beloved of all who flew them, the DH Sea Hornet (this is the dayfighter variant) had a short life aboard carriers in the days when jets were just around the corner (RN via Captain Leahy).

versions, the single-seater day fighter and the twin-seat night fighter. The former had a top speed of around 470 mph (756 kph) and a range of 1,500 miles (2,778 km) with auxiliary tanks, and made its maiden flight on April 19 1945. The first squadron, 801 (part of 1 CAG) embarked in *Implacable* in 1949 and later in *Indomitable*. This was to be the only embarked squadron, as the aeroplane was pronounced too large to operate from light fleet carriers and it was being closely followed into service by the Hawker Sea Fury with its wider role capabilities.

The twin-seat Sea Hornet NF21 was to serve three years longer (1949-54) than its single-seat stable mate. The prototype had first flown in 1946, but again only one front line squadron was so equipped—809—which took its Hornets to sea in *Vengeance, Indomitable* and *Eagle*, before reforming with the Sea Venom jet. In the single-seat, single-engine world of naval aircraft there were four types which were about to enter service in the late 1940s. Up in Yorkshire, Blackburn Aircraft Ltd had taken almost the whole war to develop the unusual Firebrand torpedo-strike fighter for the RN. Although the Mark I had carried out carrier trials in *Illustrious* in February 1943, it was not until September 1945 that 813 Squadron had re-equipped with Firebrand TF4s, two years later the squadron received the TF5 which it took aboard *Implacable* and *Indomitable* as part of 1 CAG. Meanwhile, 827 Squadron had also been equipped and it spent a year in Eagle (1952-53). The ability to carry a 1,815 lb (839 kg) torpedo and still fly at 340 mph (547 kph) was undoubtedly its finest achievement, but by 1953 it had been replaced with the equally unusual Westland Wyvern.

The former was certainly a little difficult to deck land because the Firebrand's design was such that the pilot's cockpit was over 15 feet (4.6 m) behind the single Bristol Centaurus engine, thus making the aircraft even more difficult to land on the flight deck than the Corsair. Its wing span of over 51 feet (15.5 m) also led to incidents of DLCOs taking a dive off the platform and into the specially provided nets surrounding it.

A former Firebrand pilot, who feels that he must remain anonymous, had the following to say about the aircraft: 'Being considerably larger (with a fin that looks as if it had been made in the dockyard), much heavier and somewhat slower than contemporary naval fighters, it was not popular. With some 15 feet

(4.6 m) of metal between the pilot's eye and the engine cowling it was difficult to deck land and there were many accidents. Only pilots with above average ability were appointed to the two squadrons equipped with the Firebrand. As one who flew them from fleet carriers for two years says, 11 out of the 12 squadron pilots had at least one accident each'.

The highly successful Firefly design was destined to be altered to provide three further marks of operational aircraft which served the FAA until 1956. The Mark 4, with its redesigned airframe and new powerplant, served in the immediate post-war period with the RN, the Dutch and the Canadians (825 Squadron). It was followed by the highly acclaimed and prolific Mark 5 which served in three roles: fighter reconnaissance (FR5), night fighter (NF5) and anti-submarine patrol (AS5). Again used by the Royal Netherlands Navy, as well as the RN, the type was first in action from *Theseus* when 810 Squadron (part of 17 CAG with 807's Sea Furies) launched a strike on Haeju and Chinnam-po on October 9 1950. In all, the squadron flew 1,165 operational sorties from then until April 19 1951.

The Firefly was used in a bombing role with 2 × 500 lb (227 kg) or 2 × 1,000 lb (454 kg) bombs, and in an anti-submarine role for defensive sweeps for *Theseus'* self-defence. The aircraft's ability to fly and operate through the Korean winter was really appreciated although some 'had a tendency to bounce their hooks', says former Firefly pilot, R.B. Wigg. He continues that, 'the role was interdiction—if it moved hit it; plus close air support for UN forces along the Han River'. Several awards of the illustrious Boyd Trophy were made for Korean operations and these are dealt with more fully in the next chapter.

During this conflict, however, the ultimate development of the Firefly entered service with 814 Squadron, and was exclusively an anti-submarine warfare (ASW) aircraft without gun armament. Before it was replaced by the Gannet in 1955, the AS6 was used by six front line squadrons and was embarked in several carriers including *Glory*.

The turboprop-powered Westland Wyvern has already been mentioned in this chapter—it finally entered operational service in the strike role replacing the latter with 813 Squadron in May 1953. It embarked in *Eagle* and the new light

Firebrands of 813 Squadron aboard an armoured fleet carrier. One wit, on seeing this illustration, marvelled that none of the aircraft present show signs of a 'prang': such was the aircraft's reputation! (Fleet Air Arm Museum).

fleet *Albion* and was followed by 827 Squadron (*Eagle*) and 831 (*Ark Royal*). 830 (*Eagle*) flew operational sorties during the 1956 Suez Action where two were shot down by Egyptian flak although both pilots 'ejected' safely. They used special seats which have now become the standard equipment on all military high performance jet aircraft since. One of the naval pilots sent to evaluate the Wyvern was test pilot Lieutenant (E) Nick Goodhart and although he thought it a 'marvellous aeroplane to fly', he admits 'it had a few foibles!'.

Without doubt though, the classical naval fighter of the period, and, incidentally, the fastest piston-engined aircraft to enter service with the RN, was the Hawker Sea Fury. The aircraft's other claims to fame include thousands of successful sorties over Korea, the first British naval aircraft with lowered folding wings (thus enabling deck handling to be improved) and it was the last of a long line of propeller-driven machines to fly with the FAA's fighter units. Also, as is mentioned in the following chapter, it was responsible for the destruction of a MiG-15 jet over Korea!

After trials in *Ocean* during October 1945, the Fury replaced the Seafires of 807 Squadron in its FB10 variant, to be followed by 802 with FB11s—the predominant variant. Besides a host of RN squadrons the aircraft equipped 808 (Australian) and 871 (Canadian) squadrons. During Korea, the following units were operational at various times: 801—*Glory*; 802—*Ocean*; 804—*Glory*; 805—*Sydney*; 807—*Theseus* and *Ocean*; and 808—*Sydney*. In the conflict its main role was to support ground attack missions by Fireflies, but it also used rocket projectiles and cannon to good effect on transport, railways and bridges. *Ocean*'s Sea Furies were especially noted for their exploits with 1,000 lb (454 kg) bombs.

A young Sea Fury veteran from Korea who knew the aeroplane well, having survived two ditchings and a crash landing, was Graham Swanson. This is his account of a typical launch: 'With the middle finger of the right hand "playing" the electrical priming pump, the great Centaurus coughed into life as the index finger of the same hand fired the starting cartridge. A quick cockpit check,

Unusual in that it was a propeller-driven aircraft, but equipped with ejector seats, the Westland Wyvern served aboard Albion, Eagle *and* Ark Royal *(with 831 Squadron, as illustrated, during a flying display in honour of HM Queen Elizabeth II in May 1957). Note the C Class destroyer in the 'pouncer' position on anti-submarine watch* (RN via Major Holmes).

acknowledgement of the cryptic radio check, and I was being marshalled to take my turn on *Glory*'s single catapult. I felt the hold-back strop pulling my Fury tight against the launching strop; then the Flight Deck Officer's green flag was held high, I opened the throttle to full bore, acknowledged that all was well by dropping my right hand and braced for the "kick". Down went the flag and my rocket-laden Fury was hurtled over the bows, to sink slightly as it gained lift and flying speed. Whilst winding my canopy shut, usually left open in case of ditching, I flew ahead for the predetermined time before turning and climbing to port to rendezvous with the rest of my flight as it was setting course for the target. In the light of dawn this could be a tricky manoeuvre, and it was always a relief to see the others, and on time!' Also taken afloat by RNVR units, the Fury was replaced by the Sea Hawk jet from 1953. Luckily today there are airworthy examples in Britain, Canada and America—the sound is unmistakable in its sheer beauty.

The most significant development in carrier aviation in terms of the actual aircraft was an event on December 3 1945, when 'Winkle' Brown landed a Vampire prototype jet on the deck of *Ocean* (Captain Caspar John) steaming down the Channel. The trials were very successful, but despite everything, including the fact that this had been the world's first carrier jet landing, the RN could not bring a jet into operational service before the Americans. The Vampire was, in any case, of limited value and, apart from a couple of temporary deployments, it did not see service as it was basically a navalised RAF fighter and unfit for carrier work. Many people believe, however, that if we had had more jets of the Attacker type in service during 1950-53, then we would not have fared so well over Korea. The Vampire did provide jet experience, however, and trials in approach methods were run in *Triumph* in June 1946, but the problems of slow reaction by the jet engine was destined to cause problems in these pre-angled deck days. The flexible deck trials have already been mentioned in a previous chapter and it must be remembered that again the Vampire was chosen. It also achieved, in the hands of 'Winkle' Brown again, the first British jet launch from catapult.

Following jet operations over Europe at the end of World War 2, the Meteor was being developed for the RAF and it is not surprising that schemes were afoot to adapt it for duties afloat. Unlike the later Vampire, it was a twin engine

Top right *Without doubt, the Sea Fury was a classic piston-engined naval fighter, and, being the last of her kind, she will be remembered by all who flew, or maintained, her as a real thoroughbred. Here a strike prepares for a catapult launch from* Indomitable *during the first few months of the aircraft's service life. The third aircraft, coded 152, is seen crossing the crash barrier, whilst the other two are made ready for launching* (RN via Captain McKeown).

Centre right *Gently does it, as Lieutenant Commander 'Winkle' Brown guides the specially modified DH Vampire on to the deck of* Ocean *in December 1945. This event heralded a new age in carrier flying, during a period when in terms of technique and experience, the Royal Navy led the world* (Fleet Air Arm Museum).

Right *Rather grainy, nevertheless worthy of inclusion in this account, is this photograph, taken aboard* Implacable, *of 'Winkle' Brown's classic achievement in landing a twin-jet aircraft on an aircraft carrier. Like the Mosquito four years before, the Meteor did not enter squadron service as a fleet fighter, but it paved the way for future jet designs, such as the Vixen and Buccaneer* (RAE via Captain Brown).

A range of Supermarine Attackers (the first British jet fighters embarked operationally) aboard Eagle *together with Sea Furies and Fireflies. The folding wing tips were to enable use of the flight deck aircraft lifts, which otherwise would have been too narrow* (Fleet Air Arm Museum).

design, and apart from non-flying deck handling trials in *Pretoria Castle*, it could not have been considered for carrier use until various defects in its flight controls and equipment had been remedied for carrier operations. 'Winkle' Brown carried out several tests to attempt to produce an approach and landing technique. By the summer of 1948, all was ready for the first landing of a British twin-jet aboard a carrier; the ship was *Implacable* and the date was June 8 1948. Although there were no plans to introduce the design into carrier squadrons, the Meteor did contribute to naval jet evolution and perhaps 'Winkle' should have the last word: 'You cannot navalise a land plane efficiently without designing it for the specialist job from the outset'.

In our story of early jet development, it is worth recording that the first night landings by jets were made aboard *Theseus* on June 19 1950. The need for a jet fighter capable of carrier operations was realised by the Admiralty in 1944 and a specification was issued for which Supermarines were awarded a prototype contract. They were already developing the Seafang as a Seafire replacement and in order to keep development time down, they utilised various parts in their design.

Following a maiden flight in July 1946 and carrier trials in *Illustrious* during the autumn of 1947, an order for 50 Supermarine Attackers was placed. The front-line squadron to be equipped with these jets was 800, which was commissioned on August 22 1951, and commanded by Lieutenant Commander George Baldwin, DSC+. Baldwin had already amassed some experience on the Attacker at Ford in the Service Trials Unit, and feels today that if more money had been spent on developing the Attacker into a tricycle undercarriage aircraft, it would have been better than the Sea Hawk which replaced it. It certainly seems to have been a stop gap design, even though it was produced in three marks: a fighter, the F1, and two fighter bomber variants, the FB1 and the FB2.

The Attacker first went afloat in *Eagle* during September 1952 with both 800 and 803 Squadrons being so equipped. Their deployments included exercises in Northern waters and two successful visits to the Mediterranean. The final mark, the FB2, was replaced by the Sea Hawk in 1954, but the Attacker continued to fly with RNVR units until 1957. So passed the first phase of the post-war developments of the RN's fixed-wing carriers which were luckily in a position to

Besides having the distinction of being the first aircraft to land on the newly built Bulwark, *the Grumman Avenger AS4 was introduced temporarily to the RN until the Gannet ASW aircraft were ready for service in 1955* (Fleet Air Arm Museum).

tackle the conflicts looming in Asia and the Middle East. The former was the swan-song of the piston-engined British carrier aircraft.

Another type of carrier-borne flying machine was about to take to the air and is the most significant feature of British naval aviation since World War 2. Today, rotary-wing aircraft have largely superseded their fixed-wing predecessors in several ship-borne roles, including anti-submarine warfare and air-sea rescue. The helicopter's development though, goes back to the days of the 'Stringbag'.

Interestingly enough, perhaps even ironically, the fixed-wing aircraft carrier played an important part in the development of the helicopter—variously called 'choppers' and 'helos'. In the mid-1930s, the Admiralty became very interested in the autogyro concept which differs from a conventional helicopter in that it has a free spinning main rotor to give lift, yet is propelled through the air by a fixed tractor or pusher propeller. The Italian Cievra Company supplied a number of autogyros to the RAF for evaluation by the Fleet Air Arm at Gosport and successful deck landing trials were carried out aboard *Furious* in the English Channel. The outbreak of war slowed down development but in 1941 that incomparable Fleet Air Arm pilot, Captain Caspar John (now Admiral of the Fleet Sir Caspar John) was the moving figure behind a scheme to interest the US Navy in a joint venture to use the autogyro in an anti-submarine role for Atlantic convoy protection from otherwise fixed-wing escort carriers. Trials were again successfully completed, this time aboard USS *Ranger*, and the helicopter was beginning its rise to fame.

The helicopter next figures in the fixed-wing carrier scene in 1949, when as part of a general upsurge in carrier development, a Sikorsky Dragonfly of 705 NAS was put aboard *Vengeance* for short trials. The air-sea rescue role was envisaged as the first operational use of the helicopter, especially to replace the venerable Sea Otter amphibian as a carrier's rescue plane. C-in-C Home Fleet's Flagship at this time was the *Indomitable* and a Dragonfly was embarked in early 1951. Unfortunately, the limitations of using a helicopter, still a rather fragile flying machine, were not appreciated by some of the more senior officers aboard and the Dragonfly became unserviceable when a launch was ordered with too much wind over the deck (WOD). The helicopter was, however, here to stay.

Chapter 13

Asian flash point—Korea

The aftermath of World War 2 left large areas, formally in Japanese control, untenable for the former colonial rulers such as Britain and France. The spreading of the Communist doctrine accounted for much of the unrest and nowhere more profoundly than the Korean peninsula, which separates the Sea of Japan from the Yellow Sea.

On June 25 1950 the North Koreans crossed the United Nations dividing line, drawn along the 38th Parallel, and invaded the Republic of (South) Korea. The Allies, under United Nations authority, were quick to react by sending forces to the area. The British light fleet carrier, *Triumph*, commanded by Captain A.D. Torlesse, DSO, was already at Hong Kong for air support duties and she arrived off Korea on July 2 with a dozen each of Seafire 47s (800 Squadron) and Firefly Is (827 Squadron). Under the overall command of Vice Admiral W.G. Andrewes, *Triumph* launched her first strike of 12 Seafires and ten Fireflies at 06.30 on July 3, against the industrial and rail centre of Haeju in concert with USS *Valley Forge*'s air group.

The Seafire and the obsolescent Firefly were not really suitable for the Korean conflict, but the military situation was such that the fleet carriers were retained

No identification problems with this carrier; it is obviously Theseus, *seen here leaving Japanese waters after a tour of duty off Korea. The word 'Theseus' is made up of members of the ship's company and embarked air group standing in a pre-arranged pattern. Ranged on deck are Sea Fury and Firefly aircraft complete with Korean War stripes* (RN via Rear Admiral Bolt).

in Europe and the Mediterranean waters in case of Soviet 'aggression', and the other light fleets were busy training up on the new aircraft types. Nevertheless *Triumph* gave a good account of herself and received much kudos from the US Commanders not least for her assistance at the Inchon Landings. By the autumn the ship was down to six Fireflies and three Seafires and as the Flag Officer, Second-in-Command Far East Station put it in a signal, '*Triumph* has done very well and has kept going beyond belief'. Her sister-ship, *Theseus* (under Captain 'Ben' Bolt—another World War 2 observer like Torlesse) was ready to be deployed to the Far East Fleet. When she arrived in October 1950, her air group, the 17 CAG, consisted of 12 Sea Furies (807) and 23 Fireflies (810), plus a Sea Otter amphibian for air-sea rescue duties (like *Triumph* before her). This latter was soon replaced by a Sikorsky S-51 helicopter, loaned by the USN and it was soon providing even more invaluable assistance than the latter, being able not only to pluck shot-down aircrews from the sea, but even from behind enemy lines. During her first period of operational duty, 384 sorties were flown by *Theseus'* aircraft in 13 days.

One of the major problems facing British and Commonwealth carrier captains was the distance from the aircraft maintenance units which could have been disastrous but for two things: (1) the incredibly good deck landing accident rate, and (2) the use of *Unicorn* to transport new aircraft and spares to Japan.

Admiral Torlesse, in a letter to the author during the preparation of this account, said simply: 'We could not have operated off Korea for more than a very few weeks without the invaluable services of *Unicorn*'. The closest airfield facilities were 2,500 miles (4,630 km) away in Singapore, with the UK factories being 12,000 miles (22,224 km) distant. Considerable efforts were made by the carrier captains to eliminate damage and wastage due to accident. In *Theseus*, Captain Bolt and his Commander (Air), Frank Hopkins (now Admiral Sir Frank Hopkins), decided that an incentive was necessary and champagne for the whole air group was offered for a successful spell of 1,000 accident-free landings! The results were remarkable, but shouldn't really be judged on the promise of 'champers'; only two barrier engagements which necessitated major repair were made between October 1950 and April 1951. The magic 1,000

Without the aid of the ferry carrier, Unicorn, *the sustained naval air effort would not have been possible. In Japan, a harbour crane was used to transfer repaired aircraft to the operational carrier, in this case* Ocean, *whilst those beyond local repair were shipped aboard* Unicorn *to the Royal Naval Aircraft Yard at Singapore* (RN via R.B. Wigg).

landings' barrier was broken in the period December 1 to February 1, with a grand total of 1,236 recoveries before a Firefly pecked its propeller on the flight deck. Even burst tyres were prevented!

After each operational period, the carrier would return to Japan, either Kure or Sasebo docks, to land damaged aircraft and to take on replacements which had been brought up to the port by *Unicorn*. Captain Bolt felt that, 'the support given by *Unicorn* and the Naval Air Base at Singapore was essential to the conduct of the [Korean] operations'. The main tasks of the naval forces was to blockade Korean waters, but the carrier element had given major roles: (1) to provide combat air patrols (CAP), (2) to provide anti-submarine screens, (3) to act as bombardment spotters, (4) to provide surveillance of enemy positions, and (5) to provide close air support when required by United Nations ground forces.

During their time off Korea, *Theseus'* air group flew 5,600 hours 20 minutes of operational sorties and made 2,361 deck landings. In January 1951 the 17 CAG were awarded the Boyd Trophy for 1950. This was her only stint in the Korean operation area, although she did relieve other light fleet carriers in the Mediterranean to allow them to be deployed 'east of Suez'. She did see action again, however, during the Suez Action of 1956, before being scrapped in 1958. *Theseus* was relieved by *Glory* in April 1951 and transferred several of her aircraft and experienced crews. *Theseus* retained about a dozen Sea Furies for the homeward voyage in case they were needed in the Gulf where there was trouble at Abadan. *Glory* had brought the 14 CAG with more Sea Furies in the shape of 804 Squadron and the Fireflies of 821 Squadron. Again this proved to be a successful tour and *Glory*'s air group was awarded the Boyd Trophy for 1951.

The pilot who carried out a tour in *Glory* and *Ocean* remembers: 'Korean operations, for all concerned, were very much a hot war, and even operating

A wintry scene aboard Theseus *during part of her patrol time off Korea. Severe conditions were met by all the carriers on station in the war zone, but these rarely hampered air operations. The aircraft on the flight deck are Sea Furies and Fireflies, both types being marked in the United Nations' black and white markings* (RN via Rear Admiral Bolt).

from the comparative safety and comfort of a light fleet carrier, the number of aircraft and crews lost was high. Few were lost because of the hazards of ship-borne operation; indeed, we would do hundreds of landings without incident. The only problem was that "hung-up" rockets tended to fly off on touch-down and knock off the tail wheels of aircraft in the deck park! The only dicey landings, perhaps, were during the first recovery after two weeks R & R*! A few aircraft were lost through engine failure, particularly Furies, whose sophisticated radial engines did not take too kindly to being hammered. The slightest lack of oil pressure and the sleeve-valves would protest, whilst the temperamental injector-carburettor was more suited to a transport aircraft'.

The Australians were anxious to play their part in the United Nations' action in Korea and, like the Canadians, provided warships. Unlike Canada, however, who could only supply destroyers, such as the *Sioux* and *Nootha*, Australia was able to put a light fleet carrier into the arena†. On April 20 1950, the 21 CAG had formed in the UK with Sea Furies (808) and Fireflies (809 Squadron), and in the September of the following year the parent carrier *Sydney* arrived off Korea.

The winter periods off Korea were particularly bad, and both *Sydney* and *Glory* experienced the long, cold winter blizzards, when even the sea froze. During this time, however, it was necessary to continue flying strikes against Communist forces, in support of the United Nations' ground forces. It says a lot for the skill of the pilots, the maintainers and the flight deck crews, that air strikes were able to be flown from carriers of a basic design which differed little from those before the war, and with aircraft which were still primitive with regard to modern avionics, and navigation aids.

It was now *Ocean*'s turn to move into the Korean campaign and in early 1952 she was replaced in the Mediterranean Fleet by *Theseus*. With the fighter ace, Captain Charles 'Crash' Evans, DSO, DSC, in command, *Ocean* arrived off Korea on May 9 1952 with 802 (Sea Fury) and 825 (Firefly) squadrons aboard. These two units, brought out to the Med by *Theseus*, had been worked up in 40 attacks on bandits operating in Malaya. *Glory* took *Ocean*'s Sea Otter amphibian home and it was replaced by a helicopter, now becoming a part of every carrier's standard equipment. Another Boyd Trophy winner (this time in 1952), *Ocean*'s 17 CAG operated well, achieving a record 123 sorties in one day‡, and a daily average of 76 sorties. (If one discusses this point with aircrew who also flew with 14 CAG (*Glory*), the point that the latter flew full length sectors is 'suggested' with some force).

Captain Paddy McKeown, RN (Rtd), then a pilot with 802 Squadron, spent some time talking to the author about the operations over Korea: 'The tactical lessons learnt in Korea were much the same as those which had been learnt ever since air fighting began—for example that flak gunners were notoriously inaccurate and in following a target through the sky, were more likely to hit anything behind it than the actual target. This is borne out to a certain extent by the fact that large numbers of aircraft which were damaged by flak were damaged in the tail section only. Experience showed that if the wing man of the two aircraft element, which made up the standard "finger four" tactical formation, used in Korea, hung on too closely to his leader he would be flying

* Rest and recreation.
† It should also be noted that 40 RNZVNR pilots also volunteered for duty in Korea.
‡ May 17 1952.

Aircraft of the 17 CAG (Ocean) *ranged on deck; the nearest Sea Fury is 115 of 802 Squadron which was flown by Paddy McKeown during 1952* (Captain McKeown).

straight into the flak dished up by the enemy for the lead aircraft.

'Young and inexperienced pilots were taken in hand by the older 'veterans' of the Korean campaign and taken on their first operational sweeps, looking for targets of opportunity or the designated areas of attack. The favourite amongst many pilots, and in particular the strike pilots of 802 and 825 Squadrons from *Ocean*, were bridges. Korea is a country criss-crossed with rivers and ravines, and bridges abound, but their construction in 1950-53 was such that they could easily be dealt with by 500 or 1,000 lb (227 or 454 kg) bombs from Sea Fury and Firefly aircraft. The only problem here was that the air groups were rationed to 54 1,000 lb (454 kg) bombs per patrol! There was, however, no restriction on using the smaller bombs'.

The standard patrol period in Korea consisted of four days on station with pilots flying two or three, sometimes four sorties each day, followed by a rest day when the ship would replenish at sea, from tankers and stores ships. This was followed by a further four days' action before the ship pulled out to Japan, and this pull-out period meant a further three days in transit to and from the action area. In 1952, for example, the light fleet carrier, *Ocean*, was always relieved on station by the American carrier, *Bataan*, although they rarely sighted each other as they passed in the night during their transit periods.

Graham Swanson, then a Sub-Lieutenant and now an airline pilot, describes a typical assortment of missions: 'Today's mission was an armed reconnaissance well behind the front line, with attacks on pre-briefed targets. As much of the enemy's surface transport was primitive, ox-carts and the like, so was most of their anti-aircraft fire. It might consist of soldiers aiming their rifles in the air, to send up a random spray of bullets at the command "Fire!", but of course there was plenty of the real thing too, though at least one could see this, especially the unnerving tracer, which hopefully went by on either side. The *boss* (Lieutenant Commander "Bill' Bailey) was notorious for going in very low, and by the time No 4—me—went over, the *Gooks* [North Koreans] would be well alerted. Today, however, we were all unscathed, with no bullet holes, or worse, in our Furies when we landed back on *Glory* after our 2½ hour sortie. After debriefing we would probably prepare for another mission in the afternoon.

'Whilst our companion Firefly Squadron, 812, carried out their strikes on anti-submarine patrols, we fighters had four types of assignment. Besides the armed reconnaissance (AR), we would sometimes carry out Close Air Support for the brave troops at the front line; being directed by equally courageous spotter-pilots in light aircraft. This was the most exciting, and probably the most hazardous mission, and being far from the coast, our senses were always closely attuned to the engine note until we got back to within gliding distance of the friendly "oggin". We also carried out Combat Air Patrols (CAPs), which were of two types, each consisting of two aircraft. The ordinary CAP was carried out at 20,000 ft (6,096 m) or so, under radar control, and consisted mainly of intercepting "bogies" on the director's screen. The other two aircraft of the flight would be detailed for a Target CAP (TarCAP), attacking targets as directed by the UN ships off the west coast. This was very interesting work, especially when asked to "spot" for a ship as she ranged her guns on to a specific target'.

At the end of the six month deployment off the Korean coast, the British carriers would exchange in Hong Kong, for example, *Glory* handed over to *Ocean* on May 1 1952, and *Ocean* handed over to *Glory* again on November 4 1952. At Hong Kong the incoming carrier would take on extra aircraft to make up the Squadrons to their war number of, say, 20 aircraft each. In addition they would take on extra pilots, who had joined the air group of the outgoing carrier in the middle of its tour, thus providing continuity and a cadre of experienced aircrew. The aircraft which returned to Britain were usually beyond local repair, although damage assessment teams would come on board at Hong Kong for the transit to Singapore to assess whether any aircraft could be dealt with at the Royal Naval aircraft yard on that island.

The RATOG gear was attached to the Sea Furies to provide the necessary power for the additional weight of two 1,000 lb (454 kg) bombs which were now being carried by 802 Squadron. These bombs were discovered in Singapore and they had been manufactured in Australia. When Captain Evans heard of these 'beauties' he promptly arranged for them to be brought up from Singapore. On arrival in *Ocean*, it was found that the bombs were compatible with 500 lb (227 kg) bomb-carriers and that, providing there was rocket assistance, a Sea Fury could leave the deck with full 20 mm ammunition, full internal fuel and two of the larger bombs. The RATOG system was very unsophisticated and it is a great tribute to the AEO of the Squadron, Lieutenant (E) 'Jack' Button, (now a retired Captain), and his team that the system did not have one failure whilst *Ocean* was operating off Korea.

The only apparent failure was during the first launch of RATOG + 1,000 lb bomb loaded Sea Furies and concerned the CO of 802 Squadron, Lieutenant Commander Fraser Shotton. It was normal practice to 'make' the master switch in the range on deck and so, in effect, arm the RATOG. As the aircraft, using a free take-off, moved down the deck it would pass a red flag, here the RATOG button was pushed and the system could be activated. Shotton reached the flag, but no characteristic roar and belching of smoke appeared from his Sea Fury, which promptly dropped off the bow of the carrier. To those watching, the Sea Fury seemed to disappear for minutes, and then, suddenly there it was, clawing

Like many of the light fleets assigned to Korean operations, Ocean, *which made two deployments, was commanded by a former naval aviator, Captain (later Vice Admiral Sir Charles) 'Crash' Evans, a fighter ace of World War 2, during her first period with the UN Fleet. In this photograph, a Sea Fury is prepared for launch on the only catapult* (RN via Captain McKeown).

into the air, tail down. Everybody was relieved to see that the CO was OK, but some of the pilots were apprehensive about making the launch, even though they had used RATOG ashore with complete success. It says a lot for the calibre of squadron commanders like Fraser Shotton that, once he had gained a safe height, he admitted over the radio that he had forgotten to 'make' his master switch. After that the Squadron never looked back until the 1,000 lb bomb supply had been exhausted.

The effect of these bombs was quite staggering and the squadron indulged in pre-dawn take-offs to catch the Communist road traffic while it was still moving. These early take-offs, quite unknown in light fleet carriers at that time, were another unorthodox move by Captain Evans. The first RNVR pilot to go out to Korea experienced some fun with RATOG gear because, although the system functioned perfectly, he had not been thoroughly prepared for the immense jolt and did not have the control column firmly in his grasp and pressed hard down. As a result, the Sea Fury seemed to leap vertically into the air, stalled and came crashing down, narrowly missing the carrier's super-structure. It hit the sea hard, and went straight down, again almost vertically. The pilot stayed on his oxygen supply until the momentum ceased and then he was able to swim to the surface, none the worse for wear. To everyone on *Ocean,* it seemed like an age before the little yellow Mae West popped up in the carrier's wake. The plane-guard Dragonfly helicopter then swooped in and picked him up.

Incidentally, during the whole of *Ocean's* time in Korea, despite a record number of sorties, there were no losses as a result of ditchings, even though many pilots, such as Sub-Lieutenant Graham 'Oggie' Swanson, now a Tristar Captain with British Airways, went in twice. His second 'watery escapade' is worth recording, not only because it was his last combat mission, but also because it can be regarded as somewhat typical:

'Lieutenant Bob Hallam was leader of our TarCAP, and we each carried two 500 lb (227 kg) bombs which had to be deposited on a particularly well defended target on the coast just west of Chinnampo, on the estuary of the large river leading to Pyongyang. The plan was that whilst one of us was diving in to drop his bombs, the other carried out a strafing run from the side, thus giving the anti-aircraft gunners a doubly difficult task. I still had a full load of bombs as Bob made his run, diving in towards the estuary. As I pulled out of my covering run, probably doing some 300 knots (556 kph), my cockpit suddenly filled with what seemed to be red hot smoke. I was already trying to jump when I heard Bob's voice in my ear-phones calling "Bale out! Bale out! You're on fire!", but every time I tried to get out of the cockpit the slip stream pushed me back. I could not see anything at all because of the smoke, but I knew that my only hope was to kill my speed. Although already in a climbing turn (or so I hoped!), I yanked back as hard as I could on the stick to take the speed off, but I still could not get out. Then suddenly I felt the aircraft spin violently, then it just was not there any more! I pulled my fingers across my chest, found the ripcord, and my feet seemed to touch the water as the parachute lines took my weight. Bob told me later that he thought I had "had it", as my Fury hit the water before he saw my 'chute open. Apparently the aircraft was on fire from end to end before the tail finally came off. Whether it burned off, or I pulled it off, we shall never know; it was probably a bit of both! It was the ensuing spin which undoubtedly saved my life by throwing me clear.

'Once in the water, the drill for boarding an inflated dinghy was to ensure that its stabilising pocket was full of water before entering from the opposite side. Having pushed the dinghy to and fro to achieve this, I had just heaved myself aboard when the sound of a low flying aircraft, definitely not that of a Sea Fury, together with machine-gun fire made me leap overboard. I need not have worried: it was a Corsair of the USN (and the water was only about five feet deep anyway), though I was quite a way from the off-shore island being strafed by the friendly Yank! My burns were quite painful, but salt water is a good palliative, and guided by Bob, my "personal" USN Dragonfly helicopter was soon winching me up. "What! You Again?", the crew exclaimed, as they flew me back to the sick bay of the British cruiser which had been directing our attack earlier*. Although I had seen no flames, I had bad burns everywhere that my flesh was exposed, including those two right fingers protruding from a flapping glove—the trade mark of an "experienced" Sea Fury pilot! Those priming and starting buttons were very hard on gloves'.

Many pilots were, however, able to bring their aircraft back to the ship and land on, thus providing a machine which could fly, and fight, another day. Paddy McKeown had a favourite Sea Fury, coded 115, which he landed on after an anxious double circuit of *Ocean*, with engine trouble which meant that he could not control the power on his approach to the flight deck. In carrier operations, the recovery of aircraft, especially after action, is the most tense moment of the day. Some escapes from death were awe inspiring, for example, Lieutenant Commander Peter London, who replaced the redoubtable Fraser Shotton half way through *Ocean*'s spell of duty in the Far East, complained of bad aileron control after he had landed on after a particularly hostile reception by Chinese and North Korean gunners. On examination, it was found that the

---

* The same crew had rescued Swanson a few weeks earlier after his first ditching.

main aileron control rod under the aircraft's—another Sea Fury—fuselage, was hanging on by a thread of metal; the rest having been shot away. If this thread of metal had not been there, London would not have been able to control his aircraft.

* * *

'*On top of old Pyongyang*
All covered with flak
I lost my poor wing man
*He never came back.'**

The Firefly pilots had their fun too, especially on operations like the raids on Pyongyang during a stalemate in the peace talks. R.B. Wigg, then a commissioned pilot with 825 (Firefly) Squadron, had a near miss during the raids when a pilot in the formation behind him loosed off all 16 rocket projectiles (RPs) a trifle early, ie, before Wigg himself had opened fire. The RPs went past his starboard wing tip rather close and put him off his stroke enough to delay his own firing for a second or so. Wigg and his observer got a very close look at Pyongyang marshalling yards! This was just one of 1,907 sorties flown by the squadron during their time in Korea, under Lieutenant Commander 'Chico' Roberts (now Rear Admiral), who won the DSO for his part in the Korean operations.

The most spectacular sortie of the tour must surely have been Lieutenant (now Commander) Peter 'Hoagy' Carmichael's combat with a MiG-15. Here, in his own words, is the story: 'It was on August 9 1952: my flight, consisting of Lieutenant Peter "Toby" Davis, Sub-Lieutenant Brian "Smoo" Ellis, Sub-Lieutenant Carl Haines, had been briefed at the unearthly hour of 04.00 to carry out armed reconnaissance over North Korea in the Chinnampo area. We took off from *Ocean* at first light, which was at about 05.15. We always knew that MiGs could be in the area but to date no luck.

'We had been operating in the same area for about 20 minutes when Sub-Lieutenant Carl Haines called out "MiGs 4 o'clock". I turned the formation to meet the attack and saw eight MiGs coming straight at us. The next thing that I noticed was tracer shells coming very slowly towards me and then accelerating over my wing. In fact it was 30 mm tracer.

'Lieutenant Toby Davis and Sub-Lieutenant "Smoo" Ellis broke away from my flight to fend for themselves as four of the MiGs decided to look after them. We, as usual, were flying at about 4,000 feet, and we always flew with gyro and fixed ring on the gunsight. Suddenly a MiG came down behind me: I turned towards him and as he flew past me, I noticed he had his air brakes out. He made the fatal mistake of trying to dog fight with us. I put my gyro sight on him and started to fire. At this point he realised he was in trouble and put his dive brakes in and started to accelerate like mad. I then switched to fixed ring and held him quite easily and my bullets started to hammer him. He started to roll over on his back and crashed into the ground with no attempt of baling out. Lieutenant Davis damaged a MiG during the engagement. The enemy then broke off the engagement. We then reformed and returned to *Ocean* after a

---

* From the evergreen *FAA Songbook*.

flight lasting one hour 45 minutes. On August 10 1952, at the same time, we were again attacked by 8 MiGs. I damaged one and they broke off the engagement. The MiGs were stupid in that they tried to dog fight with us instead of using the advantage of their speed and climbing. I got quite a lot of publicity for the above but as much credit goes to my "flight".

'Though, in fact, I was time expired in 802 Squadron before we sailed for Korea from Malta, Commander Barrie Nation (who did our appointments) came out to Malta and said, "Of course, Hoagy, you don't want to leave the squadron now, do you?". What do you say to that? I know what my answer

Whilst the Hawker Sea Fury carried out fighter and fighter-bomber operations armed with cannon, bombs and RPs (such as this 802 Squadron aircraft), the Firefly AS 5s (such as these snow-bound aboard Sydney) *operated anti-submarine and bomber sorties. The combination proved remarkably well adapted to the rigours of continued wartime operations and was employed by all light fleets engaged in this theatre, except* Triumph *which was equipped with Seafire 47s and Firefly Is* (RN via Captain McKeown and AWM/42855).

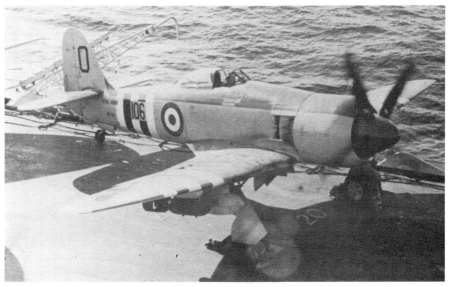

One of the favourite targets for both Sea Furies and Fireflies was bridges, which abound in Korea. Illustrated are the road bridges to To-Ko-Ri which were destroyed by aircraft of 17 CAG operating from Ocean *in October 1952. Readers may recall that the name has a familiar ring to it because in the late 1950s there was an American-made film about the 'Bridges of To-Ko-Ri'. It looks as if the Royal Navy got there first!* (RN via R.B. Wigg).

would be to that today. In view of the publicity, My Lords of the Admiralty brought me home earlier than the rest of the squadron in case of my being shot down and taken POW. They reckoned that I might have had a rough time. For this I was awarded the DSC, which I learned when reading the *Daily Mirror* in the frigate *Leeds Castle!*'

Several records were set up during *Ocean*'s first tour, including the staggering total of 123 sorties from a one catapult ship in a day, when some pilots flew four sorties and 802's Paddy McKeown flew a record five sorties that day. In all McKeown flew 178 sorties during the tour (made up of 139 offensive and 39 CAP missions), which averaged out at about two per day while the ship was on station. *Ocean*'s Captain Evans sent the following signal after the days flying on May 17 1952: 'Our pilots today have broken all existing records for British light fleet carriers in flying 123 sorties over our operating area. From dawn to dusk the area has been pounded by rocket and bomb attacks. The destruction figures include three bridges downed, four coast gun emplacements shattered, 15 ammo-laden ox carts exploded, and an oil fuel dump fired, smoke and flames have been billowing from this for most of the day. The airspot for *Belfast* scored a direct hit on a coastal battery with six-inch salvos. A total of 456 rockets, 72 bombs and 20,300 rounds of 20 mm have been consumed. Serviceability has remained excellent and we continue with 68 sorties tomorrow'.

Glory, now commanded by Captain Duncan Lewin, DSO, DSC, another of the select group of former aircrew light fleet carrier Captains, was on station again on November 8 1952, following a deployment to the Mediterranean. With Sea Furies (801) and Fireflies (821) again embarked, she remained off Korea until May 19 1953 when *Ocean* again relieved her. By now, the action was becoming even more intense, as an Armistice was about to be signed. By the time *Ocean*'s second tour had been completed in November 1953, hostilities were over and *Sydney*, the relieving carrier, was more of a guardian than a warship. *Ocean* returned home to Portsmouth after 2½ years foreign service.

Table of carrier operations in Korea

1950	*Triumph*	13 CAG	800 (Seafire)	827 (Firefly 1)
1950-51	*Theseus*	17 CAG	807 (Sea Fury)	810 (Firefly 5)
1951	*Glory*	14 CAG	801 (Sea Fury)	821 (Firefly 5)
			804 (Sea Fury)	
1951-52	*Sydney*	21 CAG*	805 (Sea Fury)	817 (Firefly 5)
			808 (Sea Fury)	
1952	*Glory*	14 CAG	804 (Sea Fury)	812 (Firefly 5)
1952	*Ocean*	17 CAG	802 (Sea Fury)	825 (Firefly 5)
1952-53	*Glory*	—†	801 (Sea Fury)	821 (Firefly 5)
1953	*Ocean*	—†	807 (Sea Fury)	810 (Firefly 5)

Without doubt the carrier air operations over Korea proved yet again the need for a mobile air striking force based on a mobile airfield—a carrier. In the limited type of war flown over Korea, the benefits of the long endurance and fuel saving propeller-driven aircraft were ably demonstrated by the Sea Fury and Firefly; America was again to learn the benefits in Vietnam when veteran Skyraider strike aircraft were brought out of retirement. Most of all though, the proficiency and weapon training skills of the FAA aircrew were shown—*Theseus*, for example, was able to operate twice as quickly as her companion USN carrier, even though she only had one catapult. The aircraft recovery interval was several times brought down below the 15 second mark, but having said all this, the limitations of the light fleet carrier with its axial deck and barriers were only too apparent. Finally, it is worth mentioning that when *Glory* brought a Dragonfly helicopter for plane guard duties from the UK it was the beginning of the ascendancy of rotary wing flyers in carrier aviation. They would not look back.

Malaya was also a prominent operations area for the FAA during the 1950s and, besides the strikes by *Ocean* in 1952, *Glory*'s air group struck at Communist villages during October. The action continued and two years later when *Warrior* came out East to relieve *Sydney* on the Korean Armistice Patrol, 825 Squadron's Fireflies were again flying ground attack sorties over the Malayan jungle. Most of the operations in this theatre were undertaken by the RAF, but the Navy did provide one of the first helicopter assault squadrons (848) equipped with Westland-built S-55 Whirlwinds.

Later problems arose in Aden which led to an eventual British withdrawal from the Indonesian-Malayan confrontation, the Kuwait Crisis 1961 and Beira Patrol. All demanded a British fixed-wing carrier presence and all were to some extent successful operations, for the RN at least.

* Part of 20 CAG also embarked.
† CAG system not employed during these periods.

Chapter 14

The new carriers

At the end of the Korean war period, the British fixed-wing carriers were little better placed than at the cessation of hostilities in 1945. The following two tables, drawn from contemporary Official Government sources, gives an impression of how the re-armament programme had fared for the Senior Service (early 1954), yet by the end of Suez (early 1957), the position had again changed:

Table 1

Operational:	*Eagle, Warrior* and *Glory*
Training:	*Indefatigable, Implacable, Illustrious* and *Triumph*
In reserve:	*Indomitable, Theseus, Ocean* and *Centaur*
Under construction:	*Ark Royal, Albion, Bulwark* and *Hermes*
Being modified:	*Victorious*
Construction suspended:	*Leviathan*
Destined for Commonwealth:	*Hercules** (RIN) and *Majestic*† (RAN)

Table 2

Operational:	*Ark Royal, Eagle, Albion* and *Bulwark*
Training:	*Ocean* and *Warrior*
In reserve:	*Centaur, Triumph, Glory, Theseus* and *Magnificent*
Under construction:	*Hermes*
Being modified:	*Victorious*
Construction suspended:	*Leviathan*
Destined for Commonwealth:	*Hercules** (RIN)

The shock of Communist aggression in Korea and elsewhere on the Asian continent led to an acceleration of the carrier building plans which had lain dormant for so long. The older World War 2 vintage carriers were becoming obsolete very quickly as the new British inventions had been readied for service. The new and larger carrier-borne aircraft and the change to a nuclear role also meant that such ships as *Illustrious* and *Implacable* were finding it hard to keep up with their American cousins in joint NATO exercises.

* Became *Vikrant* in 1957.
† Became *Melbourne* in 1955.

The new carriers were designed with a new generation of larger, jet-powered aircraft in mind; however, they could easily accommodate the old piston-engined machines like this Firefly AS6, the last of the long line of Fairey aircraft of that type (Fleet Air Arm Museum).

The larger carriers could now be replaced by the two *Audacious* Class hulls which had not been cancelled at the termination of hostilities; *Eagle* (ex-*Audacious*) and *Ark Royal* (ex-*Irresistible*) under construction by Harland and Wolff and Cammel Laird respectively. *Eagle* was the nearest to completion and she was launched by HRH Princess Elizabeth (now HM Queen Elizabeth II) at Belfast on March 19 1946 and the carrier (the largest RN warship at that time) was accepted for service by the RN on March 1 1952. In many ways, *Eagle* was an updated *Implacable* Class, but she had several worthwhile improvements to her armament and internal arrangements. Her early career was devoted to trials, both of her own equipment, which still consisted of an axial deck and hydraulic catapults, and as a floating host to the new series of naval aircraft which were due to come into service—the Gannet, Sea Hawk and Sea Venom.

Her first partial air group was composed of Attackers (800 Squadron) and Firebrands (827 Squadron) and, in July 1952, she replaced *Indomitable* as flagship of the Home Fleet's Heavy Squadron. The major NATO exercise, Mainbrace, allowed her full CAG to be embarked: Attackers (800 and 803); Fireflies (812 and 814); and Firebrands (827).

As it happens, this was not at all a permanent arrangement and several units were replaced for Arctic trials that autumn. By January 1954, after time in the Mediterranean where she was later to join 2 ACS, *Eagle* accomplished her 7,000th deck landing. It is to be remembered that her flight deck was still for all intents and purposes axial (albeit with a painted angle) and it was not until 1957 that she was fitted with a mirror landing sight and had an interim angle applied to the flight deck.

It was *Eagle*'s near sister-ship, *Ark Royal*, which pioneered the angled deck, steam catapults and mirror sight into service. The cost of these magnificent ships was staggering for *Eagle* had cost over £15.75 million in 1952 and *Ark Royal* with her many refinements cost nearly £21.5 million. Throughout the

Another famous carrier with breeding was Eagle *which, although in service before* Ark Royal, *always remained in the latter's shadow. This wintry scene shows a squadron of Westland Wyverns ranged for flying* (Fleet Air Arm Museum).

next two decades, these two ships would be rivals, for whilst *Ark* caught the public's imagination, *Eagle* is regarded by many matelots as the more 'warship-like' vessel. *Eagle*'s early days were plagued with problems, not least the idea that the ship was too big for one Commander executive officer, and so, following the USN's example, two were appointed. The Commander (XO) is responsible for the smooth running of the ship and to have this as a dual responsibility was not a workable arrangement and it was eventually stopped, much, one can imagine, to the delight of First Lieutenants who had become 'mess deck officers' in effect. *Ark*, on the other hand, developed an unenviable reputation for unserviceability and was christened 'Park Royal' by the dockyard maties at her home port of Devonport. It was hardly expected at the time that *Ark Royal*, the fourth ship to bear the name, would be Britain's last fixed-wing carrier.

The first and last commissions of *Ark Royal* were particularly notable in that there were no serious deck landing accidents. This is rather remarkable considering the problems involved. The crash ratio of fatal accidents, about two per 10,000 flying hours, remained the same throughout the carrier's existence. As aircraft power, speed and performance increased, so various aids were devised to assist the landing—angled deck, nylon barrier and mirror landing sight. This meant that more and more powerful aircraft could be used, but surprisingly the crash to landing ratio remained the same. In peace time, with an average pilot completing 2,500 hours flying, it meant that every other pilot had a chance of being killed, quite astounding when one considers that in wartime the risk would be even higher, with enemy action and the general high levels of operational expediency. In fact, the only thing that was more dangerous than carrier landings, say at night, was training for air displays where the casualty rate went up 40 times that of peace time night flying, even when one considers that much carrier flying was done especially in the 1950s and 1960s at night in 'thick' weather in the Bay of Biscay; something that no other Navy has had to put up with.

As a replacement for the *Colossus* Class of light fleet carriers, came the rather attractive 1943 war programme *Hermes* Class of which post-war cancellation had allowed four out of eight to be continued. *Centaur* was the first of the four to be launched, on April 22 1947, followed by *Albion* on May 6 and a year or so later *Bulwark* took to the water on June 22 1948. *Hermes* (ex-*Elephant*) was not launched until February 16 1953, eventually becoming the last British fixed-wing carrier to enter service. She was completed to a slightly different pattern and can therefore almost be given a Class of her own.

When *Centaur* entered service with the fleet, she was the first angled-deck carrier (although the deck was angled merely by painting the centre-line off centre) and her first operational commission, under Captain Henry Rolfe, began a 'very exciting period in naval aviation' as ship's and aircraft tactics were evolved. Initially, the air group consisted of Sea Furies and Avenger AS4s, but these were replaced by Sea Hawks (801 and 811 Squadrons) and Gannets (820 Squadron), with the most welcome continuance of the Dragonfly plane guard helicopter. Despite being engaged in these trials, *Centaur* was flagship for most of the period of the Mediterranean Fleet's Aircraft Carrier Squadron, where she was partnered by her sister-ship, *Albion*, still in those days an axial deck ship. These two later went to the Far East as part of an important flag-showing task group.

Centaur's Captain, who had been both a pilot and observer before the war, was very pleased that he had the angled deck which 'greatly increased the operational potential' of his ship. Under his guidance and that of his Commander (Air) Derek Empson (one of the two former RNVR aviators to reach the rank of Admiral), the ship explored the new concepts and the tactical use of aircraft from an angled deck, especially in the area of speeding up flight deck operations. To quote Derek Empson, 'if Nelson had "frigates" written on his heart, then Commanders (Air) of the jet age had "fuel state" indelibly inscribed on theirs!' Fuel economy was to become the pre-occupation of the

The angled decks of Ark Royal *showing the difference between the partial angle of 1961 (left) and 1971. The size of 'Flyco' and amount of radar array has also drastically altered* (RN photos).

When Lord Louis Mountbatten departed the Mediterranean in December 1954, part of the farewell tribute of the men who had been under his command was a steam past of the aircraft carriers Centaur *and* Albion. *The former was not only the Carrier Squadron flagship, but also the first angle-deck carrier to be tried operationally.* Albion *was still at that time configured in the old axial style* (RN via Rear Admiral Rolfe).

next three generations of naval aviators. Veteran aviators, like Henry Rolfe, realised very rapidly just how valuable the Cambell-Boddington design was to modern carrier operations. It had also been shown that it was not necessary to continuously alter the ship's heading to achieve safe landings. This increase in the landing rate was equalled by the introduction of steam catapults which meant that strict attention to the steam jet on the bow of a carrier was no longer necessary as again a perfect into wind heading was not imperative.

There had been, by all accounts, a considerable battle in the Admiralty to procure two cats for the class. Rear Admiral Torlesse recalls that several gunnery specialists were more interested in increasing the main batteries forward which would have meant only one catapult could have been fitted. These two factors, added to the continued development of radar, meant that a dramatic revolution was under way. For a change it was a revolution that depended on British inventive skills and engineering expertise.

Whilst *Centaur*, after these initial trials, launched into a career of showing the flag, exercises and limited operations, against such targets as arms smugglers off Aden, *Bulwark* spent some time as trials carrier relieving *Illustrious*, and was the first ship to carry out detailed trials with a mirror landing and sight deck landing aid. *Albion* was initially employed in the usual round of work-ups, trials, exercises and courtesy visits. All three carriers, however, built up a reputation for being happy ships and, despite the occasional flying accident, as safe ships.

During the 1960 commission in the Far East, *Albion* had so many aircraft embarked that the flight deck handlers had only inches to spare in order to leave room for the last aircraft to land on safely. They were under such pressure that a great cheer went up when it was announced that a Sea Hawk pilot had ejected and had been safely recovered by helicopter from the sea. They then had a few extra feet of space due to the loss of the aircraft.

The shortcomings of the armoured fleet carriers which had served so well during the war became readily apparent as the RN moved into a new age. Apart from various trials and training roles, the six ships could not contribute to the further development of the British fixed-wing carrier in their existing state. It was therefore proposed in 1948 to modernise the whole class with the possible exemption of *Illustrious*, still troubled by the unwelcome attentions of the Luftwaffe during the Mediterranean campaign. The plan was to enable them to operate 30,000 lb (13,600 kg) aircraft and that *Formidable* should be the first to go into dockyard hands. With an eye on costs and other matters, it was later decided to refit *Victorious* first. It turned out to be more than the four years' job originally planned and so it was that *Victorious* was the one and only armoured fleet carrier to be so modernised.

She was taken in hand at Portsmouth on October 10 1950 and did not recommence fleet operations until January 1958. When she did go to sea again she had been considerably altered and was the first British carrier to carry all the post-war developed aids—a fully angled deck (8¾ degrees), a pair of steam catapults, four uprated Mark 13 arrester wires and two deck landing mirror sights. Atop the island was fitted the latest Type 984 '3-D' radar which gave her a characteristic silhouette, not unlike that of *Hermes* and, later (post-1964), *Eagle*. Space was allocated for guided weapons servicing and the general handling arrangements were improved. It was necessary to equip her to operate the third generation of carrier aircraft like the Supermarine Scimitar and the de Havilland Sea Vixen, together with their new weapons such as the Firestreak anti-aircraft missile (AAM) and the nuclear bomb.

When *Victorious* put to sea for preliminary sea trials on February 3 1958 she was commanded by Captain Charles Coke, DSO, RN, who wrote, 'As Captain I took a huge pride in commanding so splendid and so successful a vessel'. Despite a fatal (and much publicised) landing accident, the initial fixed wing aircraft came aboard—Scimitars of 803 Squadron, Sea Venoms of 893 and Skyraiders of 849B Flight*. The Whirlwind plane guard and general duties helicopters were already aboard in the tradition that they came aboard first and left last during a carrier's deployment. It was during this first commission of the modernised *Victorious* that one of those notions of the then First Sea Lord, Lord Mountbatten, bore its usual fruit. A works-study group, led by Commander (E) Jack Button, a veteran of Korean operations in *Ocean*, pioneered many improved techniques around the ship including a reduction in the time necessary to rig the nylon emergency crash barrier from nine minutes to just two. In the days of the bigger jets this would be a vital contribution to the new flight safety ideas coming along. The group later took their skills to *Hermes* and *Ark Royal*. Later in the commission, 824 Squadron with anti-submarine Whirlwinds, were able to join in the fun. Various trials with Sea Vixens, Gannet AEW3s and the Buccaneer prototype were also undertaken before Taranto veteran, Captain (now Vice Admiral Sir Richard) Janvrin, DSC, took command. His Commander (Air) was another famous naval aviator, John Treacher, who went on to command *Hermes* and to attain Admiral's rank.

Sadly, despite a long refit between 1962-63 and considerable service in the East of Suez theatre, *Victorious* developed a small fire whilst in dockyard hands

* The airborne early warning squadron was 849, but to ensure continuity of command it was split into fights denoted by letters, eg 849B in *Victorious* and 849D in *Eagle*.

Left *Three fixed-wing carriers together make a breath-taking sight. The date is May 1957 and the occasion a review of the Home Fleet by HM Queen Elizabeth II. The carriers are* Ark *(leading),* Albion *and* Ocean, *the latter being on her last commission* (RN).

Below *The only armoured fleet carrier to have its career extended was* Victorious *which underwent an extended refit from 1950 until 1958. Happy* 'Vic' *is seen here during post-refit trials and her island is topped by the extraordinary Type 984 'dustbin-style' radar* (RN).

at Portsmouth and she was classified beyond repair in 1967. It has already been said that there are some ships which can be termed 'happy ships' and one such was undoubtedly the former armoured fleet carrier, *Victorious*, especially after her long refit, 1950-58. Many former carrier aviators and seamen believe that a happy ship results from, as Captain Button put it, 'a feeling which comes from the top—a good Captain and heads of departments—and which spreads on down the line of command'.

Victorious' first commission after refit was one such good start, under the almost paternal care of Captain Charles Coke. Many believe that when a ship is off on a good footing, it will stay that way and by the number of ratings who applied to return to the *Vic* tour after tour this was certainly apparent in the case of the 35,500 ton carrier. This was true of *Vic*, despite the trials and tribulations of the then new Type 984 Air Warning Radar kit, a new lower deck messing system and sea trials for the Sea Vixen all-weather fighter.

Some carriers had less happy starts and *Eagle* is often given as an example of an unhappy warship which was due, many say, to the adoption of two Commander (XO) billets in the same ship at the same time. There is, however, no doubt that after her long refit, 1959-63, *Eagle* was a happy ship and former members of the ship's company and of the air squadrons will tell you that *Eagle* had more character than any other carrier since the war, even including the ever-popular *Ark Royal*. There can be no doubt the smaller light fleet types of the *Albion* group were happy ships also, and this can be attributed, one is told, to the smaller ship's company which allowed officers and men to know each other better; on some of the larger carriers, especially with a staff embarked, it was not unusual for officers not to recognise a brother officer from the ship when ashore!

Although originally laid down by Vickers Armstrong (Barrow) in June 1944, the *Hermes* (then called *Elephant*), part of the war emergency plan for a class of improved light fleet carriers, was originally intended to be all but identical to her sister-ships, *Albion, Bulwark* and *Centaur*, but the Admiralty had other ideas. She was launched on February 16 1953 and completed in October 1959! The long delay did allow the builders, however, to complete her with the so-called modern aids, as well as the RN's second and last deck-edge lift. The first one of this design, so prevalent in the USN, was in *Ark Royal* (1955-59) but this had proved difficult to operate successfully; *Hermes'* was of a different design and as these words are written, still survives in the ASW carrier which she has become. The re-designed island also mounted a Type 984 radar similar to *Victorious'* array. When commissioned *Hermes* embarked Sea Vixen (890) and Scimitar (804) jets, Whirlwind anti-submarine helicopters and a flight of Gannet AEW3 early warning aircraft.

At the end of 1960 *Hermes* was deployed East of Suez and, in company with *Victorious*, she operated off Aden for a while. After a refit between October 1961 and 1962, *Hermes* again joined the Far East Fleet (where she relieved *Ark*) before being taken in hand for a major refit from 1964-66.

So the scene is set for the major drama of the 60-year life of the British fixed-wing carriers. First, however, we must examine the carrier-borne aircraft available in more detail and take a look at a small landing operation in North Africa.

Chaptain 15

Hawks to Vixens

The second generation of post-war aircraft had now arrived and, besides the new helicopters whose whirling blades were to make carrier operation that much safer, the new jets were entering service. Reportedly one of the most delightful aircraft to fly from a carrier was the sleek Hawker Sea Hawk. Initially designed as an interceptor, the Sea Hawk found its own particular niche in the carrier story in the ground attack role. The first production variant of the Sea Hawk F1 flew in November 1951 and was put into service, replacing the Sea Fury piston-engined fighter, with 806 Squadron (Lieutenant Commander Pat Chilton) in March 1953. Subsequent marks were the F2, the FB3/5, the FGA4 and FGA6. They flew from all contemporary operational carriers and were in the thick of the fighting, providing close-in ground support for the Allied Forces during the Suez crisis in 1956, when the following squadrons were deployed: *Albion* 800, 802* and 810; *Bulwark* 804* and 897; *Eagle* 899.

The halcyon days of carrier operations were during the Sea Hawk's service life and the rivalry between the units and ships was particularly strong. Each squadron had its own markings—a red fin for 800, a tiger's head with a scimitar in its mouth for 804, a flying fish for 898, and so on. By 1960, however, the Sea Hawk was obsolete in a front line role and, when *Albion* returned from the Far East for conversion to a Commando Carrier in December 1960, 806 disbanded. The Sea Hawk had been replaced by the Scimitar and the era of the light, 'fun to fly' jet was over.

The Navy's premier Sea Hawk unit was 800 Squadron which joined *Ark Royal* in September 1955 in her first commission, having worked-up aboard *Bulwark*. The unit was commanded by Lieutenant Commander Ray Lygo, who 14 years later commanded *Ark* and rose to the rank of Admiral before retiring in 1978. Another member of 800 was Lieutenant Ted Anson who was to become the *Ark*'s last Commanding Officer. 'The whole squadron', recalls Captain Alan 'Spiv' Leahy, CBE, DSC, 'liked the Sea Hawk very much'. Leahy, then a Lieutenant and the Senior Pilot, continues 'we found it super to fly and there was no noticeable difference between the various marks from the flying point of view, except that the newer aircraft climbed rather faster!'.

The Sea Hawk's companion in service was the de Havilland Sea Venom. This was the RN's first jet all-weather fighter but, unlike the Hawk, it was a dual seat aircraft where the observer sat beside the pilot. Three basic variants were

---

* These squadrons were destined to embark in *Ark Royal*, then under refit.

Flown by no less than 13 front-line carrier squadrons, the beautiful Hawker Sea Hawk was the RN's leading day fighter from 1953 until 1960. The larger carriers often embarked more than one squadron, whilst the new light fleets like Centaur *carried only one for normal peacetime operations, in this case 801 Squadron during 1959–60* (RN via Captain McKeown).

delivered to the FAA and all were respected for their ability to sit down 'amongst the wire in a most impressive manner . . . as good as anything seen on the deck yet', said Lieutenant Commander M.A. Birrell, DSC, who commanded 891 Squadron in *Ark.* Several early accidents did not make it that well loved by observers, although the radar was 'most satisfactory' according to accounts at the time. There were problems in early days of poor weather landings and until Carrier Controlled Approach (CCA) was improved, Birrell reckoned that 'the carrier's (*Ark Royal*) capabilities in bringing its aircraft on being very little advanced since the days of the previous *Ark Royal* and her Swordfish'. Being relatively unsophisticated, the Venom was designed to fill the gap between the Sea Hornet and the advanced Sea Vixen design of the next generation of jet aircraft. It, however, served in seven front-line squadrons from 1954 to 1959, with the following squadrons and carriers: 809 Squadron—*Albion*; 831 Squadron—Various carriers in the ECM role; 890 Squadron—*Ark Royal*; 891 Squadron—*Eagle, Ark Royal, Centaur*; 892

About to make a perfect touch-down and take a wire, this magnificent photograph of a Sea Hawk, again from 801 Squadron, illustrates the poise and grace of the little fighter (RN via Captain McKeown).

Squadron—*Eagle*; 893 Squadron—*Eagle, Ark Royal, Victorious*; 894 Squadron—*Eagle, Albion*; 895 Squadron—*Albion*. The Australians also flew the type from *Melbourne* (805, 808 and 816 Squadrons).

With a considerable number of Soviet submarines in service—about four times as many as the Germans had U-Boats operating in 1939—the FAA made a great effort to improve their anti-submarine capability. Besides the Firefly and Avenger squadrons mentioned in a previous chapter, the Navy had a new, rather unusual bird, earmarked for service—the Westland/Fairey Gannet. It carried a pilot and two observers in a tandem seating arrangement down the spine of the fuselage and was powered by a geared 'Double-Mamba' in-line engine arrangement which gave it the characteristic Gannet eight-bladed nose. Besides depth charges and other anti-submarine nasties, the Gannet, which made its maiden flight in September 1949, carried sonobuoys for locating submarines underwater, and a dustbin-like radar dome beneath the fuselage. From 1955, this 19,600 lb (8,890 kg) aircraft became the mainstay of carrier ASW operations and when one squadron (824 in *Ark Royal*) had their leg pulled about the aircraft carrying everything but the kitchen sink—they fitted one of those into the bomb bay which was denoted 'Kitchen Sink (Old Original) Mark 1'. It was recorded that the sink had a ballistic trajectory not unlike that of a brick-built chicken house!

Gannets went into front-line service aboard *Eagle* (826) and *Ark Royal* (824) in 1955 and eventually 810, 812, 814, 815, 816, 817, 820, 825, 831, 847 and 896 front-line squadrons were also equipped. Their time in service in the ASW role was limited, however, by the introduction of helicopter anti-submarine squadrons, equipped with the Whirlwind. The Gannet aircrews did not let such an event pass lightly as the *FAA Songbook* records:

'The Gannet was splendid, it went to the fleet,
It worked very well and they thought it a treat,
The Choppers went in and the Gannets went out,
Then the Choppers went in with a fine waterspout.'

This was far from the end of the Gannet story as we shall see later.

Top right *Very much the hangar mate to the Sea Hawk was the two-seat DH Sea Venom, an all weather fighter with a range of 705 miles (1,305 km) and the capability to carry bombs or rockets. Its fighter-bomber role was tested at Suez in 1956 when five Venom squadrons were committed. This aircraft, about to catapult from* Eagle *(note the 'J' on the tail), was allocated to 894 Squadron; the unit was at Suez but flew from* Albion *(Fleet Air Arm Museum).*

Centre right *Destined, like the Dragonfly plane-guard, to be replaced by Whirlwind helicopters, the Gannet provided a useful ASW capability to the fleet during a period when the Cold War was at its most frigid. Gannets frequently employed free take-offs, although they were catapult-capable as well. Note the Sea Furies parked under the lee of the island (Fleet Air Arm Museum).*

Right *The Royal Navy's carriers were provided with a stop-gap airborne early warning aircraft in 1951 by virtue of the Douglas Skyraider. This American design eventually remained on the books of 849 Squadron for nine years until replaced by the Gannet. Not only was the Skyraider capable of detecting approaching enemy aircraft and ships, but it could be used to direct strikes on shore or surface targets, as at Suez. 849 Squadron was divided into flights for embarked service and this Skyraider comes from C Flight in* Albion *(Fleet Air Arm Museum).*

The need to provide advanced warning of an air threat to the fleet was proved in the last days of the Pacific war when hastily modified Avengers were rushed into service carrying airborne radar. In the late 1940s and early 1950s, Britain did not have the radar nor the airframes available for such a role, so the RN went shopping in America (or to be more precise the Mutual Defence Assistance Programme was invoked). The aircraft was the Douglas Skyraider AEW1 (Airborne Early Warning) and commanded by Lieutenant Commander John Treacher, 849 Squadron was the the first and only front-line unit. It was, however, split into flights and three or four aircraft were detached to various carriers—849B to *Ark* for instance. This unit was also part of the FAA flypast for HM The Queen's Coronation Fleet Review at Spithead. The last piston-engined carrier aircraft, the Skyraider or 'Guppy', was phased out in 1960 to be replaced by the suitably modified Gannet AEW variant of which more later.

In the helicopter world, the success of the rotary-wing types in Korea, and at home with 705 Squadron, led to the extensive use of Westland-built Dragonfly helicopters aboard carriers as plane guards, where to some extent they supplanted the traditional plane guard destroyer which hung on to the starboard quarter of a carrier at a distance of several cables throughout the carrier's search for wind, as if attached by a string! They were used as carrier-to-shore transports and as casualty evacuation (casevac) and communications aircraft. The Dragonfly was rather small though and eventually it was replaced by the Whirlwind HAR1, but not before the type led the Coronation FAA flypast at Spithead in 1953.

The next helicopter on the carrier scene was again an American design built under licence in Britain and named the Whirlwind by the RN. Initially, American-built models, christened Whirlwind HAR21s and HAS22s, were flown by 845 Squadron. They were fitted with short-range sonar and could be fitted to take a homing torpedo—but only if the sonar was removed first! The British-built successor, the Whirlwind HAS7, was heavier and not that popular with aircrew—'it had an air intake that was placed as close to the sea as possible, and several unwary aviators experienced the predictable effect of sucking gallons of salt water into an internal combustion engine'. In fact, as many Whirlwind HAS7s were lost as the number of Dragonflies actually bought for service with the RN! Besides 845, the Whirlwind served with 814, 815, 820, 824, 847 and 848 Squadrons following its replacement of the Gannet as the carrier fleet's leading anti-submarine weapon and the formation of the naval air commando assault units. Several ships' flights were also equipped for search and rescue duties. 'The advantages of having an SAR chopper aboard a carrier were very great for not only was it a high morale factor, because it would pick up a ditched pilot rapidly, but also it was operationally good to have the pilot back aboard as soon as possible', says Derek Empson, speaking as a former Commander (Air), carrier Captain and FOAC.

The Whirlwind's replacement was the jet turbine powered Wessex HAS1 which first flew in prototype form in May 1957. It was much improved in performance and had a better endurance, being able to lift a sonar plus two anti-submarine torpedoes. Its main advance, greatly beloved of aircrews, was its ability to hover automatically at night. Eight front-line units were equipped with the Wessex, being initially shepherded into service by 815 Squadron (Lieutenant Commander A.L.L. Skinner) in July 1961. A couple of months later the unit embarked in the newly refitted *Ark Royal* (Captain Peter Hill-Norton—now

The ubiquitous Whirlwind is often illustrated in its anti-submarine or search and rescue roles, but it is illustrated here aboard Warrior *during Operation Grapple in the Pacific during the 1957 Atomic Tests at Christmas Island. The helicopters were used for liaison and communications duties* (Fleet Air Arm Museum).

Admiral of the Fleet, Lord Hill-Norton). Like its smaller brother, the Whirlwind, Wessex airframes were converted into Commando helicopters. The RAN also bought a substantial number (designated Wessex HAS31s) for service aboard *Melbourne* and when this carrier visited Spithead for the Silver Jubilee Review, there was still a Wessex aboard for plane-guard duties.

It was not long before the anti-submarine world had progressed so far that the Wessex, in its original form, was again outmoded and the RN released a substantial number of airframes for conversion by Westland. The new model, termed Wessex HAS3, was taken aboard *Eagle* by 826 Squadron in April 1969 (the unit having previously served in *Hermes* with Mark 1s). The Wessex HAS1s still formed individual Carrier's Search and Rescue Flights—the last afloat being *Ark*'s SAR Flight commanded by Lieutenant David George, RN. The Wessex 3 only served in *Eagle* and *Victorious*, finding its true home in the County Class destroyers which so often escorted the carrier units at sea. The Wessex could, it is said, be summed up as follows:

'I'm your Wessex Pilot baby, I can fly
I'm a supersonic guy,
I'm your Wessex Pilot baby, I've got speed
I've got everything I need.'

FAA Songbook (Tune: *Urban Spaceman*)

Whilst the Wessex was taking over the rotary wing side of carrier aviation, the fixed-wing element was still reigning supreme and was moving into its third generation of jets with the introduction of the Scimitar. This was the RN's first swept wing, single-seat fighter and fully loaded it weighed 40,000 lb (18,100 kg). It was also a nuclear capable strike aircraft and its development can be said to have directly influenced the angled deck principle. Without such a system the Scimitar would not have effectively been able to operate at sea. Its development

Above *The Supermarine Scimitar brought a new era of naval flying with its swept wings and trans-sonic performance. Replacing the Sea Hawk squadrons, Scimitars equipped four front-line squadrons, initially with 803 Squadron aboard the re-commissioned* Victorious *in 1958. Pictured later in the 1960s at the Fly One position, with Sea Vixen jets and Gannet AEW3s, the same unit's aircraft are parked after flying* (Fleet Air Arm Museum).

Below *Just as the Scimitar replaced the Sea Hawk, so the Sea Vixen replaced the Sea Venom. This Vixen from 890 Squadron is being washed down aboard* Ark *during a nuclear attack exercise in 1964. The long probe jutting from the wing is an in-flight refuelling probe which allowed aircraft so fitted to be topped-up with fuel by a 'tanker' aircraft, perhaps another Vixen or a Scimitar* (RN via Vice Admiral Gibson).

was almost simultaneous with the refitting of *Victorious* and it was to her that 803 Squadron was assigned. Its sea service did not start well, because having formed the first operational Scimitar unit, Lieutenant Commander Des Russell, 803's CO, was killed when landing on *Vic* in September 1958. This did not prevent three other front-line units from forming—800, 804 and 807—as well as a special in-flight refuelling evaluation unit called 800B Flight in 1964. Scimitars had several well documented occasions of having to use the emergency barrier and are usually said by those who flew them to have been landed in a 'controlled crash'.

'The Scimitar would go like a train and it could overtake anything even whilst climbing. I can remember', recalls Alan Leahy again, 'meeting a flight of F-100 Super Sabres over the Mediterranean. This supersonic aircraft was the USAF's latest toy, but we ran rings round them in our Scimitars, because the F-100s had drop tanks, even though we also had drop tanks on'. The aircraft still had a fearsome reputation, especially in smaller carriers such as *Hermes*, where Leahy was Commander (Air). 'It was unforgiving', he remembers, 'a pilot had to obey the rules especially on the approach but it was quite a step up from the Sea Hawk and the fastest British fighter before the RAF introduced the Lightning.' Its introduction into service, together with that of the Sea Vixen gave the fleet, in the words of former Carrier Captain and Admiral Richard Smeeton, 'an atomic capability and a greatly improved Air Defence'.

The new Carrier Air Groups aboard British fixed-wing carriers, which had long ago dispensed with Air Group Commanders, unlike their American cousins, would now have two new jets when they went aboard *Ark, Eagle, Hermes, Victorious* and *Centaur*. This unusual design of the de Havilland Sea Vixen with its twin booms and off-set pilot's canopy had already achieved notoriety because of the spectacular crash of a prototype (the DH110) at the Farnborough Air Show some years before the fighter entered service. Both *Albion* and *Ark* were used for trials of the pre-production aircraft, then *Victorious* and *Centaur* played host to the Intensive Flying Trials Unit (IFTU) known as 700Y Squadron in 1958. *Ark* was destined to receive the first squadron, 892, which formed in July 1959 and embarked for seven months from March 1960.

The Vixen was operational with 890, 892 and 899 Squadrons, as well as 892, in the all weather fighter role, where its two man crew could provide expert attention to the task of protecting the fleet. The observer was secreted in the starboard fuselage—in the 'coal hole' as it was known. This was not a particularly pleasant place to be during launch or recovery because there was only a small window in the fuselage and this was usually kept blacked out to allow the observer to operate the airborne radar. Not only did one feel cut off but ejection was difficult and risky—sometimes fatal. Such a feeling of insecurity could not have been helped by an inconsiderate pilot. One such pilot had a habit of talking to himself over the intercom and was heard to mutter such dire things as, 'Oh no, that's torn it' and 'that doesn't look good'. Not really guaranteed to help the observer relax! He was soon sorted out by SOBS (Senior Observer) after the latter had been subjected to such a ride!

Chapter 16

Musketeer—carrier power at Suez

Since the 19th century Britain and France had maintained a presence along the thin corridor of waterway which links the Red Sea and the Mediterranean. During World War 2, considerable effort was put into defending the 'canal' against the Axis in North Africa and the Near East. Following a revolution in Egypt during 1952, British troops pulled out of the canal zone under a promise of free use and defence of the Suez Canal. Refused financial assistance by the West, Colonel Nasser, the country's leader, nationalised the Franco-British Suez Canal Company in July 1956. The tense situation which arose was complicated by the Israeli-Egyptian Sinai confrontation which led eventually to Anglo-French forces being called in to 'save' the canal.

That is the background to what, but for the politicians—particularly American—would have been a classic carrier support operation. The politics involved are, as always, complex, but at home in Britain, Prime Minister Anthony Eden knew where his duty lay. A combined fleet of French and British warships, spearheaded by *Eagle* with *Albion, Bulwark, Arromanches* (ex-*Colossus*) and *Lafayette*, set out along the Mediterranean from the Malta area, and despite a lengthy voyage from the West, the Naval task force arrived off Port Said, the planned landing area, on October 30 1956. The landings were politically to be called an intervention—a police action—to prevent Israel and Egypt (neither of whom were friendly to Britain at that time) from destroying the canal, so vital to British interests in the Far East.

Carrier	Squadron and aircraft embarked	Carrier	Squadron and aircraft embarked
Eagle	830 Wyvern	*Albion*	800 Sea Hawk
	831 Wyvern		(destined for *Eagle*)
	849A Skyraider		802 Sea Hawk
	891 Sea Venom		(destined for *Ark Royal*)
	893 Sea Venom		809 Sea Venom
	(from *Ark Royal*)		810 Sea Hawk
	899 Sea Hawk		849B Skyraider
Bulwark	804 Sea Hawk		894 Sea Venom
	(from *Ark Royal*)		895 Sea Venom
	897 Sea Hawk		

NB *Ark Royal* was undergoing her first major refit and was actually re-commissioned the day news of the carrier strikes broke in the British press.

Still equipped with Sea Hawks and Sea Venoms some months after Suez, Albion *was one of three fixed-wing carriers in action against targets in Egypt. In this photograph the smoke around the aircraft is caused by the cartridge starters of the jet engines being fired; quite an alarming sight for the uninitiated!* (via Graham Wilmott).

Despite the fact that *Albion* was still in refit when the Admiralty began to receive intelligence that all was not well in the Eastern Mediterranean, she was readied for sea and as fate would have it, she arrived on station, to join Rear Admiral 'Lofty' Powers' other two carriers—*Eagle* and *Bulwark*—on her Captain's birthday. He was Richard Smeeton, an experienced naval aviator, who had been Captain (Air) Mediterranean only a few years before, and so was well acquainted with the political scene in the region.

Albion had on board an almost fully worked up Air Group led by 800 Squadron, fresh from the first commission of *Ark Royal*. This helped to speed up the post-refit trials period which lasted only about ten days instead of the

The main fighter support to the landing came from the Sea Hawks, like those illustrated here in Albion. *Note the group of aircraft handlers between the two catapult tracks— that could be a rather risky position at times!* (RN via Captain McKeown).

Still wearing the yellow and black identification stripes of the Suez action, this Avenger from Bulwark *is prepared for a free take-off from* Ark Royal; *the latter was re-commissioned after her first refit the day the first carrier strikes were made* (Fleet Air Arm Museum).

normal two months. Throughout the policing operation, apart from going off station to refuel, *Albion*'s aircraft were flying nearly all daylight hours. Although several of her aircraft were shot down, all the aircrew were picked up by friendly forces. After the 'action', *Albion* remained at sea for a month on ceasefire duties and the fact that she was able to do this can perhaps be attributed to the fact that Dick Smeeton 'ran a taut ship'.

Most of the aircrews had been briefed about the *Musketeer* situation in October whilst deployed in the UK and at Malta. They immediately set about brushing up their weaponry and Army co-operation roles; many of the pilots and observers had served in Korea and had done this before, albeit a little slower, in piston-engined aircraft. The air squadrons were redeployed, mainly because a continuous provision of air cover was envisaged, and the smaller carriers would need to refuel more often than *Eagle*. Most squadrons joined their carriers en route to *Point X-Ray* off Port Said and, on October 30, a pre-dawn launch was made but the strike was cancelled before the attacking aircraft reached the African coast.

On November 1 1956 it was on in earnest, and the whole circus began its operation. 809 Squadron flying Sea venom FAW22s from *Albion* were targetted for Almaza airfield near Cairo, but on arrival found that 'the birds had flown'. Lieutenant R.B. Wigg takes up the story. 'We made a rather shallow run in, pumped our rockets into the hangars and loosed off 20 mm around the place. We went down the main runway in finger four, almost, at a hundred feet (30 m) or so, and the tracers from the ground criss-crossed our path from both sides in a most spectacular fashion, much more impressive than the Korean variety, but probably less lethal'. Other airfields were attacked—Bilbeis, Cairo West, Dekheila (a famous FAA station in World War 2) and Inchas. Wigg led the second strike of the day on Almaza and they destroyed a MiG-15 and a transport on the ground. Even at this stage it was certain that ground intelligence was not as good as in Korea.

Besides *Albion*'s and *Bulwark*'s need to refuel, *Eagle* developed catapult faults during the flying operations, which led to more pressure on the smaller carriers; even so, 621 were launched on the one serviceable cat. Her Wyverns were in any case found to be vulnerable to enemy ack-ack, two being shot down, so less aircraft were tasked and ranged for each strike. The light fleet *Arromanches* was operating with Corsair fighter-bombers (14F and 15F) and they assumed responsibility for the eastern side of Port Said where oil storage and industrial targets were attacked. The attacking air groups used a common radio frequency and, as Lieutenant Wigg put it, 'when the French were engaging a target, there wasn't much room on the air for anyone else!'. The French lost a Corsair and its pilot during the strikes and all but one of the FAA pilots were rescued by Whirlwind plane guard helicopters.

At Suez, the co-operation and liaison between the British and French carrier units was particularly good and the FAA representatives who witnessed the operations from *Arromanches* and *Lafayette* were impressed by the Corsairs especially. Lieutenant Commander Leppard, who had broken his leg and so could not fly, was transferred via helicopter to *Arromanches* and even indulged in a little 'batting' for the French Corsairs and Avengers; amongst the aircrew of the latter type was Philippe de Gaulle (son of the late President of France).

On November 5 1956 came the airborne assault from Cyprus and the Army co-op bit began in earnest. Much of the FAA activity was now devoted to 'cab-rank' duties over Port Said, with strike aircraft airborne and ready to attack any target directed by the Army controllers on the ground. Fighters provided a rescap (a rescue combat air patrol) over a Sea Hawk pilot who had parachuted into the desert east of the canal, until he was picked up by an Israeli patrol.

Earlier that day, 809 Squadron was engaged in what was probably the only air-to-sea engagement in defence of an aircraft carrier post World War 2. For several nights, Egyptian fast patrol boats had been harrassing the naval task force but, on November 5, three vessels were still in sight at dawn. The morning

802 Squadron's Senior Pilot during Suez was Lieutenant Commander 'Paddy' McKeown who brought his bridge-busting expertise from Korean operations. Standing by the powder-blackened cannons of his Sea Hawk is his Pilot's Mate Leading Airman Beek (RN via Captain McKeown).

The embarked flights of Skyraiders provided airborne early warning and tactical air control for the strike aircraft (Fleet Air Arm Museum).

CAP of Sea Venoms was launched to identify them. After circling for some time, the flight was ordered to attack and sink two of them, leaving the third to recover survivors. The fleet was not bothered again. On November 6 the naval assault force arrived and 45 Royal Marine Commando was landed by helicopter at Gamil airfield. The Commando assault carriers were *Theseus* (845 Squadron) and *Ocean* (Joint Helicopter Unit) both using Whirlwinds and some Sycamores. It was all to no avail, however, as the United Nations called a ceasefire the next day.

Perhaps this was just as well because the momentum built up by the carrier would have been hard to sustain. As it was, *Albion* had been on constant patrol for 30 days and was due back in Malta. *Bulwark*, after 600 sorties, was also due back in the UK, where she arrived a week before Christmas. *Eagle*'s 'cats' were repaired in Malta where the carrier stayed until her refit the following year.

Again we must ask what did the campaign at Suez achieve in terms of carriers? It was shown, as off Korea, just how useful a carrier force could be at an international trouble spot, even one close enough for land air forces to operate. The aircraft from the carriers also supplied a continuity impossible for the RAF even operating from Cyprus. At Suez, the Fleet Air Arm put into the air a very considerable force of some 125 fighter-bombers from three fixed-wing carriers and they did this from relatively close inshore giving the Sea Hawks and Sea Venoms about an hour to an hour and a quarter over the target. This was especially important during the Army co-operation phase of the action when naval aircraft were always on call. This should be compared to the matter of minutes achieved by the RAF and French Air Force from their further flung bases.

Secondly, the use of carriers to mount commando assaults was taken to heart and it is interesting to reflect that both *Albion* and *Bulwark* were converted into commando carriers in 1961 and 1959 respectively. This is perhaps the greatest benefit. Whatever is said, however, of the tactical doctrine learned, politically, Suez was a complete disaster because, as we shall see, it gave an excuse for the eventual demise of the carrier.

Chapter 17

The carrier crisis

'It is essential in the National interest that the Royal Navy shall continue to exercise air power over the sea with fixed-wing aircraft under full Naval authority: this can only be achieved by the continuation in service of aircraft carriers.'

FAAOA pamphlet 1965

In the early 1960s the carrier was in its heyday as it provided the core of the fleet, both at home and East of Suez. Its role in the modern Royal Navy was as follows:

(1) In peacetime, especially in the days around the Cuban missile crisis, the carrier had a special role—a Cold War role—in showing the flag. This not only contributed to good relations with foreign governments and peoples, but also showed our allies that we were ready and able to come to their aid in the event of aggression by a third party.

(2) What has been described as 'Gunboat Diplomacy', ie, the presence of a strike carrier and a commando carrier, full of Royal Marine Commandos, sitting off a dissidents' coast can be very persuasive. It also had the ability to show the third party that they would risk almost everything if they tangled with a mobile air power.

(3) In limited or 'brushfire' wars to act as a mobile air base providing both offensive (strikes against enemy positions) and defensive (anti-aircraft or anti-submarine) airpower, especially at long-range. Our ground forces could then expect back-up and faster reaction times than the RAF would be capable of as exemplified by this anecdote attributed to a local commander in Aden; he is reputed to have said that whenever there was a carrier offshore and he requested air support in the Radfan, a naval presence was there within minutes. If there was no carrier available, the RAF would spend several days holding meetings to decide whether they were trained to carry out the role! Whether true or not, this exemplified the carrier's role in limited confrontations as a back-up to existing forces, or spearheading the newly arrived contingent.

(4) In a role perhaps even more prevalent today, the carrier was the ideal tool on which to base the protection of sea trading routes, especially in the area out of reach of land-based aircraft—about 98 per cent of the sea lanes! For a while the RN maintained two carriers east of Suez and they provided a presence in the choke point areas such as the Malacca Straits in the time of tension with

A strike carrier operating as part of a 'Gunboat Diplomacy' Task Group with a commando carrier, frigates and a destroyer. The strike carrier is Eagle *(nearest camera) which, together with* Albion, *is passing through the Pillars of Hercules during a Mediterranean exercise* (RN).

Indonesia. As an example of the area it was possible to cover with fixed-wing carrier-borne aircraft, during the Beira oil patrol off Mozambique, *Eagle*'s air group (Sea Vixens of 899 Squadron, Scimitars of 800 Squadron and the 'eye in the sky' Gannets of 849D Flight) covered some 200,000 square miles (518,000 sq km) per day, giving an all day and all night presence. During a 46-day stint, *Eagle*'s aircraft had 'intercepted' and identified 770 ships off Beira.

(5) The final role envisaged at this time for Britain's carrier fleet was as a part of NATO's Strike Fleet (Atlantic), a nuclear deterrent force of surface warships.

With only five fixed-wing carriers still in service, it is difficult to see how the RN would have coped in a general war, but there is no doubt that their training and equipment were second to none. The RN's carrier strength in early 1962 was five fixed-wing carriers and two commando carriers. These later ships, *Albion* and *Bulwark*, were converted from fixed-wing and were now only capable of operating helicopters. *Bulwark* was the first such ship in the world, drawing on the experience of *Ocean* and *Theseus* at Suez. In 1961, *Bulwark* was a leading light in the Kuwait crisis when she transported a full commando into position using Whirlwind HAS7 helicopters—not the best tool to use for troop transportation in hot climates! It was envisaged that she and *Albion* would alternate their stations in the Atlantic/Mediterranean and the Indian Ocean, with one always on call East of Suez.

Fixed-wing carriers—early 1962

Ark Royal (R09)	43,340 tons	Scimitar (800)
		Sea Vixen 1 (890)
		Wessex 1 (815)
		Gannet 3 (849C)
Eagle (R05)	43,060 tons	In refit (1959-64)
Victorious (R38)	30,000 tons	In refit (1962-63)

Fixed-wing carriers—early 1962 *(contd)*

Hermes (R12)	28,000 tons	Scimitar (803)
		Sea Vixen 1 (892)
		Wessex 1 (814)
		Gannet 3 (849B)
Centaur (R06)	27,000 tons	Scimitar (807)
		Sea Vixen 1 (893)
		Whirlwind 7 (824)
		Gannet 3 (849A)

Commando carriers—early 1962

Albion (R07)	27,000 tons	Wessex 5 (845)
		Whirlwind 7 (846)
Bulwark (R08)	27,000 tons	Whirlwind 7 (848)

It was obvious that the existing fixed-wing hulls were becoming tired and not sufficiently strong to operate the heavier and faster modern carrier aircraft. A new carrier class was overdue. Despite the continual refitting of the carrier fleet with the latest radar and other equipment, it was clear to the Admiralty that a new ship with the new British inventions was imperative. The need to continue with the carrier as the core of the fleet had been clearly shown and, at the time, the future political intents of the world showed that the mobile air base theory was important to combat instability in the emerging nations of the world where a 'presence' or police action could not be undertaken by regular land-based forces.

Former carrier captain and naval aviator, Rear Admiral 'Percy' Gick, CB, OBE, DSC, summed up the feelings of many of his contemporaries in this quotation taken from the Fleet Air Arm Officers' Association booklet entitled

A typical scene aboard the five remaining fixed-wing carriers in the early 1960s. On board Victorious, a Sea Vixen FAW1 leaves the port catapult as a Scimitar is marshalled on to the starboard one. Besides the three men standing there is, to the left, a rating holding a small black board, face down; this is the check-board which reminded pilots of the last minute cockpit checks, when acknowledged by the gloved hand of the pilot the launch could proceed (RNAS Culdrose).

Aircraft Carriers (c 1965): 'I am convinced', he wrote, 'that we shall need a strong carrier force for at least the next two decades. So, I believe, do all responsible politicians. I can only hope that they have the courage of this conviction, and will provide soon enough, and in sufficient numbers, the men, aircraft and ships we need to do the job they have given us'.

The Navy's plan was the CVA-01 programme for a class of radically new fixed-wing carriers containing several new British invented techniques, including a 'parallel' deck system of operation, 'round the island' aircraft manoeuvring, and water spray arrester gear. The programme was conceived by a special 'think-tank' set up in the Directorate of Naval Air Warfare (DNAW), headed by Captain Eric Brown. In this letter of appointment the phrase 'the Navy puts the utmost importance on this project' is significant.

In July 1964, the Cabinet of the Conservative Government authorised the building of a new aircraft carrier at an estimated cost of £56m* and at least three were needed to fulfil British needs and obligations in the NATO area and East of Suez. As the construction swung into top gear it could be seen that it was one which would not have an easy ride through the political scene. Besides the Duncan Sandys (1957) Defence White Paper mentality which believed that everything could be done by a missile, there were those on the left-wing of the Labour Party (then still in Opposition) who reportedly believed that the carrier was responsible for Britain's action at Suez and every other 'interference' since then. In Service terms, however, the phased retirement of *Ark Royal* and *Eagle* necessitated replacement by something of the CVA-01 ilk.

The birth of this design was initially bedevilled by the concept of shipborne vertical take-off and landing (VTOL) aircraft for fleet defence. The VTOL protagonists envisaged an escort group where each destroyer had its own VTOL fighter of the Hawker P1154 type to carry out the entire strike and defence portfolio. Luckily for the Royal Navy the FAA was able to show that the VTOL fighter of those days was not likely to attain the true capabilities of either role for at least 20 years, so gradually a more realistic atmosphere approached.

DNAW had decided that the average complement of CVA-01 should comprise Phantom fighters, Buccaneer strike and Gannet AEW aircraft. At this time, the RAF was still being offered the Hawker P1127 (the forerunner of the P1154), and was trying to persuade the Navy to standardise on this and abandon the large carrier concept in favour of the RAF island-hopping strategy.

DNAW opposed these advances and even persuaded the RAF that the P1127 could not do their job either. The emphasis then swung to the P1154, but by mid-1964, the proposed navalised version had also been rejected by the Admiralty on the recommendation of DNAW, since exhaustive and detailed investigations at RAE Farnborough had revealed the following damaging deficiencies:

(1) a performance well below the manufacturer's specified figures, and that of the Phantom;

(2) a very poor load-lifting capability in the VTO mode;

(3) severe difficulties in proposals to alleviate the payload problems by catapulting;

(4) total incompatibility with the RAF's required version;

(5) a probable, unacceptably high peacetime attrition rate due to its single-

* In 1981, a guided missile frigate cost the Navy about £125 million.

Being safely locked away in Ark*'s upper hangar is a prototype Hawker P1127. The Navy thought that the best thing for the aircraft was to lock it away, but it was the forerunner of the RAF's Harrier and the Navy's own Sea Harrier, albeit nearly 20 years later* (RN via Vice Admiral Gibson).

engine layout, exacerbated by the fact that the power plant was of untried design; and

(6) a problem, very close to a naval pilot's heart, was the fact that model tests showed poor ditching characteristics.

The argument, put forward by the then Deputy Director of NAW, 'Winkle' Brown, was that if the aircraft needed to run along the deck to achieve a realistic performance, then the RN might as well have carriers in any case. These carriers could then operate the American-built McDonnell Douglas F-4 Phantom, a conventional design of powerful potential which was highly thought of by the FAA. Captain Brown recalls that: 'the arguments in favour of a British aircraft were, of course, strong, but the Navy countered this by arguing that fitting the Phantom with Rolls-Royce Spey engines and British avionics would produce a superior aeroplane to the standard US Naval Phantom, as well as an attractive export model'.

By all accounts, the Navy found a strong ally in Sir Solly Zuckerman, Scientific Adviser to the Cabinet, who seemed more sympathetic to the logic of the Navy's arguments than those of the RAF. In January 1964 the Deputy Director at DNAW went across to America to discuss the possibility of re-engining the Phantom and later the Minister of Defence, Julian Amery, signed a Memorandum of Understanding for the procurement of the Spey-engined Phantom. By this time, the RAF had become disillusioned with the P1154 and had clambered 'aboard the Navy's Phantom bandwagon' and finally, with the axing of TSR2, they had to settle for the Buccaneer as their low-level strike aircraft as well. 'So standardisation was achieved, but hardly in the way anyone had anticipated', comments 'Winkle' Brown, somewhat wistfully.

This was the time of the public debut of Concorde and a sobering thought struck naval aviators: in the P1154 they might be capable of Mach 1.6*, whilst it

* Mach 1.0 = the speed of sound.

The great white hope of the Fleet Air Arm during the 1960s was the remarkable CVA-01 design; a world beater in true British carrier tradition. Sadly, it is only possible to illustrate the beauty by way of an artist's impression. Notice the revolutionary features such as round-the-island taxiing, open ended hangar and comprehensive point defence system (MOD).

was conceivable that their grannies could be tripping across to America in a somewhat faster Mach 2.0 airliner!

The CVA-01 design envisaged a 53,000 ton carrier approximately 900 feet (274 m) long, capable of handling the latest jets and helicopters in a design at least 20 years in advance of existing hulls. It had a single hangar, 660 feet (201 m) by 80 feet (24.4 m) and was capable of stowing two-thirds of the aircraft complement, with a unique facility to allow its engines to be run at the aft end where the hangar could be opened to the air. The flight deck design represented a 15 per cent increase in usable 'real estate' with two aircraft lifts away from the main 'runway'—one lift being of the deck-edge variety. Two new, long-stroke steam catapults were considered necessary, together with a direct-acting water spray arrester gear complex.

50,000-55,000 tons (although not greatly larger than *Ark* or *Eagle*), represented the limit to which a British warship had to be built. One only has to look at the narrow entrances to both the carrier base ports of Portsmouth and Plymouth, and the lack of large graving docks to see the wisdom of this decision. Although some people argued for a smaller 30,000 ton design, the loss of 50 per cent of the strike potential which this would have meant only saved 10 per cent of the cost. To go with the design was an integral self-defence guided weapons system and a projected class of escort guided missile destroyers (actually as large as cruisers) termed the Type 82.

In the event only one, *Bristol*, was constructed but their role would have been something like that planned for the County Class in the late 1950s. Ideally, CVA-01 would have been available in 1970-72 (replacing *Victorious*), with the other units coming along in phased replacement of the remainder of the existing carrier force, say, CVA-02 in 1974-76 *Ark Royal*, and CVA-03 in 1978-80 *Eagle*, leaving *Hermes* to be converted to a commando/ASW carrier and *Centaur* to be phased out into retirement. Although construction costs would have been high, say, £55-65 million apiece, the savings in costly refits like that of *Ark Royal* during her Phantomisation (1966-69) would have been just as great. Not only this, but the cost of each carrier over the building period would have been only £6 million per annum.

There were those in other Services, and in the Royal Navy itself, who thought the whole carrier concept outdated, notwithstanding the lessons learnt in Korea and by the USN off Vietnam. The continued building programmes of America and France, the designs of the Soviet Union and the continued use of carriers in Argentina, Australia, Brazil and India should be considered significant. *Eagle* was also undergoing a costly £31 million major refit and the RAF thought the time ripe to regain control of all aspects of strike aviation. Marshal of the RAF, Sir Thomas Pike, had put forward a scheme for a 'Pike Ship Fleet'—a concept based on the 'Woolworths Carrier' of World War 2—which postulated a large number of cheap, small carriers, operating VTOL aircraft flown by the RAF. By 1964, however, the Air Staff had made a complete Air Power 'take-over' bid and had asked for a world-wide cover to British forces, by a system known as 'island hopping'. (This was nicknamed the 'Mobile Global RAF' by the other services!)

The Navy realised that in a crisis the Air Force would have enough to think about without trying to provide fighter cover to ships at sea. Even with in-flight refuelling, the likelihood of maximum, on the spot, air cover at the right time was as unlikely then as it definitely is today. The advantages of having an air component with a fleet are many, including the fact that the F-4 Phantom could intercept a hostile target at 100 miles (185 km) from the parent carrier in about eight minutes from catapult launch! Besides the actual intercepter there was also the need for airborne early warning such as that provided by the Gannet, not to mention the anti-shipping strike capability of the newly arrived Buccaneer. On a carrier, the latter was instantly available to deal with a potential surface threat several hundred miles away—before it could reach a weapon launch position and become a real threat.

To make the island-hopping strategy appear better than in fact it was, several vital points were deliberately overlooked and in one study, a chart was shown with the distance between Australia and South East Asia reduced by 300 miles (556 km) to bring operational areas into range. Further, the political problems

Originally laid down in June 1944, launched in February 1953, completed in 1959 as a fixed-wing carrier, Hermes *was converted to a commando carrier (1971–73) and to an anti-submarine warfare carrier in 1976. With the refit to enable her to operate the Sea Harrier 1980–81, she has spent more time in dockyard hands of one sort or another than at sea with the fleet.* Hermes *is seen here on a grey Atlantic day in the mid-1960s operating Sea Vixens of 890 Squadron* (Fleet Air Arm Museum).

Plymouth's Devonport dockyard shared with Portsmouth the role of carrier base-port and shown here in Devonport, at the time of the fateful Healey White Paper, are Eagle *and probably* Centaur *(right) with* Ark Royal *in drydock* (RN via Admiral Griffin).

associated with obtaining staging rights for military aircraft had been discounted. From the strategic point of view, however, the major disadvantage of the scheme was its extreme vulnerability to every conceivable type of attack.

The change in direction and colour of the Government in 1964 led to a field day for anti-service politicians and for the carrier knockers in the Navy and other services. The days of the British carrier as the world had come to know it were numbered. Despite well reasoned arguments put forward by such eminent figures as the First Sea Lord (1SL), Admiral Sir Caspar John, and the Fifth Sea Lord, Vice-Admiral Sir Frank Hopkins, from organisations like the Navy League and the Fleet Air Arm Officers Association, and from well-informed politicians in the Houses of Parliament, the CVA-01 programme was cancelled in the Defence White Paper of 1966. Caspar John, it should be remembered, was the first, and so far only 1SL from the Navy's aviation branch and, together with former observer and carrier captain, Frank Hopkins, he had worked hard to keep the project alive.

Here, then, was the third carrier crisis* within a 20-year period and for the first time in history, it seemed that the Government had acted against the better judgment of the Senior Service. The effect of the 1966 Defence White Paper on the Navy was staggering and the magnitude of the decision to scrap the carrier force was due mainly to feeling that there would be nothing else for 20 years that could do the job in hand better.

In fact, it meant that the entire structure of the Royal Navy, except for the submarine branch, would have to be re-planned and then re-built at an astronomical cost in time, manpower and money. The main architect of this devastating blow was Defence Minister, Denis Healey, but it was not only the Labour Party who thought the carrier was dead, for several Conservatives and many Liberals believed that Britain should withdraw from East of Suez and concentrate on facing the Soviet threat in Central Europe. It was not to be the

* The crises were (1) post-World War 2, (2) post-Korea and (3) 'Healey'.

Equipped with Gannet AEW3s, Scimitar F1s, Sea Vixen FAW1s and Whirlwind HAS7s,
Victorious *lies alongside the mole at Gibraltar, the usual first and last stop of deploying fixed-wing carriers.* Vic*'s life was sadly very short after she had been modernised, although if CVA-01 had been built she would have lasted until the latter's commissioning in about 1970* (RN via R.L. Ward).

axe straight away, in the way that the RAF's TSR2 and P1154 were dealt with, but a gradual, if firm, run down. First to go was *Victorious*, on the flimsiest of excuses leading from a minor fire in a mess water heater. *Hermes* was converted into a commando carrier while *Ark* went into long refit to bring her up to *Eagle*'s standard and to enable her to operate the Phantom, Buccaneer S2 and Sea King.

Before closing this sad chapter of British naval history is is worth remembering that *Eagle* and *Hermes* remained in their fixed-wing roles for a while to ensure that the withdrawal from East of Suez, especially Aden, went well. One can ponder the fact that even in peacetime such an operation needed carriers and yet Healey's White Paper maintained that carriers were no longer necessary in the modern war environment! The Secretary of State's decision finally was, in the words of a senior officer present throughout the crisis, a classic manifestation of the old American criticism, 'Don't confuse me with the facts—my mind is made up!'.

To quote from a letter to *Air Pictorial* by Rear Admiral A.S. Bolt in 1972, 'Why an aircraft carrier should be required to cover a withdrawal in peacetime but *not* a possible reinforcement of South-East Asia or Australia in *wartime* is difficult to understand'. Also that decision caused the resignations of the First Sea Lord (Admiral Sir David Luce, KCB, DSO, OBE) and of the Navy Minister (Christopher Mayhew). Later (1968) Rear Admiral John Adams, a former captain of *Albion* and serving as Assistant Chief of Naval Staff (Policy), joined the list. The effect was felt throughout the Navy, nowhere more directly than in the Staff Divisons of the Admiralty.

Chapter 18

Carrier aircraft swansong

The evolution of the fixed-wing carrier aircraft had been short in naval terms, yet in the end it had kept up with the land-based Services; in actual fact, the naval designs of the 1960s were adopted by the air forces on both sides of the Atlantic. At the time of the carrier crisis, the FAA was probably the best equipped 'air force' in the world.

In the late 1950s, the Blackburn Company had designed the world's first low level high speed strike aeroplane, then called the NA-39, now world famous as the Buccaneer. This was a very apt name for an aircraft designed to zoom in under an opposing force's radar and carry out a 'raid'. The Buccaneer S1 was a projected replacement for the Wyvern but the latter had left service four years before 801 Squadron was formed; this unit later went to *Ark* and *Victorious*, following the type's intensive trials at Lossiemouth with 700Z Squadron, commanded by Commander Alan Leahy. 801 was followed by 800 and 809—it was 800 which achieved fame during the *Beira Patrol* in the Mozambique

'All hot to trot', this Buccaneer S2 of 800 Squadron is seen aboard Eagle *during the spring of 1971. The plane guard Wessex helicopter in the background has just given the 'Bucc' a visual inspection before the latter is catapulted off the waist catapult. Note the jet's nose high attitude and the catapult gear. The apparatus behind the Buccaneer is the projector landing sight aid (RN).*

Channel. The S1 did have its limitations, especially in the weapons carrying role and only 40 were built.

The S1 'Bucc' had a major drawback in respect of its full war-load and hot, still days in the tropics. Because of carrier catapult limitations, the way had to be found of utilising the aircraft to its full potential. The RN considered the problem and resolved to establish a tanker flight using redundant Scimitar airframes. The flight went aboard *Eagle* as 800B Flight, part of 800 (Buccaneer) Squadron. The Scimitar simply topped up a Buccaneer strike in mid-air before it went off to its target; equally in the event of a recovery mishap, suitably equipped aircraft could be kept aloft by the Scimitars with extra fuel, thus easing the situation when flying was taking place, without a diversion airfield ashore.

The Mark 2 Buccaneer was able to carry twice the offensive load from the deck of a carrier, as well as having more thrust and better fuel consumption from the Spey engines which replaced the Gyron Junior turbojets of the S1. In all 84 Buccaneer S2s were produced for the Royal Navy, equipping four operational squadrons—800, 801, 803 and 809, and flying from *Ark, Eagle, Hermes* and *Victorious.* Again 801 was the first unit to fly this latest model of the 'Bucc', an aircraft which filled the carrier role exactly.

The *Torrey Canyon* episode off the Cornish coast, allowed 800 Squadron to use live bombs on something more worthwhile than the practice ranges. This Squadron remained afloat in *Eagle* until that ship's retirement in 1972, leaving ony 809 to soldier on until 1978 when *Ark* was paid off. The Buccaneer's service life in operational squadrons was 16 years (1962-78)—somewhat of a record, especially when one considers that the RAF still use them! 'Spiv' Leahy sums up the Buccaneer very simply as being 'a tremendous step forward in naval aircraft design'.

The up-dated Sea Vixen FAW2 was popular with everyone except the observers who had to sit down in a 'coal hole' compartment next to the off-centred pilot's cockpit. This Sea Vixen FAW2 from 892 Squadron is being flown by Hermes' *Commander (Air), 'Paddy' McKeown, and is seen here overshooting the carrier along the axis of the angled deck. An easy recognition feature of the Mark 2 Vixen is the extended wing top fuel tank* (HMS Hermes).

In the mid-1960s, the Buccaneer's hangar mate aboard the fixed-wing carrier force was the de Havilland/Hawker Siddeley Sea Vixen FAW2. The initial model of the Vixen had been well established in service, when the admiralty decided to increase the fuel storage and equip the aircraft for the new Red Top anti-aircraft missile. It took two years to obtain the necessary production aircraft, at first new airframes and later using FAW1s. The Vixen's ability to fight and strike both night and day made the carrier force more versatile than ever before. In December 1964, 899 went aboard *Eagle*; the squadrons so equipped were: 890—1967-70; 892—1966-70; 893—1965-70; and 899—1963-72. Besides *Torrey Canyon, Aden* and the *Beira Patrol*, the Vixen will be remembered as the last fighter to serve aboard *Eagle*; in fact, the last British-built fixed-wing fighter aboard a conventional carrier.

The third fixed-wing type in the 1960s and 1970s was the Westland/Fairey Gannet AEW3—quite literally a radar station in the sky. The airframe had been extensively re-designed from the ASW version, and had a prominent radar dome. Deck landing trials were carried out aboard *Centaur* and *Victorious*, whilst the sole operational unit, 849 Squadron, was formed in January 1960. 849C Flight was the first to go to sea, embarking in *Hermes*, herself not long out of the builder's hands.

The squadron was divided into flights in the same way as it had been with the earlier Skyraider and although not necessarily permanently embarked in a particular carrier, four flights were initially created. The following listing shows though that some ships had only one flight ever embarked: *Ark Royal*—B and C; *Centaur*—B; *Eagle*—D; *Hermes*—A, B and C; and *Victorious*—A and B.

Again figuring in the *Beira Patrol*, the Gannet continued to prove its worth until 849 Squadron was finally disbanded in 1978, after 849B had been the sole surviving flight from 1972, when 849D was disbanded. So the airborne early warning expertise of 25 years of operational use passed from the RN. The radar

Ugly, yet beautiful at the same time, the Fairey Gannet AEW3 equipped only one squadron, like its predecessor the Skyraider. 849 Squadron's B Flight served aboard Hermes, Victorious *(above right) and later for nearly nine years aboard* Ark Royal *(below). The prominent radar radome below the fuselage shows up dramatically as 044 prepares to take the wire aboard* Ark *(Fleet Air Arm Museum & RN/Lieutenant Safe).*

domes were not sent to the scrap heap, however, as the RAF put them underneath Shackletons, but gone was the bubbling drone of the Gannet—the first fixed-wing aircraft to be launched and usually the last to be recovered during normal flying operations. In October 1968, when 892 (Sea Vixen) Squadron disbanded, the efforts of DNAW some years before were about to bear fruit. In July 1964 the Admiralty arranged for an order of 140 McDonnell Douglas Phantom fighters and, although the order was eventually reduced to 28, the RN at last had a truly supersonic bird—unfortunately fate and the Labour Party decreed that it was to be the last fixed-wing conventional fighter in the RN.

On March 31 1969, 892 Squadron recommissioned at Yeovilton with 'omega' marked Phantoms—the Greek letter signifying the end of the Naval carrier fighter which had begun with the Nieuport Nightjar and Parnall Panther 50 years before. The Phantom in British service was somewhat superior to those delivered elsewhere in the world, including American carriers, and much of this was due to the fitting of Rolls Royce Spey turbofans and British avionics. Certain other refinements had to be made, including a folding radome to allow the aircraft to use the relatively small flight deck lifts aboard *Ark* and *Eagle*. It was aboard the latter that the Phantom carried out early trials, but *Eagle* was unable to operate the aircraft without modifications to her catapult gear and flight deck jet blast deflector cooling gear. In the event, only *Ark* received a 'Phantomisation'.

Somewhere off the southern coast of France on November 27 1978, Flight Lieutenant Murdo MacLeod, an RAF exchange pilot with 892 Squadron, lit the afterburners on 012's Speys and the Phantom thundered down the long waist catapult, out over the Van Galm bridle catcher, off the forward end of the angled deck and home to Leuchars in Scotland. The last fixed-wing fighter had been launched from a British fixed-wing carrier.

In the space of 60 years, the art and science of flying aircraft from flat topped warships had improved to a state where it was almost accident free. Gone were the days of the Fairey Flycatchers roaring the hearts from their Jaguar engines in *Glorious'* hangar before leaping into the air from the lower flying-off deck.

During non-flying periods, routine maintenance could be carried out aboard carriers on the flight deck where the aircraft were always chained and lashed when not in use. Here 892 Squadron Phantoms are prepared for Ark's last 'Families Day'.

Gone too was the beautiful sound of the Merlin-engined Supermarine Seafire as it made a free take-off from an escort carrier. It was the tune of the jets which really set the fixed-wing carrier apart. The massed cartridge start of Sea Hawks and Sea Venoms in *Albion*—'enough smoke and flame to show even a half-blind enemy where the carrier was'—was the heralding of a day's flying. The ship would have already come to flying stations, and, as the pilots checked their aircraft, the plane guard helicopter would have been launched. In later-days, the smoke was gone, replaced instead by a roar and the familiar whirring sound of the helicopter that all took for granted.

Before closing this, the last chapter of fixed-wing carrier aviation, we must look at one of the finest rotary-wing aircraft ever developed—the Sea King anti-submarine helicopter. The need to have a long endurance helicopter to match the prowess of the *Bucc* and *Fox 4*, led to the procurement of the American-designed, but British-built, Sea King HAS1 (later also the HAS2 was in service with 824 Squadron). Two squadrons were formed in 1970 to fly this large hunter-killer from fixed-wing carriers—824 (*Ark Royal*) and 826 (*Eagle*). Many new refinements, as yet unseen by carrier goofers, included retractable undercarriage, a boat hull and power folding main rotors for easy handling on the flight deck. The Sea King was normally equipped with four externally mounted depth charges, but it could carry nuclear depth bombs. For search and rescue, the helicopter also carries a winch and many times during the course of the careers of both carriers, the Sea King units saved lives which would otherwise have been in deadly peril. Just another positive attribute to maritime affairs by the fixed-wing carrier.

Chapter 19

Halcyon days

In 1964 *Eagle* left Devonport—known to all and sundry as 'Guz'—following a five-year refit which provided the fleet with one of the most up-to-date weapons systems in the world, but at a cost of £30 million. The most important new features were the fully angled deck of 8½ degrees and two new steam catapults. Visually, the ship had changed considerably as well, due to the Type 984 radar 'dustbin', à la *Hermes*, on the island and the 'Alaska Highway' to starboard of the superstructure. The gun armament was almost totally removed and replaced by Seacat surface-to-air missiles (SAMs) and *Eagle* could now carry 35 fixed-wing naval aircraft plus ten helicopters.

Ark Royal, having just returned from the Far East, was put into refit at Plymouth on January 4 1964 and she stayed at 'Guz' until November. *Ark*, as well as having her major propulsion problems rectified, also lost much of her gun armament at this time, yet she was only fitted for, but never with, air defence missiles.

Victorious was duty carrier east of Suez in 1964, maintaining a presence in aid of the fledgling federation of Malaysia, then under threat from left-wing dominated Indonesia. The 'confrontation' as it was called lasted from 1962 until victory to the Allies in 1966. During this time, carrier aircraft, both fixed-wing strike and rotary-wing troop transports, provided logistical and tactical support to the combined forces of Australia, Britain and New Zealand who were engaged in a counter-insurgency operation. Despite the disparity between Indonesia and the Allies on paper, the threat of missile-armed patrol boats and air attack was taken very seriously.

Admiral Sir Derek Empson recalls that, as a carrier captain during this time, he had a couple of periods of great anxiety when electrical faults in *Eagle*'s power supply caused the ship to go 'blind' down the Malacca Straits. Bad enough for navigation even without the risk of missile attack! In the end, Britain's unsung victory was achieved by her superior resources on land, sea and in the air, aided considerably by her Allies; the much vaunted missile boat attacks never materialised.

At home, *Hermes* carried out a series of customary exercises, followed by trials with the Sea Vixen FAW2 fighter, before starting a £10 million refit at Devonport. The only remaining fixed-wing carrier was *Centaur* and she too, was east of Suez. Her days were numbered, however, and by 1966 she had reverted to being an accommodation ship at Devonport and later Portsmouth where she was used as billets for the ship's companies of carriers under refit.

Left *The fully modernised* Eagle *steams at full speed as a Buccaneer S2 of 800 Squadron makes a high pass over the carrier.* Eagle's *final air group consisted of Buccaneers (800 Squadron), Sea Vixens (899 Squadron), Gannets (849 Squadron D Flight) and Sea Kings (826 Squadron)* (Fleet Air Arm Museum).

Below *With the Sea Kings of 814 Squadron ranged on her flight deck, the anti-submarine carrier,* Hermes, *leaves Portsmouth Harbour for a training cruise to the Mediterranean with Dartmouth Cadets aboard. Note the retained deck-edge lift vertically below the funnel and pennant number R12.*

This then was the position of the Royal Navy's carrier force when the Labour Government regained office in 1964. Two years later, following that infamous White Paper, the position was to be quite different. By 1967 *Victorious* had paid off into refit but she was destined not to re-commission at Portsmouth in 1970 as originally intended; the excuse being a small fire which had broken out during the refit. As recorded above, *Centaur* was also paid off during this time.

Hermes, the newest carrier in the Navy, was still operational, but to a certain extent she was out of her depth when operating the heavier and larger jets except, perhaps in near perfect conditions, with good WOD. The problems arose from short catapults and comparatively slow operating speeds. For

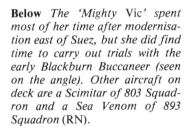

example, *Victorious* was far better equipped to operate the Scimitar and Sea Vixen than *Hermes*. One of the latter's Commanders (Air) remarked to the author that the operating 'window' in which landings could be safely accomplished was very small. Captain (then Commander) Alan Leahy remembers that he experienced several sleepless nights during calm periods, especially east of Suez. Again one has cause to lament the loss of *Victorious* before the end of her useful life. One should remember when considering the carrier scene at this time that of the four larger carriers, only *Ark* was not equipped with complex, highly advanced and comprehensive Type 984 radar and its associated display system. Meanwhile *Hermes* was still active in the

Mediterranean area and later, in 1967, in the Far East again. She spent the next 24 months operating in Home and Far Eastern waters. In July 1970, *Hermes* ended her fine career of ten years as a fixed-wing carrier at Portsmouth. Between March 1 1971 and August 17 1973 she was put into dockyard hands at Devonport and completely stripped of all her fixed-wing aircraft equipment—steam catapults, projector sight and arrester gear. For a refit costing £25 million, the RN now had a 'new' commando carrier*.

From 1960 and her emergence in the new role during 1974, *Hermes* had added 1,900 tons (1,931 tonnes) to her standard displacement but lost 210 ship's complement. Most interesting of all, however, are the data on draught:

	1960	**1974**
Draught forward	27 feet 10 inches (8.48 m)	27 feet 8½ inches (8.46 m)
Draught aft	27 feet 10 inches (8.48 m)	29 feet 6 inches (9.02 m)

Perhaps the gallant lady didn't like losing her 'cats' and felt down at heel?

In September 1967 *Eagle* completed her refit and embarked the new Buccaneer S2 naval strike aircraft of 800 Squadron, together with Sea Vixens (899) and Wessex HAS3 (826) helicopters, making her one of the most powerful ships in the Far East. Yet the writing was on the wall for all carriers and a British presence east of Suez especially. Still in accordance with tradition, both ship and air group operated at maximum efficiency until the end. *Eagle*'s last deployment to the Far East represented an equally final phase in British maritime history. On the very day *Eagle* left Singapore—October 31 1971—the British naval presence there also ceased. 'It was a magnificent sight as *Eagle*, wearing her paying-off pennant, steamed out of Singapore. The dockyard had done a marvellous job and she was beautifully painted up; it really evoked some memories for the carrier people standing by and watching history in the making', is how Keith Leppard, whose appointment as Chief Staff Officer (Operations and Training) to Commander, Far East Fleet, recalled the event as *Eagle* cleared the breakwater.

For some seemingly unaccountable reason, *Eagle* never really made the public eye in the same way as her half-sister, *Ark*; the latter 'having the advantage of a famous name, whereas nobody had heard of the previous *Eagle* until she was sunk', says Admiral Sir Derek Empson. He was speaking from some experience, having served as a young RNVR pilot in *Eagle* in the Mediterranean Theatre during World War 2, commanding the last *Eagle* (1963-65) and flying his flag as FOAC in the same carrier (1967-68).

Eagle was undoubtedly much better equipped mechanically than *Ark*, but when the time came for a carrier to be Phantomised, it was the latter which the Government chose. This decision has puzzled observers of the naval scene, because *Eagle* had already had a Phantom-capable waist catapult and was already part way to being able to use the aircraft operationally. Further, *Ark*'s hull was in a poorer shape and, had the CVA-01 programme gone ahead, *Ark* would have been replaced before *Eagle*. Some have said that *Ark*'s refit, being longer and therefore able to keep more people at the dockyard and manufacturers in employment, was politically motivated. Devonport was, and still is for that matter, a marginal seat at Parliamentary Elections. Others have found the decision stranger still considering the 'Park Royal' reputation of *Ark* with the much publicised breakdowns and malfunctions. The choice for a single

---

* This had a limited ASW capability, later enlarged in the mid-1970s.

fixed-wing carrier could only rest between *Eagle* and *Ark* because, firstly, the CVA-01 project had been cut and secondly, because *Hermes* was already finding Scimitar/Vixen operations a trial and the Phantom would have made safe and efficient flying nigh impossible. Still, in 1969, *Eagle* was the venue for a series of Phantom deck landing and handling trials because *Ark* had not come out of dockyard hands.

Taking the whole sequence of events in perspective, it is easy to jump to the conclusion that the whole episode was politically stage-managed. One has to remember that though *Eagle* did lack the flight deck alterations which would enable prolonged Phantom operations and that by the time the trials had been completed, *Ark* was ready for sea; there was only enough money in the kitty for one fixed-wing carrier to operate Phantoms. It is strange and somewhat ironic to consider that *Eagle* possessed the 984 radar which was a superior fit to *Ark*'s 965 with which the latter ended her days! Perhaps the last word on the subject should be left to one of a group of officers in the Wardroom at Yeovilton, home of the Fleet Air Arm: 'What you have to remember is that *Eagle* was a fighting ship, not like *Ark*: she was a gin palace!'.

The need to 'angle' totally *Ark*'s deck and to refit extensively the complex sensor equipment, contributed heavily to the £32 million bill presented to the Exchequer at the end of 1969. For that money, the British public then had the most powerful and flexible warship ever to serve in the Royal Navy with the world's best mini-airforce. The air group for the Sixth Commission and for the rest of the ship's career was a balanced combination of Phantom FG1s (892 Squadron), Buccaneer S2s (809), Gannet AEW3s (849's B Flight) and the Sea King helicopters of 824 Squadron. With the RN's fixed-wing aircrew training programme running down, the jet units had more than their fair share of light blue (RAF) uniforms. In real terms, of course, the first two decades of carrier aviation had seen the same phenomenon so there was no real effect on operational efficiency, perhaps just a small sag in morale?

One of the advantages of the Phantomisation aboard Ark *was the installation of the bridle-catching snoop which saved the tax-payer several hundreds of pounds per launch. This Phantom's bridle has just parted company with the aircraft and will continue to travel down the snoop to be recovered later for re-use* (RN/CPO Gilbert).

On exercise in the Atlantic as part of the NATO naval forces, Ark Royal *carries out a replenishment at sea with the oiler* Tidesurge *and, nearest the camera, the stores support ship* Lyness; *providing a very close escort is the Tribal Class frigate* Eskimo. *The problems associated with flying and loading stores can be seen from the gaping hole left by the forward lift whilst stores are transferred below* (RN).

When Captain Ray Lygo took *Ark* to sea for her first deployment after Phantomisation, it was to a very reduced operational area to that in which fixed-wing carriers had been used to venturing. Gone were the runs ashore at Singapore or 'Christmas shopping' at 'Honkers'*, for now the two remaining carriers were, following the imminent withdrawal from east of Suez, limited to the NATO arena—from the West Indies to the Eastern Mediterranean, from the north of Norway to the Tropic of Cancer. Later, with only one carrier available, it was inevitable that an even closer working relationship to the US Navy's Atlantic and Sixth Fleets would be evolved to ensure that the *Ark* was used to her maximum potential.

During the long round of exercises, operational training and flag-showing visits between 1972-78, the *Ark* was kept in full fighting trim†. To do this it was necessary to have two replenishment ships in close attendance, one to refuel the carrier, the other to act as a mobile store house. So it was that another close working relationship was built up, this time between *Ark* and the Royal Fleet Auxiliary (who man the replenishment vessels). A full-scale RAS (replenishment at sea) did mean, however, that *Ark* was unable to operate her fixed-wing aircraft, because the two large mid-flight deck aircraft lifts were used to move stores from the deck to the compartments below decks where they were kept. Ironically, the abandoned CVA-01 design had eliminated the need to use

* 'Honkers', probably an Australian term, is now a well-known colloquialism for Hong Kong.
† The full story of *Ark*'s career, in words and pictures, is recounted in *Ark Royal—A pictorial history of the Royal Navy's last conventional aircraft carrier* by Paul Beaver (Patrick Stephens) 1979.

aircraft lifts as supply routes into the bowels of the carrier, therefore ensuring that the task group could launch a strike and defend itself even during the RAS, one of the most difficult of nautical manoeuvres.

Another most difficult manoeuvre was the docking of a fully laden carrier in harbours better suited to the wooden walls of England. The last sea-going Captain of *Ark*—now Rear Admiral Edward Anson, CB—recalls a rather special docking in March 1978, after *Ark*'s last tour of the British coastline. *Ark* was preparing for her last deployment (the last deployment of any British fixed-wing carrier), after having been flagship at the Queen's Silver Jubilee Review at Spithead and following the traditional autumn exercise season. Admiral Anson takes up the story: 'After Christmas leave, a Dockyard Assisted Maintenance Period [AMP] and a Harbour Administration Inspection, *Ark Royal* sailed on February 21 [1978] for her Sea Inspection. This took place off the east corner of Scotland. A Sea Inspection differs from an Operational Readiness Inspection in that it embraces all aspects of the ship other than pure flying and includes such exercises as towing other ships. In the event, *Ark Royal* towed *Olmeda* (a RFA tanker) which represented a disabled tanker. Obviously, the opportunity was taken to fly during this period but the emphasis was on all those other aspects that any ship might be called upon to perform during a deployment.

'Families Day on March 9 was rather special as it was the last one. Accordingly arrangements were made to retain the aircraft on board so that the families could witness the launching and recovery of aircraft. There had been Families Days in the past, but very few when aircraft had been operated specially for the families—so this one was special. Unfortunately the weather was not good, but nevertheless all of the 1,500 families that came were able to witness one launch and one recovery of the aircraft—so at least they could see what the ship actually did despite the bad weather.

'As the flying display finished in the afternoon all aircraft were launched for their shore bases and the ship headed for the breakwater for subsequent passage up the Hamoaze to Devonport. As the ship passed the breakwater the visibility

Ark, truly in the public eye after the Sailor *series on BBC tv, was the star of the Silver Jubilee Review at Spithead in June 1977. As the Royal Yacht* Britannia *passed the flagship the sailors lining the sides gave three cheers for Her Majesty.*

had dropped to 1.5 miles (2.8 km) and a decision had to be made whether to continue up harbour or to secure to Charlie Buoy. Permission was granted for - *Ark* to enter harbour, so passage was continued past Charlie Buoy on to the transit for the Smeaton Pass. *Ark* was then committed to enter. She passed along the front of the Hoe, past Millbay docks, and shaped up for the long starboard turn around the Vanguard (by Drake's Island) when the visibility suddenly dropped to 260 ft (80 m)! Several people in key positions were a lot older, a lot wiser and very grateful by the time *Ark Royal* finally arrived safely alongside in her usual slot in Devonport dockyard! I mention this particular detail about the fog', the Admiral continues, 'because I later received a letter from the mother of a Royal Marine who said that she had enjoyed her day at sea but, "the highlight for her had been to see the tug take complete charge in the fog and tow the ship into harbour"! My ulcers had a different tale to tell!'.

The 'key positions' mentioned in Rear Admiral Anson's account were the same as any warship for actual ship handling, if only a little more 'key' because *Ark* was the largest warship in the Royal Navy. However, being an aircraft carrier, the ship could really be divided into two parts—the aviation side under the direction of Commander (Air) or 'Wings', a reminder of the days when carriers had 'Wing Commanders', and a seamanship side under the Commander. Both sides were again sub-divided into various departments so that the running of each component in the ship's daily routine could be achieved smoothly.

The large carriers like *Ark* and *Eagle* were floating homes for more than 2,700 men who, over a period of 60 years, had gained and inherited a vast storehouse of knowledge and experience, which enabled 'the slick performance' on the flight deck and the 'smooth operation' of the ship herself. The one aim for this

Two of the most important men aboard a carrier are 'Little F', the Lieutenant Commander (Flying) and 'Wings', the Commander (Air). During Ark*'s last years, the posts were held by Korean-veteran Pete Sheppard and by Tony Layard, respectively (FPU).*

community—so often rightly called a small town—was to provide an efficient fighting ship, nothing more, nothing less. The *raison d'être* of a carrier was its aircraft and it was the Air Department who provided this service. In many ways it was similar to that service provided at naval air stations but, instead of having many hundreds of acres of ground to play with, a modern fixed-wing carrier had only 'three acres' and somewhat less in the light fleets like *Centaur*.*

Manoeuvring the aircraft for launch and after recovery was the responsibility of the aircraft handling team of surcoated ratings under the Captain of the Flight Deck who reported to the 'Fido' or Flight Deck Officer. Whilst any aircraft were in the launch, recovery or circuiting modes, they were the responsibility of Lieutenant Commander (Flying)—Little 'F'—who reported directly to Commander (Air). Both these officers, who would have been former naval aviators themselves, either pilots and/or observers, occupied the Flying Control Position (known as Flyco) adjacent to the bridge but jutting out over the flight deck. Another team under the Hangar Control Officer would manage the parked aircraft on deck or in the hangars below, and this was another slick operation, almost an artform, because the right aircraft had to be positioned at the right place at the right lift at the right time for a sortie without interfering with other operations on the flight deck. It is worth noting here the sterling work provided by the Carrier Controlled Approach Room (see Chapter 11) and the Meteorologists, from their little office under the bridge.

To keep a complex piece of hardware like a Sea Vixen or a Phantom airworthy required detailed knowledge and considerable resources. The individual air squadrons, through their own air engineering officers (AEOs), could undertake a certain amount of maintenance, but all large scale work was carried out by the ship's AEO and his team. The AEOs had a convoluted reporting procedure to the Captain, either via the Squadron CO through Commander (Air), or directly via the Commander (AEO). The above departments were unique to aircraft carriers of whatever size. Even the smallest merchant and escort carriers had some semblance of the system, albeit with one officer or even a senior rating holding down several jobs. For example, Vice Admiral Gibson, when CO of 802 Squadron with the rank of Lieutenant in *Audacity*, did several air-orientated jobs, as well as commanding his squadron of five Martlets. Often during the carrier story, the individual job titles and responsibilities changed with circumstances and experience gained, but the expertise was always there.

The other departments normally found aboard HM warships—marine engineering, weapons electrical, communications, operations and supply—were just as much part of the carrier scene as that of any destroyer or frigate. What did differ was the scale of the responsibility and of the task involved. Imagine having a fault in the refrigeration plant with 10,000 lb (4,536 kg) of meat in store and being 2,000 miles (3,700 km) from the nearest supermarket with 2,700 hungry mouths to feed!

The marine engineers in a carrier, besides keeping the propulsion system operating at its optimum, a task quite special to carriers where the ship's speed through the water was used to provide wind over the deck, were responsible for the flight deck equipment. The Marine Engineering Officer (MEO), usually a

---

* This account has been written in the past tense for obvious reasons, but much of the information is equally applicable today to the *Invincible* Class.

senior Commander in large carriers, would have the care of the steam catapults and arrester gear within his department. In the last ten years of fixed-wing carrier aviation, a 25 ton (25.4 tonnes) aircraft arrived on the deck at 150 mph (241 kph) and needed to be stopped in 200 ft (61 m) by a steel cable stretched across the deck. To make sure that this and every other system functioned correctly the marine engineers worked around the clock.

In the weapons electrical (WE) department, a carrier carried air electrical engineers. In the early days, aircraft and radar maintenance was simple, because there was very little complex gear fitted to aircraft. One must bear in mind that ASV (anti-surface vessels) radar only came into being in the early part of World War 2. Following that conflict, however, a mass of electrical and electronic gear started to appear in aircraft and in carriers, part of a general technological revolution.

As the use of aircraft at sea developed it became increasingly important for command to be able to direct aircraft from the carrier to carry out the appointed task or to carry out some task other than that originally briefed. In the early days, even the first few campaigns of the war, it was not possible to give the aircrew a great deal of after-launch assistance. Early naval aviators nearly all required an observer or TAG to operate a morse-type radio and it was not until after several tragic losses that carrier-to-aircraft voice radio began to be an equal partner in carrier life. We have seen how fighter direction 'took off' during World War 2, especially in the vast tracts of ocean where the BPF operated. In later years, electronic counter measures and radar surveillance all played their part in making the Communications Department, the nerve centre of the ship, and consequently of the fleet.

To keep the whole system of carrier, aircraft and men functioning required stores and spares. Without food and pay, the men could not function in a peacetime Navy and the ship just would not have gone anywhere. One evening aboard *Ark*, the author encountered a choice of 18 main dishes in the galley—for if an Army is said to march on its stomach, then a Navy certainly swims on one! Due regard must be paid to the Seaman Department who made the carrier 'an efficient base for the aircraft' in the words of an MOD (N) release. The Medical and Dental Departments, whose services were happily needed less and less as flight safety improved, were still in evidence. Many old and bold (or just plain old) aviators can thank the rapid attention of the flight deck doctor for their still being alive to tell the tale.

The men's education was also provided for and several ships had, in later years especially, their own TV station giving the messdecks (crowded as they were) a feeling of being more like home. In action, instructor officers were available to carry out functions both on the flight deck and in the operations room.

So when the final demise came to fixed-wing carriers, one chilly December morning in 1978, the Royal Navy said goodbye to a remarkable weapons system, a way of life which had been born a cinderella to become in its maturity the core of the ocean-going fleet. Carrier aviation is and was an institution, a matter of teamwork. Now the large warship has all but disappeared from the Royal Navy, its passing is felt with regret by many, both civilian and service man alike.

Chapter 20

A new dawn

As many a tear was being shed for the demise of *Ark Royal (IV)*, the last of her kind, a new dawn was breaking for the Fleet Air Arm of the Royal Navy. Despite the loss of conventional fixed-wing aviation, the fleet was to operate jets again, albeit in a small, far from conventional, way. When the Hawker P1127 leapt into the air from its Surrey home in November 1960, Britain led the world in the development of vertical take-off and landing (VTOL) jet aircraft. By 1963, trials had been carried out aboard *Ark Royal* and, in 1964, an improved version, the Hawker Siddeley Kestrel, had been developed from which sprung the BAe Harrier ground attack fighter for the RAF. In the meantime, the RN was considering the introduction of the Hawker P1154 as a supersonic VTOL fighter for fleet defence, but as has been mentioned previously in this book, it turned out to be anything but the right tool for that job.

Then, in 1966, there came that so-called 'misguided political axe', when the Government of the day published its White Paper on Defence, hacking the Navy's morale with more effect than the sinking of the *Hood* two decades

The forerunner of the Sea Harrier FRS1 (now in service aboard Hermes *and* Invincible*) was the Hawker P1127, which carried out trials aboard* Ark Royal *in Lyme Bay during February 1963. Today vertical take-off flying is quite commonplace, but then, judging by the 'goofers', it was a very special occasion indeed!* (RN courtesy of Vice Admiral Gibson).

The majority of carrier flying in the late 1970s and early 1980s was taken on by the various Sea King squadrons. This crowded hangar scene was taken aboard Bulwark *(then converted for anti-submarine and commando duties) some months before her demise in March 1981.*

before. The development of land-based VTOL aircraft did continue though in the shape of the Harrier. For many years observers wondered when or if a navalised version would be made available for service on the proposed 'through-deck' cruiser design which had become fashionable as the Navy's capital surface ship replacement for fixed-wing carriers.

The need for air defence at sea is today more vitally necessary than it was 20 years ago, because the last two decades have seen the propagation of the Soviet maritime presence world-wide, but especially in the North Atlantic, NATO's own back door. The 'pond', as it is often called, represents the major supply line to Europe in the event of war with the 'East' and the current and projected Soviet maritime aircraft available could, it is conceived, saturate any ship-borne defence in mid-Atlantic and any RAF/NATO land-based air defence within the Continental Shelf area. The main role of a fighter at sea then would be to destroy snooping intelligence gatherers, missile guidance aircraft and conventional maritime strike bombers. Where does one base such a defence aircraft? On carriers was the obvious answer, but did the USN (the only NATO partner with fixed-wing aviation at sea) have enough to go round? No, came back the answer again. So what was to be done?

Between 1969 and 1976, successful trials were carried out aboard several carriers to prove that standard land-based VTOL aircraft were capable of limited operations from a deck at sea. Carriers in which these demonstrations were carried out included the former British light fleet *25 de Mayo (Venerable), Vikrant (Hercules)* and *Melbourne (Majestic)*, plus RN warships such as *Eagle* and *Bulwark*, the latter having been converted to the role of commando carrier by this time.

Both the Spanish and US Navies had an export version of the Harrier design, known as the AV-8A Matador, afloat by the time that the RN was in a position to order the British Aerospace (BAe) Sea Harrier FRS1 for service aboard the

20,000 tons (20,320 tonnes) through-deck cruisers of the *Invincible* Class, now known as light anti-submarine aircraft carriers. Although the staff requirement appears to have been written in 1969, it was not until May 1975 that an order for 34 single-seat and two twin-seat Sea Harriers was forthcoming. Later, in June 1978, a further ten were ordered but the first operational squadron was not formed until April 1980 (800 Squadron), followed by 801 Squadron in February 1981. These two units were dedicated to *Invincible, Illustrious* and *Hermes* (assuming that one is always in refit); the envisaged third squadron will not now be formed for service in the third *Invincible* Class carrier. These warships, although operating jets and helicopters, cannot be called conventional fixed-wing carriers, no matter how hard one stretches one's imagination.

In terms of flight deck space, a VTOL aircraft is more efficient but when fully loaded, the Sea Harrier would need catapult assistance to get off the deck. Without the provision of a costly, and for that matter, top-weight heavy, catapult system, the operational effectiveness of any contemporary VTOL fighter/strike aircraft is reduced both in terms of payload and endurance, the latter due to the reduced fuel load.

Fortunately for the new generation of Sea Harrier pilots flying from *Invincible* and the refitted *Hermes*, a serious incident occurred on the fleet carrier *Victorious* during the so-called Indonesian confrontation in the Far East. It was September 1964, when there was still concern about Indonesian fast patrol boats with missile armament, plus Russian-built bombers of the Indonesian Air Force being a threat to British and Commonwealth warships in the area. On the Type 984 radar plot there appeared a 'bogey' which brought the ship rapidly to action ships. As usual there were two Sea Vixens (890 Squadron) at readiness and these were immediately brought up to the steam catapults for launch. The day was hot with little wind, typical in fact for that part of the world, and the heat had caused the metal of the deck to expand, thus closing the narrow

One of 801 Squadron's Sea Harrier FRS1 V/STOL fighters lines up on Invincible's *flight deck before a normal ski-jump launch. The ship carried out the first of the class trials in November 1980 and embarked 801 Squadron soon after, the latter re-commissioned in February 1981. By 1983,* Invincible *will be joined by her sister-ship,* Illustrious, *to whom the retiring* Hermes *will transfer 800 Squadron (Stephen Wolf).*

The bridge of a modern carrier is well laid out and air-conditioned. On a typical day during the 'Orient Express' deployment, Invincible's *bridge party include a lookout (left), the rating officer-of-the-watch, the helmsman, the communications (tactical) rating and the second OOW at the binnacle* (HMS *Invincible*).

catapult tracks. For all intents and purposes *Victorious* was now defenceless—the weak point of this highly efficient weapon was a small area of steel. The 'blip' on the air defence plot, had it been found hostile, would have found a large and vulnerable target.

Needless to say, the Flight Deck Engineering Officer promptly took the initiative and ordered large quantities of sea water to be pumped over the deck, thus returning the shape of the catapult tracks to their normal dimensions. Eight years later, this same officer, Lieutenant Commander Doug Taylor, began a research fellowship at Southampton University which led to what has been called the most revolutionary carrier development since the angled deck, over 30 years before. The development was the 'ski jump' or ramp now built into the four remaining carriers—*Hermes, Invincible, Illustrious* and *Ark Royal* which is being built.*

The ski jump prototype ramp was completed on land at the Royal Aircraft Establishment at Bedford in June 1977 and by 1980 trials with gradients of 6 degrees to 17.5 degrees had been carried out. So successful were these tests that completion of *Invincible* had to be further delayed so that a 7 degree ramp could

---

*The 1981 Defence Review indicated that only two *Invincibles* would be retained with the third, later identified as *Invincible* herself, being sold; this was not to be (see page 229).

Watchkeeping for the engineering department of a modern aircraft carrier no longer means a noisy engine room, but the ship's control centre (SCC) instead. The panel to the right is used to control the four Rolls Royce Olympus engines which power Invincible *(*HMS Invincible*).*

be installed by British Shipbuilders. *Hermes*, then in long refit was also taken in hand for a 12½ degree ramp, with which *Ark Royal* was built; *Illustrious*, however, retains the 7 degree ramp at present.

A remarkably simple piece of engineering, the ski jump makes it possible for aircraft to be launched in any wind and during any point in the ship's pitch cycle. A launch is now that much safer and easier. The idea is not completely new as three* of the pre-war conventional carriers were equipped at various times with a ramp to assist the launching of their respective aircraft. The new ramps, unlike the wooden ramps fitted in *Furious* do not actually extend the length of the flight deck. Commander Taylor originally envisaged calling his invention a 'runway in the sky' and thought of using a system of elevated catapults rather than an extension of the runway-like flight deck which today allows for free take-offs.

It is interesting to note that during the attack on *Tirpitz* in 1944, Barracudas embarked in *Furious* were able to take off with a full fuel load and 1,600 lb (726 kg) of ordnance, by virtue of the wooden ramp. This is in stark contrast to the 4,500 lb (2,041 kg) of ordnance carried aloft by the Sea Harrier in *Invincible* and her sister-ships. A further extension of the ski jump principle could well be

*Courageous, Furious and Glorious

When Invincible *arrived at Portsmouth in March 1980, a 'New Dawn' was heralded throughout the Navy following the darkness after* Ark's *decommissioning in December 1978. The new concept of operating V/STOL aircraft in a maritime environment was to be the spearhead of the Fleet Air Arm in the 1980s and 1990s.*

the use of container vessels on the so-called 'Arapaho' scheme at present being studied on both sides of the Atlantic. The scheme, somewhat reminiscent of World War 2 MAC-ships, calls for the deployment of a Sea Harrier and its associated gear using a portable ski jump to launch and a small landing pad for recovery on the deck of the merchant ship.

Without doubt, whatever happens in the field of ship design or operation technique, the overriding need for naval aviation, especially in NATO, is for a supersonic VTOL aircraft, carried in suitable numbers in modern warships. The new *Invincible* Class of carrier has a design complement of five Sea Harriers together with nine Sea King HAS5 or EH-101 helicopters. Critics of the concept have said that *Invincible* is little better off for air defence than *Audacity* was in 1941. The disbandment of 849 Squadron and the phasing out of the airborne early-warning (AEW) Gannet in 1978 left a major gap in the Royal Navy's umbrella which just could not be filled by land-based maritime or AEW aircraft, especially the very limited numbers available in time of war. That gap was readily confirmed in May 1982 with the sinking of the guided missile destroyer *Sheffield* and the introduction a few weeks later of the airborne-early warning version of the Sea King helicopter, giving yet another element to the versatility of the helicopter at sea.

By late 1985, the *Invincible* Class aircraft carriers were able to field an improved team of Sea Harrier FRS 1 and Sea King AEW 2 during exercise Ocean Safari and prove that the light aircraft carrier has a valuable role to play in the defence of the North Atlantic.

Chapter 21

Carriers go to war

When the first *Invincible* Class light aircraft carrier, now designated CVS in NATO parlance, was commissioned into the Royal Navy in 1980, nobody could have believed that she would be sent into action not in the North Atlantic as was her design concept, but 8,000 nautical miles to the south, off the Falkland Islands. The South Atlantic conflict of April-June 1982 made two out of the three British-built carriers involved household names in the English speaking world—*Invincible* and *Hermes;* the third flew the naval ensign of the *Armada Republica Argentina* and was called *25 de Mayo*, after the date when Argentina was granted independence from Spain.

When Argentine marines invaded the British dependency of South Georgia and, almost immediately afterwards, the Falkland Islands proper, *Invincible* had been exercising in Northern Norway with the Royal Marines, and on returning to Portsmouth sent her company on Easter Leave. *Hermes*, too, was at Portsmouth, undergoing a refit but, more to the point, with her boilers stripped for maintenance. The marshalling of supplies, men and equipment for the South Atlantic Task Force which was to be led by Flag Officer First Flotilla, Rear Admiral 'Sandy' Woodward, called for major effort from all concerned. Undoubtedly, the speed with which the ships were assembled and made ready for the voyage 'Down South' delighted Britain's NATO allies and amazed those not so well disposed towards us. It has emerged since that the Argentine Government did not expect Britain to stage a counter operation immediately.

For several years, the debate about the Sea Harrier's operational ability from the CVSs had been raging fiercely in Whitehall and the Navy. As events were to prove, the combination was probably the best mix of aircraft and ships available to any navy in the world. The Sea Harrier and the carriers certainly won their spurs in the Falklands.

A general call went out in early April for all available Sea Harrier and other aircrew. It had been decided to embark five Sea Harriers of 800 Squadron in *Hermes*, together with seven of the same type from the Operational Training Unit, 899 Squadron. In addition the Royal Navy's largest ship was to take nine Sea King HAS5s of 826 Squadron and nine Sea King HC4 helicopters from 846 Naval Air Commando Squadron. *Invincible*, being smaller, embarked only eight Sea Harriers, (five from 801 Squadron and three from 899) plus the nine Sea King HAS5s of 820 Squadron, amongst whose pilots was a certain Sub-Lieutenant HRH The Prince Andrew MVO RN.

The carriers, with several escorts and Royal Fleet Auxiliaries, sailed from

Left *The conflict in the South Atlantic saw the first operational use of the* Invincible *Class carriers when* Invincible *was deployed with the Task Force. The campaign also showed up the lack of close-in weapons and when the carrier returned to Portsmouth, she was refitted with Phalanx and 20 mm Oerlikons. Here she is on her way south* (Fleet Photographic Unit).

Below Invincible *in her South Atlantic paint scheme with all black areas painted grey to reduce the risk of being observed. The Lynx on the flight deck is equipped with 'Orange Crop' ESM to 'decoy' possible Exocet missile attacks* (Fleet Photographic Unit).

Portsmouth after a tremendous send-off on April 5 1982 and began the vital task of shaking down the new, enlarged air groups. The Sea Harrier squadrons had to reflect that amongst their numbers were every available airframe and pilot, not to mention maintainers. The intelligence estimates also gave food for thought—12 Argentine fighters and strike aircraft to every one Sea Harrier; two Argentine air superiority aircraft to every one SHAR (as the Royal Navy's fighters are generally called aboard ship). *Hermes* had been chosen as Flagship for the Task Force since her high powered communications suite was considered more suitable for the operations Rear Admiral Woodward had planned. The ship's captain was Captain (now Rear Admiral) Lyn Middleton, a former pilot and the one who had previously commanded 809 Squadron aboard *Hermes* in 1966/7. *Invincible*, although more modern, had less accommodation and therefore was probably more suited to the role of air defence co-ordinator, under Captain (now Rear Admiral) Jeremy Black. After the completion of 'Operation Corporate', as the British called the liberation of the Falklands, stickers appeared all over the ship, inscribed 'There and back with J.J. Black'; such was the esteem in which he was held. After a stop at Ascension Island (used mainly to transfer personnel and distribute the overload of Royal Marines to the Assault Ships), almost midway between the United Kingdom and the Total Exclusion Zone (TEZ) created around the Falklands, the Force sailed south into the South Atlantic.

On the other side of the fence, *25 de Mayo*, built as a Light Fleet Carrier just after the Second World War (see page 119), had already been in action, ferrying and landing the assault troops at Port Stanley. The troops, specialist assault marines, were ferried ashore by four Sikorsky SH-3 Sea Kings and several smaller helicopters, as well as by landing craft. With no real defences available to the islanders, the carrier was able to come close inshore. After the landings, she returned to her base port and prepared for air strikes, should the need arise. Her regular complement of A-4 Skyhawk strike fighters were in the process of being replaced by the Dassault Super Etendard naval fighter, purchased from France and armed with the AM39 Exocet missile. This combination was to prove rather deadly later on in the conflict, but throughout the war the Super Etendards were not operating from the carrier's deck. There have been several opinions given for the lack of air action by the newer fighters, including the need to strengthen *25 de Mayo*'s steam catapult and arrester gear. However, it now seems clear that it was not intended that the French-built jets should be anything but shore-based, such were the problems of integrating the Exocets with the aircraft. When the Argentine carrier did sail again, in a pincer movement designed to trap the carrier battle group (CVBG), she was again fully operational with A-4 Skyhawks embarked. They were armed with conventional iron bombs with retarders and their crews were highly trained in anti-ship operations, as was shown when they operated against the British in San Carlos Water and the Falklands Sound in May 1982. Here they caused the loss of at least one frigate, the Type 21 *Ardent*, It is, therefore, certain that had a strike been launched against the CVBG on May 2 and had some of the Skyhawks managed to penetrate the SHAR defensive screens, considerable damage would have been done. As luck would have it for the Argentines, when launch time for the strike came, there was no wind across the deck and the Skyhawks could not be launched. *Invincible* and *Hermes*' Sea Harriers, however, because of their unique design and the ability of the ski-jump ramp on each carrier's bow, were able to fly. They did not seek out *25 de Mayo* but concentrated on the enemy positions ashore instead.

After the cessation of hostilities, the United States Navy produced a report which said, very broadly, that had an American carrier task group been in the area instead of the British, they would have been able to operate more aircraft, carry out more roles and provide excellent airborne early warning of air strikes. Although there can be no disputing the latter, it is quite possible that *no* aircraft would have been able to operate for much of the time because the flight decks of the large carriers would have been 'out of limits' for the large jets with their conventional launch and recovery patterns. *25 de Mayo*, being midway in size between *Hermes* and *Invincible* would also have been limited thus by the bad weather and heavy seas—in the same way as she was on a calm day. In any case, the matter became academic because, following the sinking of the Argentine cruiser *Belgrano* by a British nuclear-powered submarine, the major surface combat units of the *Armada Republica Argentina* were loath to leave port. Actually, it appears that *25 de Mayo* remained at sea until May 8 when she landed her aircraft.

Meanwhile, the Sea Harriers embarked on the British carriers had been in

The most potent weapons system aboard the new class of British aircrft carriers is the Sea Harrier, seen here launching from the ski jump ramp, carrying two AIM-9L Sidewinder missiles for a patrol during the Falklands conflict. This aircraft will be updated to keep pace with modern equipment and remain with the 'Invincibles' until at least 2000 (HMS *Invincible*).

The heart of the ship's aviation side is the hangar where the new scissor lifts are making the movement of aircraft considerably easier. Pictured here around the after lift are the Sea King HAS 5 helicopters of 820 Squadron (HMS *Invincible*).

action for the first time. On May 1, Rear Admiral Woodward opened his air operations with a strike against Argentine positions, flown by nine SHARs from 800 Squadron (the 899 aircraft having been temporarily absorbed into the other two units) who successfully toss bombed their targets. Six Sea Harriers from *Invincible* provided air cover against possible counter attacks by the Argentine forces. On returning to *Hermes*, the 800 aircraft were reconfigured on deck to the air defence role. In the air defence role, the Sea Harrier carries the advanced American-designed AIM-9L Sidewinder missile, which can lock onto a target from almost any angle. To back up this primary system the aircraft are also armed with two 30 mm Aden cannon under the belly. During the Falklands conflict both systems were used to destroy enemy aircraft and the Sea Harriers suffered no losses in air-to-air combat with Argentine Mirage, Dagger or Skyhawk jets. May 1 was the day of the first aerial engagements for the Task Force when Sea Harriers from 801 Squadron made the first kills against Mirage IIIs of *Grupo* 8, Argentine Air Force—one of the two was actually finally destroyed by the guns defending Port Stanley; in fact, by its own side!

The Argentine Navy has possessed submarines for some decades and even though one of their four had been sunk in South Georgia only weeks before, two were at sea in early May looking for the carriers. Had one of these West German-built boats managed to hit and even just cripple a carrier, the liberation

The tightly packed Sea Harrier parking area and the chaff rocket stains show that Invincible *has been in action. This photograph was taken in May 1982, during the carrier's operational duties in the TEZ. The lighter grey SHARs are part of the squadron flown south midway through the conflict* (HMS Invincible).

of the Falklands would have been made impossible. In fact, Argentine sources still maintain that one submarine did manage to fire a salvo of torpedoes at *Invincible*, but that they failed to detonate. Those aboard *Invincible* at the time cannot recall any such incident. Nevertheless, it was important for the resident Sea King squadrons to put in maximum effort in terms of an anti-submarine screen around the carrier group. The technique of providing a constant number of helicopters, usually three on station in the screen at any one time, is called 'ripple' flying. Each carrier had to provide sufficient helicopters to put nine Sea Kings on the screen at any one time, which meant that 12 crews had to be available. For each Sea King this is a total of three officers (two pilots and the observer) and an aircrewman. Each helicopter has a four-hour task, although it is possible to change crews and refuel in-flight from smaller ships on the 'screen' thus allowing a quicker, more efficient turn around. The Sea King support helicopters were also busy with covert landing operations on the two main Falkland Islands, inserting members of 22 Special Air Service Regiment and naval gunfire support directors from a specialist commando-trained unit of the Royal Artillery, with Special Boat Squadron personnel protection parties. The intelligence that these men were able to obtain made the eventual landing operation safer and easier than might otherwise have been possible. Using *Hermes* as a base, this information could soon be passed to the Flag and to London.

During early May, both carriers in the British task group continued to fly aircraft around the clock in the Combat Air Patrol (CAP) and strike/reconnaissance roles. However, they still kept the decks clear for helicopter operations in connection with, for example, the evacuation of wounded from the disabled destroyer *Sheffield*, 'ripple' anti-submarine operations and the raid on the Argentine radar and air base at Pebble Island. The Pebble Island raid represents an example of one of the most daring and politically important events in the conflict giving, as it did, a tremendous boost to the morale of the British forces and, one imagines, somewhat worrying the Agentines in view of the ease with which task force helicopters were able to land SAS and SBS personnel. The raid was carried out without loss and incredibly, involved only two Sea King HC4 helicopters flying from *Hermes*, which had moved closer to West Falkland to launch and recover the aircraft. During this pre-landing period, considerable work was being undertaken in the United Kingdom to transport aircraft to the TEZ and to prepare the second *Invincible* Class carrier, *Illustrious* for sea.

The role of the chartered container ships, typified by the ill-fated *Atlantic Conveyor*, was not to act as flying platforms, as their normal decking would not take the weight of regular flying operations anyway, but to act as transports and repair depots. When *Atlantic Conveyor* was lost to an attack of Exocet missiles, launched from two of *25 de Mayo*'s Super Etendards, it was not so much the ship whose loss was grieved but the support helicopters and equipment being carried. Nonetheless, the success of *Atlantic Conveyor, Atlantic Causeway* and *Astronomer* has resulted in the Royal Navy taking a more positive line on the use of merchant hulls for carrying and operating aircraft, which is discussed a little further on. *Atlantic Conveyor* also brought to the TEZ a number of RAF

Standing guard on Invincible's *bridge top during the hours of daylight to form a last ditch defence against air attack. In the background,* Hermes *changes course to recover her aircraft* (Fleet Photographic Unit).

Harrier GR3 ground-attack fighters which were deployed from No 1 Squadron RAF to take over the ground-attack role, for which they were optimised, from the Sea Harriers who were needed for air support. This was especially true following the loss of several Sea Harriers from either ground fire or flying accidents. By May 18 1982, *Hermes* had embarked six Harrier GR3s which were recovered aboard with some skill as the pilots had not been previously deck qualified. In addition to the extra Harriers, the Royal Navy had reformed 809 Squadron at RNAS Yeovilton to go south with every last available Sea Harrier and pilot. The eight aircraft were ferried to Ascension and trans-shipped to the TEZ; four embarked in *Hermes*, with the same number in *Invincible.*

As the pre-landing phase of the conflict progressed, the Sea Harriers continued to fly regular CAPs but without encountering significant opposition from either the Argentine Air Force or the country's naval arm. Unfortunately, there were not enough SHARs and they lacked the range to prevent resupply operations to Port Stanley, Goose Green and Fox Bay by Argentine aircraft up to the size of Hercules transports. However, the use of the runway at Port Stanley had been denied to jet aircraft by the world's longest bombing raid by a single RAF Vulcan bomber from Ascension Island. Despite this the Agentines still had sufficient aircraft capable of using Falklands' airfields and attacking the carriers at sea.

On May 19, *Hermes* was the launching point for what has become a celebrated operation and one over which there has been much speculation (all unconfirmed by the Royal Navy). A lone Sea King HC4, actually the first production model of the type, departed the carrier, staged through the patrol vessel *Dumbarton Castle* and apparently deposited a troop of SAS on Argentine soil to report enemy air activity. The crew then flew the helicopter to Chilean soil, destroyed it and gave themselves up, having given the SAS time to 'dig in' first. The trip has all the hallmarks of a one-way mission, but this will not be confirmed until official papers are released in 2012!

The CVBG and the Amphibious Group, sailing from Ascension and South Georgia, were now ready for the landing operations—Operation Sutton. Undoubtedly the vulnerability of the carriers was a problem facing Admiral Woodward and his staff at this time. The CVBG, with its escorts, had to operate east of the Falklands, out of range of the Exocet-carrying Super Etendards, yet close enough inshore to provide adequate cover for the amphibious operations, As luck would have it, and probably as a result of the Pebble Island raid and other diversionary tactics, the Argentine high command looked upon the first reports of landings at San Carlos and Ajax Bay as exaggerated. This gave the troops time to get ashore and become established.

The carrier aircraft support for the landings and the beach-head commenced with CAPs being flown by pairs of Sea Harriers, directed by radar controllers in warships offshore; but they were always conscious that the position of *Hermes* and *Invincible* could be given away to the Argentines' Westinghouse radar installed above Port Stanley, for it was simply a matter of tracking the SHARs home, unless they flew low level under the radar cover. The distance and time

Opposite *The CVBG moves towards Port Stanley at the cessation of hostilities;* Hermes *is just visible behind the three Royal Fleet Auxiliaries which have supported the two carriers with all solid and liquid requirements* (Fleet Photographic Unit).

factors involved meant that there were fighters being launched from the carriers every 30 minutes or so during the hours of daylight. The Sea Harrier maintained combat air patrols south of the Fox Bay area on West Falkland, as well as on the Argentine side of that island, with the third figure-of-eight patrol line to the north of Pebble Island. The aircraft were free to range across the islands, always excepting the missile engagement zone around the beach-head at San Carlos. The holding patterns were flown at medium altitude. After the successful landings, the Royal Engineers built special landing pads on the North Shore of San Carlos Water to be used as a Forward Operating Base by Sea Harriers and Harriers alike. The idea was to extend their range and time on task by allowing them to refuel, but not re-arm, after a first sortie, returning to their parent ships after the second sortie or when weapons had been expended. Sea Harriers also used *Fearless* and *Intrepid* for landing platforms, although neither Assault Ship had been previously cleared for such operations. After the landings, the Argentine Air Force and Naval Air Arm launched several heavy raids against the British warships and auxiliaries in what was to become known as 'Bomb Alley'. Despite great gallantry, some skill and several losses to the Royal Navy, the Argentines were unable to gain air superiority, nor were they able to dislodge the amphibious forces.

British Aerospace, the manufacturer of both the Sea Harrier and the Harrier, have released figures which indicate that some 2,000 sorties plus were flown, the bulk by the Fleet Air Arm. The Sea Harriers were airborne for approximately 55 hours per aircraft per month, flying up to six sorties a day. At the height of the operations the pilots were averaging three to four sorties every day and spending up to ten hours a day in the cockpit, either flying or at alert. It is interesting to reflect that the Sea Harriers, despite being embarked in the carriers far from their main maintenance bases, were serviceable for nearly 90 per

Illustrious *relieved* Invincible *in the South Atlantic in September 1982 and was herself relieved on station by RAF Phantoms based at Port Stanley that December. She is pictured here returning to Portsmouth, having flown off her air group to Culdrose and Yeovilton* (Fleet Photographic Unit).

cent of the time and only one per cent of the planned sorties could not be flown because of unserviceability. Although no real dogfighting developed in the battles over the Falklands, the Sea Harriers claim 31 out of the 120 fixed-wing aircraft and helicopters destroyed or captured during the 74 day conflict. Later the British Government White Paper on the conflict reported that 103 aircraft had been destroyed, 14 probably destroyed and 15 captured. Other sources give the numbers as 117 destroyed and 32 captured. It seems likely now that 16 Skyhawk and Mirage/Dagger jets were destroyed in combat with the Sea Harriers, with an additional seven other types of aircraft. This makes a total of 23, of which seven were by the fighters' Aden cannon; in all 27 Sidewinder missiles were launched by the British jets.

From the carriers' point of view, the prolonged period at sea was beginning to take its toll on the ships, their men and equipment. Some statistics from *Invincible* make interesting reading: from April 5 to September 17 1983, the ship spent 166 days at sea (a world record for continuous aircraft carrier operations), steaming 51,660 nautical miles (95,674 km), or twice around the world at the Equator, consuming 30,196 tonnes of diesel fuel and supplying 7,620 tonnes of aviation spirit to aircraft. The Sea Harriers of 801 Squadron flew 1,437 sorties of which 950 were for combat air patrol and fighter sweeps, during which time they accounted for seven enemy aircraft destroyed and three probably destroyed with a dozen Sidewinder missiles being fired. The aircraft flew for a total of 1,580 hours, which is three times the normal flying rate and one pilot even spent nine hours in the cockpit. The Sea Kings, by their very nature, flew more hours, 4,700 in fact, although the actual number of sorties was only 1,650. 820 Squadron engaged mainly in active (dipping) and passive (sono-buoy) anti-submarine warfare, also managed to spend time exercising with friendly submarines, searching for surface contacts and providing *Invincible* with helicopter delivery service (HDS). Although the official reports show that no submarine contacts were positively obtained, the nine Sea Kings did release six torpedoes at possible targets and in addition dropped ten depth charges. The statistics can be meaningless to those unconnected with flying, but to give an idea of Sea Kings flying hours it must be realised that they flew the same number of hours as would five members of the squadron had they been airborne for the entire time the ship had been at sea with the Task Force.

Despite the cessation of hostilities on June 14 1982, the British Government decided to keep one carrier at sea in the TEZ until a permanent fighter air base could be established ashore. Even though she had already undergone two changes of gas turbine engines, *Invincible* was by far the best choice to remain on station. *Hermes* was sent home to Portsmouth to a hero's welcome and *Illustrious* was speeded through her sea trials to rendezvous with *Invincible* in the TEZ on September 17.

Illustrious brought south two new helicopter variants as part of her air group which also included the Sea Harriers of 809 Squadron and the Sea King HAS5s of 814. The latter helicopters were Sea Kings which had been converted to carry the Thorn EMI Searchwater radar, a variant of which is also carried in the RAF's Nimrod long maritime patrol aircraft. The sinking of the *Sheffield* has been attributed to the lack of airborne early warning (AEW) capable of detecting low flying strike aircraft 'over the horizon' of a ship's own radar, a role carried out by the Gannet AEW3 in *Ark Royal* and previous aircraft carriers. Westland and Thorn EMI managed to test fly the Sea King AEW in a matter of weeks and

Illustrious proved a very useful test bed for sea trials, remaining in the South Atlantic until December 1982 and only being withdrawn when the RAF set-up an air defence unit at Port Stanley, flying Phantoms.

It is strikingly obvious that the Falkland Islands could not have been liberated without the aircraft carriers *Hermes* and *Invincible* and, in particular, their Sea Harrier fighters. The British Government's White Paper, entitled, *The Falklands Campaign: The Lessons* is a little more restrained in its praise saying that the carriers 'were effective and flexible command ships and provided good platforms for air operations', though the Sea Harriers and Harriers are described as 'a major success'. It was discovered, however, that the *Invincible* class was in need of close-in weapons and all three—*Invincible, Illustrious* and *Ark Royal*—have been fitted with new small calibre naval guns and counter measures dispensers. Although the light aircraft carriers and the Sea Harrier have had their critics, the combination proved highly successful in this limited war at least. Changes in the design of both the ships and the aircraft have followed from the experience gained but this will only strengthen their ability in their 'real' role in the North Atlantic.

The Royal Navy has also grasped the idea of using converted container ships as platforms to operate helicopters from as a supplement to, but not a replacement for, aircraft carriers. This scheme, known as SCADS (Shipborne Containerised Air Defence System), uses the United States Navy's Arapaho concept, as can be seen in the converted container ship *Astronomer,* which was renamed RFA *Reliant* in January 1984. The present design can accommodate five Sea King helicopters and has already been put to use in the Eastern Mediterranean to support British troops in the Lebanon. A whole range of helicopter operations could be supported, with the work undertaken by British Aerospace Dynamics Group and Cammell Laird involved in the addition of 55 ISO containers for support and domestic facilities, as well as a hangar structure on the main deck. A helicopter flight deck has also been included in the design, with surveillance radar and counter measure facilities. The equipment has autonomous power generation, distribution and communications. A development of the design, which may well come about with the experience gained in *Reliant*, would include facilities to support commando and amphibious landing operations, airborne early warning, search and rescue and anti-shipping operations. Although there is a general reluctance to use merchant ships for naval operations, this might well prove to be a cheap and cost-effective alternative to building helicopter cruisers. In addition, being compatible with other merchant ships, a SCADS ship could sail with a convoy to give support and protection. There is even a design for a Harrier Carrier variant using a Fairey Engineering Containerised runway and ski-jump and Seawolf air defence missile systems. The designers believe that almost any modern container ship could be converted to an operational Harrier Platform within 48 hours.

The idea of a Harrier Carrier is not new. In the last ten years or so there have been several designs for aircraft carriers which warrant mention in a book devoted to the British Aircraft Carrier, especially after the success of *Invincible* (and to a lesser extent, *Illustrious*) in the South Atlantic. There they proved that they did indeed rate the nomenclature of aircraft carrier.

One of the first designs suggested for carrying Sea Harriers to sea was a small and cost-effective design from Vosper Thornycroft, part of the nationalised

A view of the future? Perhaps, but only as part of a team which must continue to include aircraft carriers. This is one of British Aerospace's containerised defence systems, which includes the Sea Harrier (BAE).

British Shipbuilders combine. The 'Harrier Carrier' was to be 8,000 tonnes (this being the smallest ship capable of carrying aircraft) and would have a speed of 25 knots. The air group was a suggested mix of eight Sea Harriers and two Lynx helicopters for 'plane guard and HDS. Alternatively, eight Sea King anti-submarine helicopters could be embarked, giving the possibility of operating two carriers together in task group or as convoy escorts, with one covering the anti-submarine side and the other the air and surface threats. There was, however, no interest in the designs, especially from the Royal Navy who were still having a hard time to justify the Sea Harrier as part of the 'armament' of the *Invincibles*.

Another British Shipbuilders subsidiary, Vickers Shipbuilding and Engineering Limited, who had completed the first of the new 19,500 tons CVS and decided to put their expertise to use in the market for the replacements for the existing fixed-wing carriers. Especially important in this market were Australia (whose Light Fleet Carrier, *Melbourne*, was finally scrapped in 1984), Argentina, France, Brazil, Spain and India. With the advent of the Sea Harrier, it would be possible to build a warship of 23,000 tonnes for convoy escort and task group roles. The Helicopter Escort Carrier Concept 1 would have 25 knots maximum speed and range of 10,000 nautical miles at a cruising speed of 18 knots. Powered by four Rolls Royce Spey gas turbines or four Pielstick medium speed diesels, the 662 ft ship would be capable of embarking either 18 Sea King-type helicopters for anti-submarine warfare, or 15 Sea Harriers and two Sea Kings. British Aerospace Seawolf could be provided for close range defence and the total complement would be 650 men. Although no unit costs were ever published, the design would have been in reach of those larger navies outside the exclusive 'Carrier Club'. HEC Concept 2 was for a carrier of the same size, but with a smaller displacement, with the object of taking a worthwhile number of anti-submarine helicopters to sea, together with fuel for escorts in a convoy situation. There were no helicopter control facilities in the design as these were to be designated to one of the escorts. Nine to 14 Sea King-type helicopters could be carried but the ship would only be powered by two diesels, having a maximum speed of only 23 knots, but adequate to operate helicopters.

Also moving in the direction of providing cost-effective platforms for aircraft, particularly helicopters at sea, Vickers commenced a design study in the middle 1970s for Maritime Area Control Ship—or MAC Ship. This idea is not to be confused with the Merchant Aircraft Carriers mentioned earlier in this book, but it was based on the premise that a navy might want to control both sea and land areas. These options called for the broadening of operational requirements as compared with other earlier designs. Vickers believed that any navy wishing to purchase what must have been, in 1978 terms, a £100 million ship would need to make sure that several roles could be carried out. The MAC Ship's intended roles were described as anti-submarine, area air defence, surface air strike, surveillance, landing operations, tactical support for land forces, tactical command, disaster relief and large scale civilian evacuation. The design was certainly flexible, allowing five Sea Harriers and nine Sea Kings to be embarked. The specification published was for a ship with an overall length of

Caught in the evening sun of the Indian Ocean, Invincible *is a fine ship and along with her two sister-ships is the largest vessel in the modern Royal Navy. It is doubtful whether a larger ship will ever be built again* (RN).

594 ft, a displacement of 13,000 tonnes, a maximum speed of 28 knots and a range, at 18 knots, of 7,000 nautical miles. A combined diesel and gas turbine propulsion system was suggested and because of the merchant ship type of design, the MAC Ship had a low cost, about two-thirds the price of a carrier built to full Naval specification.

There were no takers for this design either, nor for the Vickers Versatile Aircraft Carrier (VVAC) which also had been designed to merchant ship standards. Having approximately the same dimensions and a similar displacement, the VVAC would have a diesel propulsion system, giving a maximum speed of around 26 knots. For comparison, *Invincible* and her sister ships are capable of a speed in excess of 30 knots in good sea conditions. The typical aircraft mix proposed would have been 12 Sea Harriers and two Sea Kings, although any navy would be free to amend the mix, depending on the circumstances. Close-in defence would be provided by three Phalanx-type gun systems situated on the fo'c'sle and at either end of the superstructure. In common with all the British Shipbuilder's designs, the carrier's superstructure was positioned on the traditional starboard side island.

Despite the success of *Invincible* and *Hermes* in the South Atlantic, and the American aircraft carriers during the Grenada invasion (1983) and off the Lebanon (1982-84), there has been very little interest in the larger, or even the middle-sized navies purchasing new aircraft carriers or area control ships, other than from their own yards. Both Italy and Spain have important programmes for light aircraft carriers, the former may purchase Sea Harriers and the latter already has a maritime version of the Harrier GR1 at sea; however, both the hulls came from domestic yards.

We have seen that the Argentine Navy has already completed the re-furbishment and re-equipment of *25 de Mayo,* whilst Australia's Air Force has won the competition amongst that country's armed forces for new equipment. It is perhaps a little ironic that *Invincible* should be the carrier chosen to lead the Royal Navy's 1983-84 Group Deployment to the Far East and visit Australia on a number of occasions, considering that but for the Argentine invasion of the Falklands and, perhaps, pressure from other NATO alliance members, *Invincible*, by now, would have been *Australia* of the Royal Australian Navy. The 'Orient Express' deployment which sadly ran into so many problems with engineering faults, did at least demonstrate that it is possible for a navy to operate a group of ships, based around a light aircraft carrier, so far from home ports. India has also refurbished *Vikrant* (see page 119) to enable that nation's Fleet Air Arm to operate Sea Harrier fighters, Alize anti-submarine aircraft and helicopters. Brazil has decided to refit *Minas Gerais* again but there must be some doubt as to her future, especially as the new Agusta AS-61D Sea King helicopters, delivered in 1983-84, are shore-based for anti-submarine duties.

Although there now appears to be very little interest in the light aircraft carrier, more from the funding point of view than any other, Vickers still have a design study progressing for a Light Fleet Carrier, designed using the expertise from *Invincible*'s construction for Flagship operations with comprehensive command, communications and sensor capability, in addition to a complement of eight Sea Harriers and nine medium helicopters of the Sea King type. Vickers see the need for a carrier with six operating positions and a 525 ft runway, ending in a 12 degree ski-jump. There would be two lifts for aircraft handling and self-defence by means of a close-in weapons system (CIWS). The specification envisages a 24,000 tonnes ship (a slightly greater displacement than the *Invincibles*) with gas turbine propulsion giving about 26 knots maximum or a cruising speed of 18 knots. The range at the cruising speed would be 6,500 nautical miles. To reduce costs, the hull structure has been designed to merchant ship standards, using the hull form of a twin-screw passenger liner.

There are many who believe that the *Invincibles* are likely to be the last aircraft carriers to be designed and built as such for the Royal Navy and that future designs, although they may still operate jets and helicopters, will be smaller and less able. The cost of the Royal Navy being a full-time member of the 'carrier-club' is expensive and certainly it will never be possible for it to acquire the large CVs of the United States Navy, nor the types currently under construction for the Soviet Red Banner Fleet.

This, of course, has been said before and although it is true that a supersonic STOVL (short take-off and vertical landing) fighter could be considered an important addition to the Fleet, the updating programme for the existing Sea Harrier will certainly see the present combination of jet and carrier in service until the end of the century. Yet that time frame is shorter than the period from the time of writing to the Carrier Crisis of the 1960s. As the Falklands conflict proved, the aircraft carrier is still important to British and NATO maritime policy, although only three carriers, with one in refit or under maintenance, is barely adequate for modern operations, both within NATO and 'Out of Area'.

Chapter 22

The future of the British Aircraft Carrier

It seems incredible that a conflict far from both the United Kingdom and main area of British maritime interest (the Eastern Atlantic) can have caused such an interest and re-awakening of confidence in British aircraft carriers. It was not of course solely due to the ships themselves, nor the men who man and fight them, but the aircraft which these carriers now carry. The Falklands' conflict proved the ability of the Sea Harrier and confirmed that modern naval and land engagements cannot be fought without helicopter power.

In the previous chapter, the actual combat in the South Atlantic and the immediate results are described and the proposals for 'Harrier Carriers' and other mini-carrier ideas discussed. It only remains to note that the Indian Navy purchased the decommissioned *Hermes* in April 1986. Since the Falklands, the Royal Navy has commissioned the third and last *Invincible* Class CVs, *Ark Royal (V)*, and she was declared operational in 1986 following Atlantic and Channel trials.

The new *Ark Royal* has been built with the experience of wartime operations and prolonged sea time from the Falklands and the Group Deployment (1983-84) taken into account. It is consequently a better ship than the first two of the class, but they too will be updated during the planned two-year refits, the first of which was commenced on *Invincible* in 1986. Trials with a steeper ski-

Ark Royal *on sea trials in June 1985, immediately prior to acceptance by the Royal Navy. Note the port quarter sponson position but the lack of armament* (Swan Hunter).

jump at RNAS Yeovilton proved that 12 degrees was the optimum for the Sea Harrier; *Invincible* and *Illustrious* were commissioned with 7 degree ramps and *Hermes* was refitted with a 7½ degree ramp in 1980.

Ark Royal was built on Tyneside by Swan Hunter Shipbuilders Ltd and proved to be a very successful project for the yard, because even with the updates resulting from the South Atlantic experience, especially in regard to close-in weapon systems, the ship was completed some four and a half months ahead of the contract time.

Ark Royal (V) was commissioned in November 1985, in the presence of her sponsor, HM Queen Elizabeth the Queen Mother, and entered service with the most advanced and sophisticated command and control facilities in the Royal Navy and certainly within the top ten of any warship in the world. On commissioning, the ship was given the five principal roles of her two sister ships:
(1) to provide a platform for Command, Control and Communications of maritime forces;
(2) to deploy anti-submarine warfare helicopters in support of a force at sea;
(3) to deploy STOVL (Short Take-Off and Vertical Landing) aircraft for air defence, surface strike and reconnaissance duties;
(4) to deploy amphibious units and their logistical support, especially in the 'quick dash' role for the NATO flanks and Out of Area operations;
(5) to contribute to the area air defence of a naval force with the Sea Dart GWS 30 missile system.

The major differences from *Ark Royal* as built and her two sister ships include the extension and lengthening of the ski-jump ramp, with its 12 degrees slope and extra clearance of the Sea Dart missile launcher. The forecastle has been given more flare and the area re-arranged to provide a location for the bow close-in weapon system (CIWS). Under the ski-jump, extra accommodation for junior rates has been built. A second CIWS has been positioned on the island superstructure, protecting the starboard side of the ship left vulnerable with the re-positioning of the after CIWS into a sponson below the port side of the flight deck. With both *Invincible* and *Illustrious*, there was concern about the Phalanx position and the protection of the port beam and quarter.

To provide extra defence against low flying aircraft and sea-skimming missiles, the Royal Navy has equipped *Ark Royal* with two 30 mm Oerlikon

The primary role of the CVSs will be centred on the Eastern Atlantic in support of NATO, using such naval bases as Gibraltar. This is Illustrious, *photographed in late 1985* (HMS *Illustrious*/LA Phot Cowpe).

Several times in her first commission, Invincible *practised a secondary role in defence of the Northern Flank, including carrying Royal Marine Commandoes to Norway in the 'quick dash' configuration. Even in this role, air defence by Sea Harrier and ASW defence by Sea King HAS 5 is still carried out* (HMS *Invincible*/PO Phot Kent).

GCM gun mountings, one on the starboard side of the flight deck, on a sponson abeam the island and the port mounting a deck below the flight deck. The smaller calibre 20 mm defences of the first two in the class have been retained.

From the point of view of naval aviation, it is the hangar deck and other internal re-arrangement which is most important, especially because it will be carried forward to the refits of *Invincible* (1986-88) and *Illustrious* (1989-91).

As part of the new Admiralty policy to keep two aircraft carriers at sea and one in refit/reserve, *Invincible*'s refit began following a spell as the Dartmouth training ship, which included a cruise to the Western Atlantic. *Invincible* then carried out some important trials on structures and systems before being put into the dockyard's hands at Devonport for a £100 million refit to bring her to the standard of *Ark Royal*, especially in terms of the electronics suite, both for warfare tasks and command and control communications.

The largest item in the refit programme is however the overhaul of the Action Data Automatic Weapons Systems (ADAWS) which was installed to Mk 6 standard, based on two Ferranti FM1600 computers to provide data and calculations for fighter direction and data linking, as well as the integration of the Sea Dart GWS 30 guided missile system. *Illustrious* was also fitted with ADAWS 6, but *Ark Royal* has entered service with ADAWS 10, the last of the 'family' of such suites, but a culmination in both sophistication and central computing size. It is thought that when *Invincible* emerges from her refit in mid-1988, she will be fitted with a Computer Assisted Command System based on the high technology FM1600E computer and the Admiralty Surface Weapons Establishment Serial Highway for the rapid desemination of data from a variety of sources. CACS systems are already in service with Type 22 Batch 2 frigates and have been ordered for the Type 23 frigates.

Internally, *Invincible* will be modified to carry an uprated air group of eight Sea Harrier FRS 1 (later FRS 2) strike fighters, nine (maximum of 11 in wartime) Sea King HAS 5 (later either HAS 6 Advanced Sea King or the EH 101) and three Sea King AEW 2 helicopters; all stowed in the hangar deck with

An unusual sight for an Invincible *Class is the embarkation of Westland Lynx AH 1 helicopters of the 3rd Commando Brigade Air Squadron which operate in support of the Royal Marines ashore. The helicopters are optimised for storage below decks (below) in the single hangar deck* (HMS *Invincible*/PO Phot Kent & Stewart Antrobus).

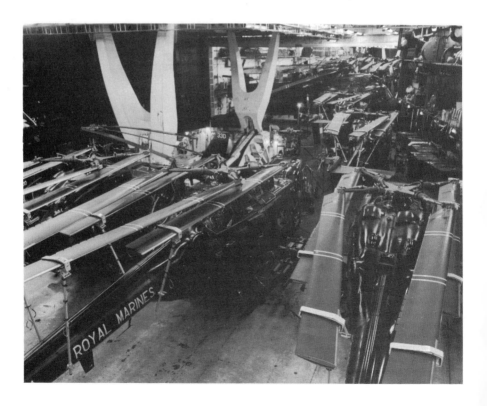

the accompanying maintenance facilities. The new hangar will have a mezzanine deck forward for stores and offices, and a mezzanine aft for extra accommodation for the air group. The air group's magazines will be enlarged to give about 50 per cent more stowage space, used for Marconi Underwater Systems Limited Stingray lightweight anti-submarine torpedo and the British Aerospace Sea Eagle long-range anti-shipping missile which will equip the Sea Harrier by the end of the decade.

The ship's own self-defence systems will be greatly improved by the provision of the Anglo-Dutch Goalkeeper close-in weapons system. The Goalkeeper is an automatic seven-barrelled 30 mm gun system with a rate of fire of 4,200 rpm which uses a Signaal radar to acquire and track an incoming low level aircraft or missile target for the American-designed GAU-8 cannon to engage with a 'wall of lead'. Three sets will be fitted to *Invincible*, presumably in the same positions as the Phalanx CIWS currently installed in *Ark Royal*. To assist with the ship's defences, the Sea Gnat countermeasures launcher system, for both flares and chaff, will be fitted in place of the US Navy's Super RBOC launchers previously carried since the post-Falklands weapons update.

The above-water sensor package will include the first of the new Type 996 three-dimensional air surveillance radar sets—the first 3-D sets at sea since *Hermes* ceased fixed-wing flying in the early 1970s. Type 996 will replace the existing Type 992 and 1022 sets. The medium-range, hull-mounted anti-submarine sonar which was fitted during the ship's building, Type 184, will be replaced with Type 2016 which is already operational with many frigates and *Ark Royal*.

Invincible will emerge from refit with accommodation, both in new messes under the new ski-jump and in the mezzanine flats to cater for the full ship's complement and increased air group of 1,400 men. Currently, especially in the light of the defence spending situation in the late 1980s, there is not room in the Defence Budget, according to the Government, for a third air group to be formed, giving one group to each carrier. This confirms the policy of keeping one carrier in reserve or refit, whilst the other two operate aircraft.

The new generation of aircraft will be the British Aerospace Sea Harrier FRS 2, the Westland Sea King HAS 6 and the Sea King AEW 2, the latter having already joined the Fleet with the formation of two flights of 849 Squadron, A and B, in 1985 and 1986 respectively. These aircraft will keep the carrier air groups viable until the mid 1990s when the Supersonic STOVL fighter, the subject of a Memorandum of Understanding between British Aerospace and McDonnell Aircraft will begin to take shape. At the same time, the Anglo-Italian EH 101 medium ASW helicopter will be entering service with the small ship flights and if a dipping sonar is fitted in the eventual production model, it could be ordered for carrier service.

The Sea Harrier FRS 2 is a remarkable refit package designed to take advantage of the advances in avionics and weapons technology since the aircraft entered service in 1980. The idea is that all 44 aircraft currently in service (the last nine will be delivered before the end of 1988) will be taken in hand by British Aerospace and the Naval Air Support Units in 1988 for the update programme; the first FRS 2 aircraft will be re-entering service in 1989/90. The new programme has six main areas of technological change which will give the pilots a better environment in which to work and fight, as well as improving the aircraft's combat effectiveness.

Left *Amongst the modifications which will be carried out on the CVSs during their planned first refits is the removal of the starboard quarter Phalanx gun to a position to port, thus clearing flight deck space.* Illustrious' *'runway' shows up well in this picture* (HMS *Illustrious*/PO Phot du Fue).

Below *Current anti-submarine warfare equipment is based around the Sea King HAS 5, seen here in the process of 'dipping', carrying four Mk 46 lightweight torpedoes. The helicopter is from 820 Squadron, then embarked in* Invincible *but currently part of* Ark Royal's *air group* (Westland).

Below right *A new dimension to the post-Falklands air group is the Sea King AEW 2 helicopter used for airborne early warning using the Searchwater radar seen extended on the helicopter's starboard side. Each active carrier has a flight of three of these helicopters embarked* (Westland).

Replacing the Sidewinder guided missile system, the AIM-120 AMRAAM (Advanced Medium Range Air-to-Air Missile) will be introduced. This missile is capable of engaging enemy aircraft at ranges beyond that of the pilot's vision and it has been designed to give greater immunity to enemy countermeasures. The system is linked to the new radar, developed from the existing Blue Fox by Ferranti. The new radar is of pulse-doppler type, capable of look-down, shoot-down operation against multiple targets. It is called Blue Vixen and flight testing began in 1986.

To protect the aircraft from counter-attack, an improved and still secret radar warning receiver will be fitted, linked into the centralised weapons management system of sensors, displays and controls. Another high technology system being developed for the aircraft is secure voice and special data links, which will enable the pilot to talk freely to the controlling ship or aircraft and to exchange information from radar and other sensors. The American JTIDS (Joint Tactical Information and Distribution System) is to be used for this function.

Finally, the pilot's cockpit systems will be enhanced with a proven head-up display, optimism pilot's controls in two systems—HOTAS (Hands On Throttle And Stick) thus allowing the systems to be worked during combat manoeuvres without the pilot taking his hands off the two most important aspects of his agility, and UFC (Up-Front Controller). Despite these changes, the Sea Harrier FRS 2 will remain the Royal Navy's air defence, maritime reconnaissance and maritime strike aircraft.

By 1987, the Royal Navy will be equipped with 90 Sea King medium anti-submarine warfare helicopters, two squadrons of which or about 20 machines will be operated from the *Invincible* Class aircraft carriers. Before 1990, it is planned to enhance the ability of these helicopters with better radar, control

systems especially for the sonobuoys, plastic (advanced composite material) main rotor blades and perhaps uprated engines. The result will be called the Sea King HAS 6 and most, if not all the existing Sea King ASW fleet will be modernised to that standard.

The third aircraft in the air group of the future will be the existing Sea King AEW 2, with updated control and countermeasure systems developed as a result of the experience amassed so far. It is unlikely however that the Thorn EMI Electronics Searchwater radar will be replaced unless the helicopter continues in service past 2010. The most serious deficiency is the lack of self-defence, either radar warning receivers or lightweight 'fire and forget' missiles.

In general terms, the Royal Navy is content that it has achieved the best possible arrangement from the limited resources at its disposal. The fact that the third air group is lacking will doubtless be overcome if the carriers are to remain totally viable, but with the current reduction of defence spending in real terms, this will take some time. Much interest will be focused in the next few years on the development of merchant-hulled helicopter support and training ships, such as *Argus*, manned by the Royal Fleet Auxiliary but having Fleet Air Arm personnel embarked. The successful future of the Aircraft Carrier is a vital contribution to Britain's defence needs, in NATO and for Out of Area operations.

The reader is left with this sobering thought of Soviet Naval C-in-C, Admiral Gorshkov: '...The Soviet Navy will no longer be confined to its home waters, but will exploit the freedom of the seas and through its global presence in peacetime will spread Communist influence outside the borders of the USSR. Sea Power without Air Power is senseless'.

A first for Invincible—*civilian pilots from Helicopter Club of Great Britain visit the ship in Portsmouth harbour. Note, below the departing Hughes 300C helicopter, the flight deck equipment parked at Fly One* (HMS *Invincible*/PO Phot Kent).

Appendices

A Carrier Flight Deck Codes (from 1945)

Since the publication of the first edition of *British Aircraft Carrier*, a number of amendments and additions to the listing of aircraft carrier flight code letters have been received and in addition, considerable original research work by Ray Sturtivant in h s book *The Squadrons of the Fleet Air Arm* (published by Air Britain (Historians) Ltd, 1984) has allowed a revised list to be checked. This list is not complete but should provide a useful reference for readers wishing to distinguish between the various ships and their embarked aircraft.

Albion	Z (1954-57); A (1957-72)
Ark Royal	O (1955-57); R (1957-78)
Ark Royal (CVS)	R (1985-)
Arromanches	H
Bonaventure	22
Bulwark	B (1954-81)
Centaur	C (1953-70)
Colossus	C (1945-46; J (1946)
Eagle	J (1953-57); E (1957-72)
Formidable	X (1946-47)
Glory	R (1946-54)
Hermes	H (1959-84)
Illustrious	D (1946-53); Y (1953-55)
Illustrious (CVS)	L (1982-)
Implacable	A (1946-47); C (1948-51)
Independencia	J and VI
Indefatigable	B (1946-53)
Indomitable	A (1947-55)
Invincible	N (1980-)
Karl Doorman	D
Magnificent	X (1948-49); 21
Melbourne	M and 21
Minas Gerais	M
Ocean	O (1945-57)
Sydney	K (1949-58); S (1958-69)
Theseus	T (1946-56)

Triumph	P (1946-55)
Unicorn	U (1946)
Venerable	B (1945-46); V (1946-48)
Vengeance	Q (1946-57)
Victorious	V (1945-68)
Vikrant	V
Warrior	W (1945-48); J (1953-54)
25 de Mayo	D

B   Carrier terminology, abbreviations and expressions

Alaskan Highway   Clear way behind island—a later development in carrier design which would have led to the Alaskan Taxiway in the cancelled CVA-01.

Angle   Angled deck.

Assault guide   Rating who leads commando teams to their aircraft—mainly used on commando carriers.

ACR   Aircraft Control Room—from here the exact position of every aircraft aboard was plotted.

AWD   All Wheel Drive tractor—used for aircraft handling.

Accelerator   Forerunner of the catapult.

ASW   Anti-submarine warfare.

AS   Anti-submarine.

AEW   Air-borne Early Warning.

Bridle   Wire which connects aircraft to catapult.

Badger   Flight deck engineer.

Bombhead   Flight deck ordnance rating.

Bolter   Aircraft which missed arrester wires and went round to land again.

Barrier   Wire or nylon barrier across the flight deck to protect aircraft parked forward. The angled deck did away with this device.

Booster   Catapult.

BPF   British Pacific Fleet.

Batsman   DLCO (qv)—pilot used to give incoming pilot indication of attitude to deck.

Chockhead   Aircraft handler.

Cat Walks   Walkway around, but beneath flight deck level.

Commander (Air)   Officer in charge of the aviation side of a carrier.

Chopper   Helicopter.

COD   Carrier On-board Delivery.

CAP   Combat Air Patrol.

Catapult   Device for launching heavy aircraft from carrier deck.

Cut   Signal given to aircraft by batsman (qv) when in correct position to land safely.

CAG   Carrier Air Group—administrative unit from 1946-54, thereafter still used to indicate the squadrons embarked in a carrier.

Deckape   Aircraft handler.

DLPS   Deck landing projection sight (replaced the mirror).

Donkey's Tail   Centre line continuation lights over rounddown to give perspective.

DAX   Direct Acting arrester wires.

DLCO   Deck Landing Control Officer or batsman.

Elephant Tango   Aircraft taxiing under power.
Fireball   Mobile powder fire extinguisher.
Flyco   Flying control position—adjacent to the carrier's bridge.
Fido   Flight Deck Officer.
FDO   Fighter Direction Officer/Flight Deck Officer/Fighter Direction Office.
Fly 1, 2, 3 and 4   Flight deck parking areas.
Fence   Barrier.
FGA   Fighter Ground Attack.
FAW   Fighter All Weather.
FB   Fighter Bomber.
F   Fighter (usually day fighter only).
FG   Fighter General.
Goofer   Person watching flying.
Goofers   Position from which flying can be watched.
Greenie   Flight Deck Electrician
Grubber   Aircraft Mechanic.
GPI   Glide Path Indicator.
Graveyard   Parking area for damaged aircraft.
Glasshouse   Flying Control Position.
HCP   Hangar Control Position—from here the marshalling of the aircraft in the hangar was controlled, particularly in regard to availability of the next day's flying.
Howdah   Retractable catapult control position.
Heavy   Fixed wing aircraft.
HAS   Helicopter Anti-Submarine.
HAR   Helicopter Airsea Rescue.
Helo   Helicopter.
Island   Superstructure on starboard side of carrier.
Jumbo   Aircraft handling crane—mobile.
Little F   Lieutenant Commander (Flying)—responsible for aircraft at launch, recovery and whilst in the carrier's circuit.
Meatball   Amber centre light of the DLPS (qv) which signified that the aircraft was 'go' for landing.
Mirror Sight   Early landing aid (replaced by the DLPS (qv)).
MAC-ship   Merchant Aircraft Carrier.
NATO   North Atlantic Treaty Organisation.
Ops   Commander (Operations)—responsible for the tasking, etc, of the aircraft.
Oleo   Load-bearing strut of undercarriage.
Plane guard   Either a destroyer or (later) a helicopter which would rescue aircrew during launch and recovery.
PLOD   Personnel Logistics On-board Delivery.
RN   Royal Navy.
RAN   Royal Australian Navy.
RCN   Royal Canadian Navy (now Canadian Forces).
RNR   Royal Naval Reserve.
RNVR   Royal Naval Volunteer Reserve—many World War 2 flyers were RNVR; RAN/RCN/RNZN also had VR.
RNZN   Royal New Zealand Navy.
RP   Rocket Projectile (unguided missile).

RT   Radio Telephone (voice communications).

Roundown/Round-down/Rounddown/Ramp   After end of flight deck.

Ramp   Ski jump—*Invincible, Illustrious, Ark Royal* and *Hermes.*

Roofrat   Aircraft handler.

Range   Aircraft parked on deck prior to launch.

Snoop   Bridle catcher at end of catapult.

SATCO   Senior Air Traffic Controller.

Stovie   Fixed-wing pilot.

Stick   Passengers in an aircraft—especially Marines for an assault.

Stickorbat   Assault plan.

SAR   Search and Rescue.

S   Strike (aircraft, eg, Buccaneer).

Talking ballast   Rating aircrew/observer.

TAG   Telegraphist Air Gunner.

Wedge Technician   Aircraft handler.

Wings   Commander (Air) (qv).

Wave-off   Order from batsman (qv) to go round again.

W/T   Wireless Telegraphy (morse key).

C   Carrier flag officers—Home Waters

Admiral Commanding Aircraft

Rear Admiral Sir Richard Phillimore	March 15 1918
(Appointment lapsed in 1919)	

Rear Admiral Aircraft Carriers (RAA)

Rear Admiral R.G.H. Henderson	Sept 21 1931
Rear Admiral Sir Alexander Ramsey	Sept 15 1933
Rear Admiral N.F. Laurence	Feb 16 1936
Rear Admiral G.C.C. Royal	July 27 1937
Vice Admiral L.V. Wells	June 26 1939
Rear Admiral Lumley Lyster	Aug 19 1940
(Squadron transferred to the Mediterranean Fleet, Sept 1 1940)	

Vice Admiral Aircraft Carriers

Vice Admiral Lumley Lyster	July 11 1942

Rear Admiral Aircraft Carriers (RAA)

Rear Admiral C. Moody	May 21 1943
(Squadron transferred to the Eastern Fleet, Dec 1 1943)	

Rear Admiral Escort Carriers

Rear Admiral A.W.Le T. Bisset	Oct 28 1943
(Squadron transferred to the Mediterranean Fleet, July 1944)	

Flag Officer 3rd Aircraft Carrier Squadron

(NB: 1 and 2 ACS were deployed to the Mediterranean and Pacific)

Rear Admiral M.J. Mansergh	July 19 1948
Rear Admiral Charles Lambe	Sept 8 1949
Rear Admiral Casper John	Jan 15 1951

Flag Officer Heavy Squadron

Rear Admiral Casper John	Jan 1952
Vice Admiral J. Hughes-Hallet	July 11 1952

Rear Admiral W.T. Couchman   Dec 8 1953

Flag Officer Aircraft Carriers
Rear Admiral W.T. Couchman   Oct 1954
Rear Admiral A.R. Pedder   Dec 21 1954
Vice Admiral M.L. Power   May 15 1956
Vice Admiral Sir Alexander Bingley   Jan 6 1958
Rear Admiral C.L.G. Evans   Jan 13 1959
Rear Admiral R.M. Smeeton   Mar 1 1960
Rear Admiral F.H.E. Hopkins   Jan 22 1962
Rear Admiral D.C.E.F. Gibson   Jan 25 1963
Rear Admiral H.R.B. Janvrin   Apr 1 1964
Rear Admiral W.D. O'Brien   Feb 1966
Rear Admiral L.D. Empson   April 1967
Rear Admiral M.F. Fell   June 1968

Flag Officer Carriers and Amphibious Ships
Rear Admiral M.F. Fell   Sept 1 1968
Rear Admiral J.D. Treacher   July 1970
Rear Admiral R.D. Lygo   May 1972
Rear Admiral A.D. Cassidi   Feb 1974
Rear Admiral J.H.F. Eberle   May 1975
Rear Admiral W.D.M. Staveley   March 1977
Rear Admiral P.G.M. Herbert   July 1978
(Appointment lapsed Dec 31 1978 on establishment of Flag Officer
Third Flotilla on Jan 1 1979)

Subordinate Commanders for Specific Operations
Commodore T.H. Troubridge, Naval Commander Centre Task Force,
North Africa   Nov 1942
Rear Admiral Sir Philip Vian, Flag Officer Force 'V' (Salerno)   Sept 1942

It should be noted that in Far Eastern waters, carriers tended to come under the direction of Flag Officer Second-in-command, Far East Fleet (FO2FEF) who usually took charge from about Aden, leaving FOAC/FOCAS to concentrate on the western hemisphere. There seems to have been no firm dividing line and at least once FO2 requested that FOAC take over when the fleet had a carrier almost permanently off Aden.

D   Carrier organisation

1930s
Captain [RN]
|
Wing Commander [RAF]
|
Squadron Leader (Flying) [RAF]
|
Flight Commanders [RN/RAF][1]
Squadron Leaders [RN/RAF][2]

NB   Pre 1938, naval pilots had dual RAF/RN ranks, but were always graded lower than their RAF land-based colleagues.

1   Pre-1933.
2   Post-1933, when embarked flights became squadrons.

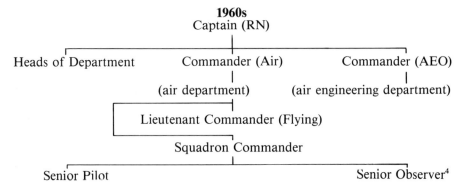

1960s
Captain (RN)

Heads of Department   Commander (Air)   Commander (AEO)

(air department)   (air engineering department)

Lieutenant Commander (Flying)

Squadron Commander

Senior Pilot   Senior Observer[4]

3   Usually included a commander of an AEW Flight of 849 Squadron.

4   Where applicable (fighter squadrons with single-seat aircraft did not have observers in their complement).

E   Carriers compared

	Argus	*Courageous*	*Ark Royal*	*Formidable*
Launched	Dec 2 1917	Feb 5 1916	April 13 1937	Aug 17 1939
Completed (as carrier)	Sept 16 1918	May 5 1928	Nov 16 1938	Nov 24 1940
Builder	Beardmore	Harland & Wolff	Cammell Laird	Harland & Wolff
Standard displacement	14,000 tons	22,500 tons	22,000 tons	23,000 tons
Overall length	567 ft	786 ft 6 in	800 ft	753 ft 6 in
Beam (at widest)	79 ft 6 in	90 ft	94 ft 9 in	95 ft 9 in
Draught (mean)	22 ft 6 in	28 ft	23 ft 9 in	29 ft
Aircraft carried	12-20	33-42	54-70	33-72
Complement	760	840	1,575	1,392 (1940)
Speed	18.75 knots	31 knots	30.75 knots	31 knots
Fate	Scrapped 1946	Sunk Sept 17 1939	Sunk Nov 14 1941	Scrapped 1953

	Vengeance	*Eagle*	*Hermes*	*Invincible*
Launched	Feb 23 1944	Mar 19 1946	Feb 16 1953	May 3 1977
Completed (as carrier)	Jan 15 1945	Oct 31 1951	Nov 18 1959	Mar 19 1980
Builder	Swan Hunter	Vickers Armstrong	Vickers Armstrong	British Shipbuilders (Vickers at Barrow)
Standard displacement	13,190 tons	43,000 tons	23,900 tons	16,257 tons
Overall length	695 ft	811 ft 9 in	744 ft 3 in	677 ft 6 in
Beam (at widest)	80 ft 3 in	112 ft 9 in	90 ft	90 ft
Draught (mean)	21 ft 3 in	36 ft	29 ft	21 ft
Aircraft carried	37-48	44-60	28-40	14
Complement	1,076	2,750	2,100	903
Speed	25 knots	31.5 knots	28 knots	28 knots
Fate	Still serves as *Minas Gerais*	Scrapped 1979	Converted to commando carrier	First of a Class of three

Eagle 1964.

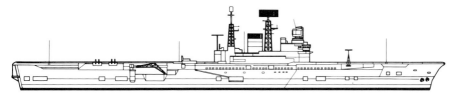

Invincible 1986.

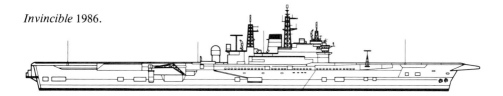

F Naval aircraft compared

Carrier-borne fighters

Type	*Sopwith Pup*	*Fairey Flycatcher*	*Hawker Nimrod*
Service dates	1918-20	1923-32	1932-39
Max speed (at alt)	74 knots	102 knots	169 knots
Endurance	3 hours	1.82 hours	1.65 hours
Wing span	26.5 ft	29 ft	33.52 ft
All-up weight	1,225 lb	3,028 lb	4,258 lb
Weapons	1 × Lewis gun	2 × Vickers, 2 × 20 lb bombs underwing	2 × Vickers, 2 × 20 lb bombs underwing

Type	*Blackburn Skua*	*Supermarine Seafire IB*	*Seafire FR 47*
Service dates	1938-41	1941-42	1948-52
Max speed (at alt)	195 knots	317 knots	393 knots
Endurance	4.5 hours	1.6 hours	1.1 hours
Wing span	46.17 ft	36.67 ft	36.92 ft
All-up weight	8,228 lb	6,700 lb	11,615 lb
Weapons	4 × Browning guns, 1 × Lewis gun for observer, 1 × 500 lb + 8 × 30 lb bombs	2 × 20 mm cannon, 4 × 0.303 guns	4 × 20 mm cannon, 8 × 60 lb rockets, 3 × 500 lb bombs

Type	*Hawker Sea Fury*	*Hawker Sea Hawk FGA 6*	*Supermarine Scimitar F1*
Service dates	1948-53	1956-60	1960-66
Max speed (at alt)	400 knots	455 knots	617 knots

Type	Hawker Sea Fury	Hawker Sea Hawk FGA 6	Supermarine Scimitar F1
Endurance	1.7 hours	1 hour	2.4 hours
Wing span	38.4 ft	39 ft	37.17 ft
All-up weight	12,500 lb	16,200 lb	40,000 lb
Weapons	4 × 20 mm cannon, 12 × rockets, or 2 × 1,000 lb bombs underwing	4 × 20 mm cannon, 10 × rockets, 2 × 500 lb bombs	4 × 30 mm Aden cannon or 4 × AIM-9 Sidewinder missiles, or 12 × 2 in rockets/ 4,000 lb of bombs

Type	DH Sea Venom FAW 22	DH Sea Vixen FAW 2	McDonnell Phantom FG 1
Service dates	1957-60	1964-72	1969-78
Max Speed (at alt)	430 knots	550 knots	Mach 2.1
Endurance	1.75 hours	2 hours	1 hour
Wing span	42.83 ft	51 ft	38.5 ft
All-up weight	15,800 lb	37,000 lb	56,000 lb
Weapons	4 × 20 mm cannon, 8 × 60 lb rockets	4 × Red Top, 14 × 2 in rockets, or 2,000 lb of bombs	4 × Sparrow, 4 × Sidewinder missiles or 10,000 lb bombs

American-built fighters

Type	Grumman Wildcat V	Grumman Hellcat II	Vought Corsair I
Service dates	1943-45	1943-46	1943-46
Max speed (at alt)	287 knots	322 knots	325 knots
Endurance	4 hours	6.5 hours	2.7 hours
Wing span	38 ft	42.83 ft	41 ft
All-up weight	6,100 lb	13,753 lb	11,800 lb
Weapons	6 × 0.50 calibre	6 × 0.50 calibre, 6 × 60 lb rockets or 2,000 lb bombs	4 × 0.50 calibre

Torpedo bombers

Type	Blackburn Ripon	Fairey Swordfish I	Barracuda III
Service dates	1929-34	1936-45	1943-53
Max speed (at alt)	103 knots	112 knots	178 knots
Endurance	6 hours	5.25 hours	4 hours
Wing span	44.83 ft	45.5 ft	49.17 ft
All-up weight	7,405 lb	9,250 lb	14,100 lb
Weapons	2 × machine guns, 1,650 lb torpedo/ bombs	2 × machine guns, 1,610 lb torpedo/ bombs, 60 lb rockets	2 × machine guns, 1 × 1,620 lb torpedo/ bombs

Type	*Grumman Avenger I*	*Blackburn Firebrand 5*
Service dates	1943-46	1946-53
Max speed (at alt)	225 knots	295 knots
Endurance	5.8 hours	2.9 hours
Wing span	54.17 ft	51.29 ft
All-up weight	16,400 lb	17,500 lb
Weapons	2 × 0.50 calibre machine guns, 1 × 1,921 lb torpedo, or 2,000 lb bombs, 8 × 60 lb rockets	4 × 20 mm cannon, 1 × 1,850 lb torpedo or 2 × 1,000 lb bombs or rockets

Anti-submarine aircraft

Type	*Grumman Avenger AS 4*	*Fairey Gannet AS 1*
Service dates	1953-55	1955-58
Max speed (at alt)	227 knots	245 knots
Endurance	4.3 hours	4.9 hours
Wing span	54.17 ft	54.33 ft
All-up weight	16,761 lb	19,600 lb
Weapons	2,000 lb of bombs/depth charges or 8 × rockets	2,500 lb of ordnance, or 16 × 60 lb rockets

Strike aircraft

Type	*Fairey Firefly FR 5*	*Westland Wyvern S 4*
Service dates	1948-55	1954-58
Max speed (at alt)	330 knots	300 knots
Endurance	6.5 hours	2.6 hours
Wing span	41.17 ft	44 ft
All-up weight	16,096 lb	24,500 lb
Weapons	4 × 20 mm cannon, 16 × 60 lb rockets, or 2,000 lb of bombs	4 × 20 mm cannon, 16 × 60 lb rockets, or 3,000 lb bombs

ASW Helicopters

Type	*Westland Whirlwind HAS 7*	*Westland Wessex HAS 1*
Service dates	1957-60	1961-67
Max speed (at sl)	60 knots	120 knots
Endurance	3.8 hours	2.5 hours
All-up weight	7,800 lb	12,600 lb
Weapons	1 × ASW torpedo	2 × ASW torpedoes

Type	*Westland Wessex HAS 3*	*Westland Sea King HAS 2*
Service dates	1967-83	1969-84
Max speed (at sl)	110 knots	144 knots
Endurance	1.5 hours	5 hours
Weapons	2 × Mk44/Mk46 torpedoes, or 4 × Mk11 depth bombs	4 × Mk44/Mk46 torpedoes, or 4 × Mk11 depth bombs

Invincible **Class air group**

Type	British Aerospace Sea Harrier FRS 1	Westland Sea King AEW 2	Westland Sea King HAS 5
Service entry	1980	1982	1980
Max speed (at sl)	625 knots	110 knots	112 knots
Endurance	2.25 hours	4.5 hours	5 hours
Wing span	25.26 ft		
Weapons	4 × Sidewinder missiles, 2 × 30 mm cannon, up to 5,000 lb of bombs underwing	None (carries Searchwater radar)	4 × Mk46/ Stingray torpedoes, or 4 × depth bombs

Note Data above has been abstracted from *Encyclopaedia of the Fleet Air Arm, 1945 to the present* and *Encyclopaedia of the Modern Royal Navy: Third Edition,* both published by Patrick Stephens Limited. The historical aircraft data has been checked with sources at the Fleet Air Arm Museum, RNAS Yeovilton.

G   Carrier sensors

The development of the aircraft carrier's own sensor suite has paralleled that of other surface warships although there has been an obvious plan to ensure that the aircraft direction and control sensors have been optimised for the ships' roles. Underwater sensors—sonars—have played a less important part in the sensor suite development programmes because the ships have been designed to carry aircraft, initially fixed-wing and later helicopters, with proficient systems for anti-submarine warfare. Emphasis has therefore been placed on the long range warning, surveillance and air control radar systems; thermal imagery (for low light conditions) and electronic warfare system have been comparatively recent developments.

Pre-World War 2 carriers

These vessels carried basic radio direction finding equipment to intercept and plot enemy radio traffic and gun battery directors, relying on optical sighting systems and primitive mechanical computer systems for 4 in (102 mm) batteries.

In the late 1930s, a long range air warning radio direction and ranging (radar) system had been perfected for naval use, and the Type 79, with a range of over 75 nm (140 km) was introduced. Most of the *Illustrious* Class were designed with the system in mind.

By the outbreak of war, gunnery radar (Type 285) was being introduced to the Fleet and fitted to most carriers, including *Furious*, for anti-aircraft defence.

World War 2 developments

The rapid technical development of radar and radio direction finding systems was important for aircraft carriers although operational tactics, following the losses of carriers sailing alone, would mean that the carrier could also rely on cover from escorts' systems as well. Early warning sets included Type 290 fitted in *Eagle* and the first height finding sets, such as Type 277. Later in the war, American technology was being developed for use by the Royal Navy, including the adoption of USN's SM-1 fighter control radar.

For self-defence gunnery, the Type 282 set was fitted to several ships, providing good gun direction information to targets within about 5 nm (9 km) of the ship, supplementing the Type 285 already in service for high angle defence.

The Escort Carriers commissioned during the war seem to have been fitted primarily with High Frequency/Direction Finding (HF/DF) gear for the British-built ships, but the American supplied vessels came with Types 79/279 and the characteristic lattern surface warning sets, like Types 271/272. Merchant aircraft carriers (MAC-ships) were generally fitted with surface warning and air warning sets placed high on the single masts of the small island superstructure.

By the time that the *Colossus* Class Light Fleet Aircraft Carriers were being built, radar was a standard fit from new, including the Type 79 (in several modifications with new aerials and processors) for long-range air warning. Fighter control sets had been developed although one carrier was still fitted with a heavy, but effective SM-1. As the Pacific War progressed, it was obvious that good, long range radar coverage of the air threat was essential as the Japanese launched raids aimed against the aircraft carriers alone; radar picket destroyers were introduced to protect the carriers which led to the development of the airborne early warning aircraft within the decade.

For the design of the new Fleet Carriers, *Eagle* and *Ark Royal,* serious attention was now paid to the sensor suite, allowing for all weather operations, night and day, against comprehensive threats. Long range air warning radar was now capable of reaching out to 150 nm (278 km) in optimum conditions, with associated systems providing height information and fighter direction and control. Gun directors had become sophisticated, especially with the introduction of several USN systems USN systems, like Mk 37.

Post-war improvements

The immediate post-war period saw the introduction of the fruits of wartime research on both sides of the Atlantic for surface warning (like Types 293 and 982) with ranges approaching 60 nm (111 km). With the advent of jet-powered aircraft in air groups (and as adversaries), sensor performance improved to match the air power requirements. When *Victorious* was taken in hand for modernisation between 1950-58, she emerged with some interesting systems, including Type 984 (three-dimensional long-range radar), 974 (surface warning) and 293Q 30 nm (26 km) height finding systems, useful for carrier-controlled approaches. Carrier Controlled Approach (CCA) allowed for low light, adverse weather recoveries of jet aircraft without their own radar systems.

Eagle emerged from her refit in 1959, with Type 965 long-range 'bedstead' air warning radar on a new high lattice mast, supplemented by the 3-D 984 and CCA system, Type 963. As *Eagle* and subsequent carriers now sported Seacat short-range air defence guided missile systems, the directors were also fitted; initially these were optical guidance only but radar control options were offered later, *Ark Royal* appeared in 1969, ready for Phantom operations with Type 965

AKE-II (double bedstead), 982 (height finding) and 983 (height finder) in the same system, and CAA.

Albion and *Bulwark* were fitted with Type 960/982 air warning radars, 983 height finders and 277Q fighter direction sets during their lives as fixed-wing Light Fleet Carriers, whilst their near sister ship *Hermes* was completed with the 3-D radar also fitted to *Victorious* and *Eagle*.

CVA-01 would have mounted an impressive suite of Anglo-Dutch Type 988 search, tracking and illumination systems, 909 for the Sea Dart missile control and CCA. When the programme was cancelled and later the *Invincibles* were partly substituted, the radar suite was altered to reflect the basically helicopter (VTOL) role of these new ships—they retain the 909 Sea Dart system, but have been fitted with 1022 (another Anglo-Dutch development) for long-range air warning, 992Q for target indication and surface warning, using the 1006 for navigation and helicopter control. Electronic warfare suites include Abbey Hill and UAA-1 ESM (electronic surveillance measures); during refits, 1022 will be replaced by 996, a 3-D radar from Plessey. For Sea Harrier and certain helicopter operations, the MEL MADGE micro-wave landing system has been developed.

Sonar systems have included the Types 184 and 2016 in the *Invincible* CVSs to reflect the carriers' anti-submarine role; other previous carriers designs have basically relied on the surface escorts and air groups for such data. *Hermes* in her ASW role was also fitted with 184.

H   Carrier defensive weapons

Although primarily designed to operate aircraft, both in offensive and defensive roles, the aircraft carrier has always carried some form of defensive armament. As the threat environment grew and changed, so the weapons systems carried were amended, improved and upgraded to meet that threat, some times not as successfully as others. There has always been a problem of accommodating the weapons and their directors at the expense of deck space and top weight.

Early carriers

The first ship designed to carry aircraft, *Ark Royal*, was armed with conventional 12 pounder guns to defend itself against surface threats because in 1914 when the ship was purchased, the air threat had yet to be fully realised. In fact, the first carriers were primarily concerned with being attacked by surface ships rather than either submarines or aircraft. It took just a few years for the air threat to be recognised so that by the time *Furious* was commissioned as an aircraft carrier, 4 in (102 mm) anti-aircraft gun batteries had been fitted but the 12 pounder guns were retained.

In the early 1920s, the multi-barrelled pom-pom 2 pounder mounting provided the first real air defence system to support the less rapid 4 in guns. Following her 1934 refit, *Hermes* was fitted with 50 calibre (12.7 mm) machine gun mountings with four barrels and at the same time, most carriers were being refitted without the larger calibre surface gunnery systems, such as the 5.5 in (140 mm) low-angle guns.

World War 2

With the loss of *Courageous* to a submarine in the early days of the war, the decision was made to protect aircraft carriers within task groups but the air threat had yet to be fully envisaged. Nevertheless, the Admiralty had begun to fit medium and close range air defence batteries, including the fitting of high-angle gunnery directors. *Ark Royal (III)* was built with six 2 pounder and eight multiple 12.7 mm mountings around the flight deck, in addition to 16 4.5 in (114 mm) mountings. The same weight of defensive gun power was designed into the *Illustrious* Class.

Rearming the carriers with the highly effective 20 mm Oerlikon cannon (still in use in the 1980s) and the 40 mm Bofors gun proved a reliable and effective mix for close-range defence. *Victorious* boasted 45 of the Oerlikon guns and 21 Bofors by the time she sailed for the Pacific in 1945.

The armament of the Escort Carriers was primarily made up of 20 mm mountings with three 4 in guns, mounted fore and aft. In the Pacific War, the aim became the classic wall of lead technique which seems to have proved effective in the Falklands conflict. The 4 in gun continued in service for some time, although the *Colossus* Class were fitted with 2 pounder pom-poms and a selection of different 20 mm mountings, dependent upon availability; the design for this class had restricted the defensive armament to anti-aircraft close-range only, the first carriers to be so armed.

The design of *Eagle* and *Ark Royal*, the 1942-type Fleet Carriers, included 4.5 in (114 mm) weapons as well as the now-standard 40 mm mountings, although the armament changed as the design progressed after the initial early peacetime delay. The pom-pom was going out of favour and being progressively replaced by the single 20 mm (60 in the *Eagle* design), the 40 mm and the twin 20 mm. By the end of the war, the six-barrelled 40 mm mounting had appeared, linked to good gunnery directors.

Post-war systems

As the Fleet Carriers were refitted in the course of their post-war service, the 4.5 in and 40 mm systems were reduced and then deleted. This not only saved top weight but eventually allowed for the fitting of a surface-to-air guided weapon system, Shorts Seacat. When *Hermes* was commissioned in 1959, her defensive armament had been reduced to ten 40 mm guns, showing how much the defence of the carrier had been shouldered by the escorts and the air group.

Victorious was rearmed during her modernisation in the 1950s, receiving 40 mm guns and 12 3 in (76 mm) mountings, which guns she kept until decommissioned prematurely in 1967. The post-war Light Fleets generally carried 40 mm guns for self-defence.

When CVA-01 was designed in the early 1960s, the area air defence missile, Sea Dart was proposed for the ship, linked to the Type 909 missile control radar. The aircraft carrier had moved into the missile and in no way could be considered a stand alone ship. Sea Dart was the primary weapon system designated for the *Invincible* Class, but originally close-range Sea Wolf point defence missiles were to have been fitted; in the South Atlantic, a close-range defence system was found most necessary. In 1982, *Illustrious* and then *Invincible*, were fitted with additional 20 mm Oerlikon guns, countermeasure launchers and the American Phalanx gatling gun close-in weapons system. *Ark Royal (V)* will be fitted with the Goalkeeper system after she becomes fully operational.

Index

Carrier aircraft